RESIGNATION IN PROTEST

By Edward Weisband

Turkish Foreign Policy 1943–1945: Small State Diplomacy and Great Power Politics
The Ideology of American Foreign Policy: A Paradigm of Lockian Liberalism

By Thomas M. Franck

Race and Nationalism
The Structure of Impartiality
Why Federations Fail
Comparative Constitutional Process

By Thomas M. Franck and Edward Weisband

Word Politics: Verbal Strategy among the Super Powers
Secrecy and Foreign Policy
A Free Trade Association

EDWARD WEISBAND
THOMAS M. FRANCK

RESIGNATION IN PROTEST

Political and Ethical Choices
between Loyalty to Team
and Loyalty to Conscience
in American Public Life

GROSSMAN PUBLISHERS
A DIVISION OF THE VIKING PRESS
NEW YORK
1975

First published in 1975 by Grossman Publishers
625 Madison Avenue, New York, N.Y. 10022
Published simultaneously in Canada by
The Macmillan Company of Canada Limited
Printed in U.S.A.

Library of Congress Cataloging in Publication Data

Weisband, Edward, 1939-
    Resignation in protest.

    Includes bibliographical references and index.
      1. Cabinet officers—United States—Case studies.
2. Cabinet officers—Great Britain—Case studies.
3. Loyalty—Case studies. 4. Political ethics—Case
studies. I. Franck, Thomas M., joint author. II. Title.
JK611.W44   172'.2'0973   74-32343
ISBN 0-670-59527-6

This study was undertaken with a Guggenheim Fellowship which enabled Mr. Franck to devote the year 1973–74 to research and writing. An earlier summer grant from the New York University Law Center Foundation made possible the English interviews.

The authors also benefited from the research assistance of the following fellows of the New York University Center for International Studies:

RESEARCH FELLOWS:
Nigel Rodley, 1969–72
Joseph Dickinson, 1971–72

JUNIOR FELLOWS:
Carol Christensen, 1969–70
Donna L. Johnson, 1969–70
George Aron, 1972–73
James Enelow, 1972–73
Joseph H. Moskowitz, 1972–73
Bertram I. Spector, 1972–73

We are also particularly indebted to Professors Albert O. Hirschman and James C. Thomson, Jr., for sharing with us their seminal work and thoughts in the field of resignation ethics and practices. Thomas L. Hughes gave us invaluable critiques which strengthened the final draft, as did Judith Friedlaender and James C. Amon. Joan E. Murtagh, Judith Chazen, and Rochelle Fenchel, through their steadfast assistance, helped free us from some office chores so we could flee across the campus and into the library. The nearly 100 living "resigners" we interviewed in the United States and England were invariably generous with their time and memories. To all these we are deeply grateful. A special decibel of

130802

appreciation is reserved for Phyllis B. Goldberg, administrator of the Center for International Studies of N.Y.U., for myriad forms of skilled and good-humored support for this enterprise. Her stenographic, editorial, and administrative skills insured the safe navigation of thousands of floating footnotes and unhinged paragraphs from draft to draft.

For
JAMES JOSEPH BAECHLE

As Queen Victoria remarked to Arthur Balfour: "We are not interested in the possibilities of defeat."

CONTENTS

Twice in eight years, scandal has forced an American President to retire from office. The Vietnam debacle rent the fabric of American politics so deeply that Lyndon B. Johnson had to withdraw what would otherwise have been his certain candidacy for a second full term. Richard M. Nixon's role in the Watergate and related "horrors" ended with his presidency being crushed under the weight of outraged Congressional and public opinion.

Today there is a widespread tendency to look for the resurrection of the body politic. The hope is abroad in the land that Watergate is a watershed. People talk of a "post-Watergate morality." The "openness" of the Ford White House is approvingly noted and contrasted with the "closed" administrations of his two predecessors.

But there is also much cynicism, a weary tendency to conclude that politics will forever be politics and power must inevitably corrupt. A mere change in Presidential style and rhetoric at the beginning of a new Administration epitomizes Aristotle's solitary swallow that does not make a summer.

Both the optimists and the pessimists are partly right. The domestic and foreign-policy disasters of the Johnson and Nixon administrations have so profoundly cracked the *status quo* as to raise at least the possibility of fundamental change in America's way of government. But such change is not achieved just by fielding a new team of players at the White House. What is required is a basic change in the rules by which the game has so long been played—and lost.

In order to know which rules of the game need to be changed, it is necessary, first, to spell out the old rules and to identify those which bear particular responsibility for the way things were. Accordingly, a Senate Committee has already examined those infamous practices of electoral strategy—the dirty tricks—which had become almost the accepted way of debasing the democratic process. Others have introduced federal and state legislation to alter the overly permissive rules and practices of campaign financing. The system of government secrecy classification has been reconsidered and modified both by Congress and the courts.

These efforts are laudable. They give us reason to hope for basic change because they make a start on constructing the durable framework for a real post-Watergate morality.

But the rules of the game that most need scrutiny and revision are those that govern the relationship between the President and his own advisers: the White House counselors and staff, cabinet members and the subcabinet. Probably neither Vietnam nor Watergate could have been prevented by a more honest system of election and financing practices, but the policies that led to the morass might have been arrested earlier by courageous public defection of key disaffected members of the Johnson and Nixon administrations. In each instance there was some halfhearted private questioning of policy, but when that failed, the overriding rule, devoutly adhered to, was: loyalty and team play above personal conscience.

It is to this rule that our book is addressed—not, however, a social or constitutional abstraction. Such a rule is part of the social environment in which real people live. When it compels an individual to subordinate one of his private moral values to some other, allegedly higher, group value, you have the making of an intense personal dilemma, which, in the most sensitive, attains the proportion of a crisis of conscience. What follows is testament to the validity and pain of that experience.

E. W.

T. M. F.

*The master no longer says: "You shall think
as I do or you shall die"; but he says: "You
are free to think differently from me and to
retain your life, your property, and all that
you possess; but you are henceforth a stranger
among your people. You may retain your civil
rights, but they will be useless to you, for
you will never be chosen by your fellow citizens
if you solicit their votes; and they will affect
to scorn you if you ask for their esteem. . . ."*

—*Alexis de Tocqueville*, Democracy in America

*Even a fool, when he holdeth his peace, is
counted wise: and he that shutteth his lips
is esteemed a man of virtue.*

—*Proverbs 17:28*

To think is to say no.

—*Emile Chartier*, Le Citoyen contre les Pouvoirs

RESIGNATION IN PROTEST

≷ 1 ≷

The Insider's
Inner Conflict

THIS BOOK is about the individual at the breaking point. It is about protest resignations compelled by unbearable misgivings; about men and women who disagree with what they see going on around them in the labyrinths of power and who resign in order to be free to tell their story.

It is also about top officials who disagree profoundly with key government policies, but who keep silent, placing loyalty to the team or careerism ahead of loyalty to principle and to the public. It is about men and women in power who wrestle mightily with their consciences—and win.

And, since silent acquiescence, getting along, became so much the order of the day in government, this book examines the costs of a system based above all on the value of "team play." Men and women in places of power and responsibility who choose not to pay the price of personal integrity merely succeed in shifting those costs to society as a whole. America, in the era of Vietnam and of Watergate, has been paying the price of a political tradition that fosters conformity rather than conviction, group loyalty rather than individual accountability, that borrows its terminology from the language of corporate athletics—in which a man's willingness to "play ball" is his true measure—rather than from moral ethics. One price is the widespread popular cynicism toward "politics" and the development of a political countersystem that operates in the streets and in the popular press, outside the systemic channels of the White House and Congress. Another, more ominous cost has been the extraordinary growth of Presidential power in an environment of toadies.

The senior federal executive who opposed the escalation of the Vietnam war in private but refrained from rocking the boat, or who witnessed the events popularly lumped together as "Watergate" but knew better than to make a fuss, is symptomatic of a serious crisis in the quality of American public life. Although this is a study of the behavior of senior government officials, the crisis of the breaking point is not an experience unique to this rarefied group. Twentieth-century America is a nation of men and women enrolled in organizations: industries, businesses, law firms, universities and schools, chambers of commerce, churches, and Rotary clubs. Americans are a team-playing people, a "house of peers." These teamlike peer groups and organizations, however "participatory" their process of making decisions, invariably have a leader and subleaders who exercise power and assume responsibility. To take and hold power the leaders must be able to command the loyalty of subordinates. Loyalty is power; loyalty is effectiveness. Without the cohesive force of habitual loyalty, the organized team becomes a feckless rabble.

"Efficiency" and its sibling, "order," are high values in all organized, technocratic societies—indeed, they lay claim to being the highest or most fundamental survival values. "At present, the technologically advanced societies such as our own," David Riesman has observed, "have reached a situation of interdependence analogous to that of the Hopi, who will all die if they do not collectively preserve the rainfall."[1]* In a society which, as William H. Whyte has pointed out in *The Organization Man,* the "organization ethic" is the transcendent social imperative, the individual really comes to believe that he does not merely work *for* or *with* the organization but belongs to it and derives his meaning from it. "Of himself, he is isolated, meaningless; only as he collaborates with others does he become worth-while, for by sublimating him-

*Numbered reference notes begin on page 207.

self in the group, he helps produce a whole that is greater than the sum of its parts."[2]

The person who sacrifices team loyalty in order to pursue a competing value, such as integrity, is likely to have brought to bear against him the coercive weight of that society's historically conditioned sense of self-preservation. Societies, groups, organizations systematize the process of making value-judgments. Indeed, they systematize the very process of perceiving reality. Woe to the individual who contradicts the organization's values and perceptions.[3] The member of the tribal council who insists on shouting "the dam is out" when the chief has said the dam is safe is in serious trouble either way: whether it is or isn't. He is embarked on a "no win" enterprise. If the dam is safe, he will look ridiculous and be chased into the desert. If it is crumbling, he will probably drown with everyone else—unless he has already been stoned to death for confronting the chief, the embodiment of the collective wisdom of the tribe. No wonder few men and women choose this unprofitable role except under the severest demands of their inner voice.

Thoreau grumbled that "The mass of men serve the state . . . not as men, mainly, but as machines . . . there is no free exercise whatever of the judgment or of the moral senses. . . . Others—as most legislators, politicians, lawyers, ministers, and office-holders— . . . rarely make any moral distinctions. . . . A very few, as heroes, patriots, martyrs, reformers in the great sense, and *men,* serve the state with their consciences also, and so necessarily resist it for the most part; and they are commonly treated as enemies by it."[4] A bit pungent, perhaps. But getting truer, it seems, by the week.

The need for efficiency and order is a powerful weapon against the obstreperous individual's conscience striving to maintain ethical autonomy. By *ethical autonomy* we mean the willingness to assert one's own principled judgment, even if that entails violating rules, values, or perceptions of the organization, peer group, or team.[5] An individual is ethically autonomous to the degree that he "sticks to his guns" about what he thinks, hears, sees, feels, or knows, even when to do so puts him in conflict with society's, or his team's, conventional wisdom and with such social values as conformity, loyalty, and institutional efficiency. As we use it, the term *ethical autonomy* is not, however, meant to imply approval of the individual's judgment, nor that we believe the individual's ethical standards in any particular instance are "better" or "higher" than those of society or his team. The social importance of ethical autonomy lies not in what is asserted but in the act of asserting.

This is because the ethical autonomy of the individual is an institution's safety valve, a corrective that protects against its own malfunctions. These malfunctions occur, for example, when a group's way of seeing, evaluating, and deciding cease to be based on a free and open flow of information from outside the group and, instead, reflect what some dominant persons within the group prefer to think is so. The ethically autonomous individual, in such circumstances, will risk great unpopularity and may even leave the group in order to challenge what the psychologist Irving Janis has called "groupthink."[6]

The pressures to conformist "groupthink," Janis finds, as do we, operate even at the highest level of national policy-making, among top officials, "no matter how mindful they may be of their exalted national status and of their heavy responsibilities. . . ."[7]

◇

Wayne Chatfield Taylor is a case in point. As Assistant Secretary of the Treasury, he had become sick and tired of being sick and tired. For months he had resisted, argued against—but utterly failed to impede—the implementation of a series of government initiatives that seemed to Taylor not only imprudent and contrary to the will of Congress but also unconstitutional. President F. D. Roosevelt and Treasury Secretary Henry Morgenthau, Jr., he feared, were hell-bent on involving America in European politics and, ultimately, in a European war.

Finally, at noon on February 7, 1939, Taylor crossed his

personal Rubicon and marched into the Secretary's office. He handed the astonished Morgenthau a letter of resignation. In tones no one could construe as excessively moderate, it discussed the policies which Taylor opposed. Specifically, the letter took aim at key foreign commitments currently being negotiated: to provide U.S. warplanes for the French government and to bail out Loyalist Spain and Nationalist China by buying up their silver on favorable terms and by extending them credit. In particular, there was a galling matter of a $25-million Export-Import Bank loan to a Spanish regime of which Taylor disapproved for its Leftist, anticlerical proclivities. "If I had been Secretary of the Treasury I would not have initiated any of [these] negotiations," he had written.

> In the case of the Chinese and Spanish transactions, I feel that the actions which were taken violate the spirit of our neutrality legislation which represents the . . . expressed opinion of the American people on . . . aid . . . to belligerents. In the case of the aeroplane purchases by the French, I do not feel that the Secretary of the Treasury should devote his time to matters which so obviously fall outside the jurisdiction of the Treasury Department.[8]

Morgenthau quickly surmised that it was the writer's intention to make this damaging letter public. He urged that Taylor take twenty-four hours to think it over, an invitation the agitated Assistant Secretary hotly declined.

Yet he did not send the letter that evening.

At 9:30 the next morning, Morgenthau bustled over to the White House to warn Roosevelt of what was afoot. In the neatly understated words of Morgenthau's diary, the President "was considerably annoyed with Wayne Taylor."[9] Between them, they set him up for the old one-two punch. First the Secretary summoned the would-be defector to tell him that his letter was unfair and untrue and that if he would not withdraw its allegations, he could expect a public fight.[10] This rocked Taylor. Now it was he who asked for a little time to think it over. He did not, however, get it; within half an hour, he was called to Roosevelt's office, where he endured a vigorous lecture on team play and the need to "go along."[11]

A little over an hour later, Roosevelt called Morgenthau and, together, they reviewed the impact they were having on Taylor and his "dirty letter."[12] They briefly considered offering him an appointment somewhere else, just to keep him quiet for a few months, before kicking him out. But this proved unnecessary. At 5:00 P.M., Morgenthau again saw Taylor. "You know, Wayne, things are very difficult," Morgenthau began, "and once the President says 'That is the policy' then we all have to go down the line. He is the quarterback. He gives the signals and we have to carry out his orders."

"Nobody realizes that more than I do," the hapless Taylor replied.

Twenty minutes after this encounter had ended, Morgenthau was able to report victory to Roosevelt: "I had a long talk with Wayne and his whole attitude is changed," he said. Taylor "is quite affable. One of the things I talked about was my secrecy in connection with the French airplanes. He is willing to change his letter, but wants a chance to think about it overnight."[13]

The next morning Taylor's surrender to Morgenthau was sealed. "The President gave me some advice," he confided to the Secretary, "and I intend to follow it."[14]

And follow it he did, to the letter, which when published on February 17 is a model of the smarmy tone and sphinxlike discretion which "team players" are expected to employ when resigning. It exemplifies the decline and fall of the Organization Man's ethical autonomy.

> Dear Mr. President:
>   I regret exceedingly that circumstances have arisen which make it desirable for me to resign my post.
>   I shall always consider it the greatest privilege to have had the opportunity of participating in the work of your Administration, and I wish to assure you that if, in the future, you should have occasion to find my services useful in some other capacity,

I would welcome the opportunity of again serving my Government.

With deep appreciation of the thoughtful understanding which you have extended to me, believe me,

Faithfully yours,

Wayne C. Taylor[15]

Roosevelt may not have believed Taylor, but he was satisfied with the outcome and knew how to express his satisfaction in currency that would be appreciated. Almost immediately, he scouted the possibility of an ambassadorship to Venezuela, but Sumner Welles at State was less than enthusiastic: "That is simply terrible," he replied to White House feelers, and he insisted privately that as long as he was there he would see that Wayne Taylor never got anything.[16] But loyalty must be rewarded and consent behavior reinforced. Eighteen months later, Taylor was found a comfortable slot as Under Secretary of Commerce.

Taylor had done what, by Washington standards, is the correct thing. And as G. B. Shaw has Lord Summerhays observe in *Misalliance,* "the correct thing depends for its success on everyone playing the game very strictly." Taylor's little, lost battle for ethical autonomy is poignantly relevant to us all, whatever our team, our role. Members of even the best-run organizations cannot always escape moments of profound crisis, when they must break faith either with the team or with themselves. These crises occur when the leadership of an institution suddenly—or gradually— embarks on a course of action incompatible with a member's private ethical standards or judgment. If the member has previously tried to change the policy from within, using the approved procedures, but has failed, should he, then, quietly go along with "the team" or should he dissociate himself from it? Does a member, merely by staying on the team, assume personal responsibility for the very decisions he opposes? And if the dissident decides to exit, is his duty to his conscience discharged by dropping out quietly, or is he ethically required to make a disagreeable public fuss?

◇

Few of us who work in organizations have escaped having our moment at this ethical breaking point; and the experience has inevitably, profoundly, if sometimes only subtly, changed us. "'Play up! play up! and play the game!' shouts the captain and the team mates."[17] To quit, and to take public issue with the way the game is being played, is bound to affect our subsequent careers. On the other hand, each time we acquiesce, by "playing up" rather than speaking up, we raise the threshold of our moral outrage, thereby becoming more inured, less vulnerable, better team players, less autonomous beings. If we chose to resign and speak up against the organization we may have branded ourselves as "the kind that won't play ball." Such a public-protest resignation may thrust us into a brief moment of popular adulation. Our blowing the whistle may help force a change in the organization's behavior. But it may also be shrugged off as a hollow gesture, the act of an eccentric, bad-mannered, ungrateful exhibitionist.

William L. Cary, a chairman of the Securities Exchange Commission, has asked with the hindsight of Watergate revelations: "Isn't there some basis for hoping that resignation and independence can become respectable?" But, in reply, he also notes that if a top official had shown more ethical autonomy "unfortunately people in this country would look upon him as a quitter, rather than a man of principle."[18]

The historic record indicates that ostracism, rather than respectability, is the probable reward for ethical autonomy. And ostracism—which makes strange bedfellows—could propel us into new alliances of necessity, or unwelcome identification in the public mind, with others of the ostracized. We might even find ourselves enrolled in a new team that confronts us with worse ethical dilemmas.

When William Jennings Bryan resigned as Secretary of State in 1915 to campaign publicly against what he believed to be the hawklike tendencies of the Woodrow Wilson Administration, he had the greatest difficulty dissociating himself from the pro-German sympathizers in the U.S. who were only too happy to adopt him. They at first offered him large and enthusiastic audiences. At a massive rally in Madison Square Garden, just after the resignation, a fellow speaker remarked approvingly on the "German atmosphere"[19] and, outside, satellite rallies were being harangued in German. As Bryan, at subsequent appearances, strove to make clear that he blamed Germany as much as the Allies for the unnecessary European war, he found many of his early supporters defecting. The Sons of Teutons canceled his Chicago rally because he insisted on talking about "peace" rather than against the export of U.S. ammunition to Britain and France.[20] But the nation's press continued to dwell on Bryan's German supporters, implying that he had become the captive of a "disloyal" element.

Bryan's was the common conundrum of the individual who is unwilling to play ball in a ball-playing society. Yet America is more complex than that. It is also a society which celebrates its Puritan ethical origins, which clings precariously to a residual faith in individual initiative and personal responsibility. Twentieth-century American society is experiencing a profound and sometimes tense state of transition. An earlier, primarily Judaeo-Christian—and particularly Puritan—ethic imposed inescapable individual moral responsibility, an autonomy of moral obligation, that is enshrined in the Bill of Rights and has been made operational in the lonely, exciting adventure of pioneering the frontier. Today, this is in the way of being displaced by a new ethic that reflects the needs and conditions of an industrial urban age.

The organization ethic demands loyalty and acceptance of institutional tactics and policies in return for companionship, security, advancement, and the shared adventure of the common enterprise. The Judaeo-Christian-Puritan ethic demands a willingness to be alone and to go it alone. Both belief systems are formulated as ethical imperatives and it is in this excruciating tension between irreconcilables that individuals find themselves when they are at the breaking point.

At the political level, however, the dilemma of the individual at the breaking point is not only poignant but also becomes socially

significant. The most powerful of all teams is the group that popu-
lates the top policy-making echelons of the national executive. In
some countries this group is the cabinet, in others it is the executive council or secretariat of the all-powerful political party. In the
United States it is a small circle grouped around the Presidency:
senior cabinet and agency officials and White House aides who
owe their positions to Presidential favor, not to an election, nor, in
most cases, to any active role in party politics. The members of this
inner circle are not only the most powerful team in the world but,
usually, the most cohesive. How they behave at the breaking point
casts a revealing light on the current state of America's values and
on the condition of its government. When these officials cease to
see themselves as individually accountable to themselves and to
the public, the stage is set for the unchecked stumbling of the
Presidency from delusion to disaster.

Most American senior officials at their breaking point do not,
like Wayne Chatfield Taylor, march determinedly up the hill and
down again. They do not suffer the pain of backing down because
they do not write such a rash letter as Taylor's in the first place. If
they are tempted to speak up publicly, their temptation is stifled
before breaking the façade of equanimity modern men at the top
wear like impregnable armor. Moral outrage stands no chance
against the layers of conditioned bonhomie.

We have made corporate bonhomie central to our individual
self-definition, a defense against the terrors of anomie. And we
have made it the highest virtue of men who govern. Dean Acheson's early career is illustrative. Roosevelt had given him the post
of Under Secretary of the Treasury and he was a member of
F.D.R.'s inner circle of advisers with Rexford Tugwell, Raymond
Moley, Lewis Douglas, Charles Taussig, and Adolph Berle.[21] In
November 1933, however, Acheson and Roosevelt parted ways
over the President's gold-buying plan, a dollar-devaluating maneuver that required the complicity of the Treasury. "The action I was
asked to take," Acheson thought, "was without legal authorization."[22] In other words: illegal. He resisted it within the Adminis-

tration until F.D.R. decided to rid himself of the recalcitrant Under Secretary. Did Acheson then blow the whistle on the President? Unthinkable. The letter of resignation he wrote Roosevelt studiously avoided any trace of public dissent, noting, instead, that Treasury Secretary William H. Woodin's health would require him to take a long leave, and that the President "should have complete freedom of choice as to whom you will place in charge at the Treasury." This was sheer invention to cover up any public sign of disagreement, a calculated collusion in an act Acheson thought illegal. The letter speaks copiously of its author's appreciation for the opportunity to serve with Roosevelt, the many kindnesses bestowed on Acheson, and tenders "most sincere good wishes for the success of your administration in the years that lie ahead."[23]

As a model of discretion, the resignation was almost faultless.[24] The public came to hear that the Under Secretary of the Treasury had thought the government's gold transactions were unlawful only because a zealous partisan leaked some key office memos in the time-honored tradition of the U.S. political counterculture, a counterculture which flourishes because there is a demand for an element of honesty and integrity in government which the mores of ritual political behavior wholly fail to satisfy. Acheson, himself, was genuinely appalled when the truth was leaked, went out of his way to abjure responsibility for informing the public, and gradually persuaded F.D.R. that it was not he who had violated the team rules.[25]

When another official resigned less graciously, Roosevelt is reported to have growled to Steve Early, "Tell that man to go see Dean Acheson to learn how a gentleman resigns."[26] Acheson, hearing the story, thought it the greatest imaginable accolade since, to a man of his political tradition, "being a gentleman" was the most important of all qualifications for public service. In 1941, Roosevelt rewarded Acheson appropriately by making him Assistant Secretary of State.

Acheson had obviously been conscious of having confronted a serious question of principle; otherwise, he would not have resigned. Yet he so defined his ethical responsibility as only to require that he dissociate himself from the wrongdoing. He did not feel compelled to alert the public or openly to disavow the wrong-doer. It is this uneasy ethical compromise that is inherent in "resigning like a gentleman." For most Americans it comes easily, usually after only a few years in high office. If they want to leave a situation they find ethically untenable, they simply declare a need to replenish health, purse, or family life which has been exhausted in the public service. Often these standard reasons are part of the truth. But even if untrue, gentlemen swallow hard and recite, as convincingly as possible, the litany of bland resignation.

Only in rare cases does this practice, even when blatantly designed to deceive the public, appear to give the conscience or temperament of the departing official much difficulty. Yet it raises a question central to democracy. If a course of action is perceived to be so wrong, so unethical or ill-advised, as to warrant a person separating himself from those embarked upon it, is it not wrong—and undermining of faith in the whole system—to leave in such a way as to give the public the impression that all is well? The high government official who sees serious wrongdoing may justify staying on if he can thereby mitigate the effects of the evil. Or he may quit and "go public." But to resign in silence or with false reassurance to the public that there is nothing wrong may be the least ethically defensible course of all: the buying of a separate peace at the expense of the entire process of responsible government.

2

Fighting Back by Going Public

WE HAVE RECENTLY witnessed a dramatic instance of how a public-protest resignation can bring about important changes in government.

For three months, President Richard M. Nixon had steadfastly refused to allow tape recordings of key conversations held in his White House office to be released. The refusal applied equally to the Senate Watergate Committee, the Special Prosecutor in the Justice Department, the defendants in Watergate-related criminal actions, the federal grand juries investigating Watergate and campaign contribution abuses, the grand jury, prosecution or defendants in the ITT case, and even Federal District Court Judge John J. Sirica, whose right to the tapes had been upheld by the Federal Court of Appeals. Once Nixon chose not to appeal that judgment to the Supreme Court, his refusal became a violation of the law. Still the President stood firm.

But on October 23, 1973, he seemed to capitulate.[1] The White House suddenly decided to comply with the Sirica order. "This President," his counsel stated unblinkingly, "does not defy the law."[2]

This was a stunning abandonment of the hitherto stoutly defended claim of Executive Privilege. Out went the argument that the President has a historic duty to defend the privacy of the office as well as the confidentiality of the advice he receives. Gone was the claim that turning over the tapes would undermine this constitutional independence of the executive branch.

◇

This radical reversal was the climax of a dramatic week culminating in the "Saturday Night Massacre" of October 20–21, 1973. Three men—Special Prosecutor Archibald Cox, Attorney General Elliot L. Richardson, and Deputy Attorney General William D. Ruckelshaus—had openly defied the President in matters relating to the tapes. Cox had been fired, Richardson and Ruckelshaus had resigned. All three then publicly and clearly stated their case against the President.[3]

Richardson not only used the occasion to lay out his specific legal and political disagreement with the President for a vast television audience but located his resignation squarely in the broader context of maintaining "the very integrity of the governmental process."[4] In the final analysis, he said, his commitment to that integrity, which included a commitment to the independence of the Special Prosecutor, had to take priority over his duty to carry out Nixon's order to dismiss Cox. To this Ruckelshaus added that anyone in public life must always keep open "the option to resign" when there is "a fundamental disagreement" and that "there has to be a line over which any public official refuses to step." That line is inevitably reached when you are asked to do something "that your conscience simply will not permit. . . ."[5]

Richardson's resignation was not lightly entered into. Earlier, as Secretary of Health, Education, and Welfare he had seen his draft legislation—in the words of a close associate—"gutted" by the White House. Yet he had loyally soldiered on, fighting to get the best deal for his three subdepartments that an economy-minded President would support. Now, in the tapes crisis, it took Richardson two hours and a wastebasket full of false starts before he was satisfied that his resignation statement exactly expressed his feelings and beliefs.[6]

An estimated 3 million letters and telegrams reached Congress and the White House in support of his position, an unprecedented response which no one, including Richardson, had thought possible. This he attributed to a "hunger for a demonstration of willingness to draw a line on an issue of principle."[7]

But, in resigning, Richardson, while resisting efforts to make him say things more sensational than he intended, also had had to contend with the Administration's efforts to have him say nothing at all. These were not crude threats to his political future but much more effective appeals to the very sense of personal ethics which was prompting the resignation. Subtly calling on loyalty and gratitude, the President let Richardson know that he had been on the short list of five persons who would have been acceptable nominees for the Vice-Presidency. Nixon also saw to it that Richardson was shown the ultraconfidential Brezhnev letter that had triggered the world-wide armed forces alert of October 25, 1973. If he felt he must resign, Richardson was admonished, he must do so silently. This was a moment of great peril. The nation must not be divided nor the Presidency weakened. To Richardson, however, it was inconceivable that he should stay on, or leave without public utterance, when the ethical and constitutional issues were so great. Important principles have too often been sacrificed for the sake of "national security." Indeed, it was that sort of thing that had triggered Watergate. Furthermore, if it was so important to maintain unity in a world crisis, why had Nixon chosen this moment of Middle East war to fire Cox?

In the weeks that followed, Richardson spoke out forcefully about the "frightening glimpse of the abuse of power." As investigators "peeled back" the "layers of secrecy" it had become clear that the republic must act forcefully to stop the "embezzlement of political trust." He called for greater and unequivocal investigative efforts to account for the "gaps and omissions" and for a series of far-reaching but specific reforms to protect against "the invasion of privacy," the "improper use of political influence," as well as to make criminal the so-called pranks and dirty tricks which had become commonplace campaign abuses. He called for a Presidency of persons who were politically accountable to Congress and the people, rather than the present "excessive reliance on political amateurs who have not yet learned that it is not always smart to be smart."[8]

Ruckelshaus, too, had to assert his ethical autonomy against strong pressure to "play by the rules." Presidential Assistant Alexander M. Haig told him, in words recalling Morgenthau's lecture to Taylor, that "the President is Commander-in-Chief and all of us subordinates have to go down the line." He added: "It's your duty to fire Cox. Besides, how can you do this to the President, given the extreme danger the nation is facing in the Middle East?"[9] Like Richardson, Ruckelshaus was not intimidated.

Certain factors help to explain why the public-protest resignations of Richardson and Ruckelshaus were so successful in compelling the President to retreat. For Nixon, it was the beginning of the end. By October 1973, he was a wounded, vulnerable Chief Executive. Then, too, it helped that the issue precipitating the resignations was a relatively clear and straightforward one, readily understood by the public. Being intimately related to the Watergate scandal, the resignations also encountered no difficulty in attracting extensive media coverage. Since the central issue of the resignations was so directly within the resigners' area of responsibility and expertise, their views carried particular weight. Perhaps most significant, the circumstances under which Richardson and Ruckelshaus resigned made clear that they were not acting out of self-interest. They had not, themselves, been directly attacked but were sacrificing their careers to defend a colleague and, more important, a principle. Their evident integrity of purpose created an ideal backdrop for an appeal to the public conscience.

Even so, there were costs to be paid. Sudden withdrawal from a senior government post can cause a case of the sociocultural "bends." Life is not quite the same when there are no more important decisions to be made. When the chauffeured limousine no longer hovers at the door, doubts about the future creep in. Are the political bridges burned? What job out of government could replace the challenge of a cabinet post? Worst of all, there are the rumors that undermine the resigner's credibility. To balance all this, however, Richardson and Ruckelshaus had a very rare, quite solid achievement to their credit. They had asserted their ethical autonomy on a question of principle. They had succeeded in achieving, through public protest, a change in Presidential policy. And they had, at least for a moment, reasserted the integrity of the public political process.

There is only one other instance in the twentieth century of a public-protest resignation that compelled a President to retreat. Early in 1946, Interior Secretary Harold L. Ickes encountered what he believed to be an egregious breach of principle by the government of which he was a part. He resigned to take his fight before Congress and the people. Briefly, the issue arose over Truman's nomination of Indiana oilman Edwin W. Pauley to be Under Secretary of the Navy. Ed Pauley was an old Truman crony. A former treasurer of, and large contributor to, the Democratic party, he had led the dump-Wallace movement, thereby giving Truman his big chance at the Vice-Presidency. The reward was to be substantial. It was clear that the Under Secretaryship was only a first step. Truman intended Pauley soon to succeed Secretary James V. Forrestal.[10]

Ickes had made a great reputation in the Roosevelt Administration as the fearless, curmudgeonly defender of the public interest. As Secretary of the Interior, he had maintained a near-obsessive interest in the expansion and protection of public lands and a concomitant deep aversion to oil interests. It was Ickes who had initiated the federal government's battle to establish its title over the petroleum-rich tidelands, a move opposed by the producers who preferred to deal with more complaisant state governments. He was not pleased at the prospect of having an oilman in the cabinet at the very time when the tidelands fight was reaching its political and judicial climax.

On February 1, Ickes testified before the Senate Naval Affairs Committee on the Pauley appointment. Asked by Senator Charles W. Tobey, New Hampshire Republican, whether Pauley had ever tried to pressure Ickes to drop the tidelands suit, Ickes said "yes." He ostentatiously avoided endorsing Pauley's nomination.[11] Returning for further testimony on February 5, the Secretary revealed that Pauley had lobbied for tidelands oil interests even in the railroad car returning from Roosevelt's Hyde Park funeral the previous April, calling it the "rawest proposition that has ever been made to me." He also reported that Pauley had dangled a $300,000 offer from California oilmen before the Democrats in exchange for a promise to discontinue the tidelands litigation.[12]

Truman was furious. Here was a virtually unprecedented instance of a cabinet member obstructing the President's efforts to choose the members of his own Administration. The new President, in any case, was finding himself increasingly out of sympathy with the "ultra-liberal prima donnas" he had inherited from Roosevelt. And Ickes, in particular, he believed to be "no better than a common scold,"[13] an incorrigible gossip, and prime source of the detailed and all-too-accurate reports of cabinet meetings that filled Drew Pearson's newspaper column.[14] At his next press conference the President strongly backed Pauley, refused to withdraw the nomination, and said Ickes was plainly mistaken.[15].

Ickes, thus rebuffed, wrote a letter of resignation. Truman said it was "the sort of resignation a man sent in, knowing it would not be accepted"[16] and that "Honest Harold," who was always firing off letters of resignation, first to Roosevelt, then to him, was surprised when it was seized with alacrity. Denying Ickes' request for a six-week phase out, the President informed him "he could leave the next day."[17]

Ickes' resignation letter of February 12 is extraordinarily long. On seven pages of single-space typescript, it conjures up the Teapot Dome scandal to explain his opposition to Pauley. The "Department of the Interior must always be on guard," he wrote, "against any association of money with politics, and even over-zealous by the standards of some men, in defending the Government's legal proprietary rights." He spoke of "sinister pressures" and the need to protect the public "treasure."[18]

Instead of waiting for the White House to announce the resignation, Ickes called a press conference that was attended by 450 reporters, "the biggest ever."[19] The same evening at 10 o'clock he broadcast to the nation. "So, men and women of America," he said, "this is the way in which the problem presented itself to me. Should I have put the country first or the Administration first?"[20] He added, "I have to spend the rest of my life with Harold L. Ickes, and I could no longer, much as I regret it, retain my self-respect and stay in the cabinet of President Truman."[21] Referring to his Congressional testimony, he growled, "I don't care to stay in an Administration where I am expected to commit perjury for the sake of the party."[22] Truman, he reported, had told him before his appearance before the committee: "You must tell the truth, of course, but try to be as gentle as you can with Ed Pauley."[23]

The Chief Executive replied one day later that he could not believe that Ickes "had dared" to impugn his integrity.[24] Ickes' feisty reply: "I would dare to dispute the integrity of the President on any occasion that my country's welfare demanded it." A President "is neither an absolute monarch nor a descendant of a putative Sun Goddess."[25] He went on to criticize the President's "lack of adherence to the strict truth."[26]

The Pauley nomination, having become intensely controversial, was being discussed widely in the nation's press. Public attention focused on the conflict of interest that might arise if Pauley, as Assistant Secretary of the Navy, were in charge of buying large quantities of oil for the government. Also now widely debated were the larger questions of coastal conservation and the struggle between Washington and the states for control of the tidelands.

As the Senate hearings continued, Ickes broadened his offensive. In another broadcast he lambasted "the average class of appointments we have been getting lately" in government, adding, "we can't hope for very much in the way of leadership or good government"[27] from this Administration. He testified again before the Senate Committee about Pauley's "false statements under oath."[28]

"No honest man withdraws under fire," the embattled Pauley told the Committee on March 8,[29] but five days later, President

Truman withdrew the nomination, attributing his retreat to "the current hysteria."[30] It had become clear that the Committee would not vote its approval. "Your honor, integrity, fidelity to duty and capacity for public service have been completely established,"[31] Truman wrote Pauley, but clearly it was Ickes who had won. Pauley had to content himself with an ambassadorship to the Philippines.

Ickes' courage may, in part, be attributed to the fact that, at the age of seventy-one, he had little reason to fear the effects of his behavior on his future career. His was the sort of last hurrah Dylan Thomas might have had in mind when he wrote, "Old age should burn and rave at close of day." Had he been forty-five, the pressures to conform would have been far greater. Then, too, Ickes, who had behind him a long career of devoted service to President Roosevelt, had never quite transferred this loyalty to his new master.

Yet, briefly, America was treated to the edifying experience of a senior federal official publicly opposing the President in a matter of conscience and in a bold public assertion of his individual ethical responsibility. If there were a tradition of such behavior—and if it were expected that men would do their duty *first* to their consciences, *then* to the public process of the democracy, and only *third* to their political Commander-in-Chief—would the Presidential decisions pertaining to Vietnam and Watergate have been publicly challenged by those best positioned to challenge them? And would such challenges have helped save "the system" from its present public disrepute?

As in the case of Richardson and Ruckelshaus, the success of Ickes' resignation in forcing a change of policy was due, in part, to the favorable conjunction of circumstances in which the crisis arose. In 1946, Truman, too, was not a President with strong public support. The issue between him and Ickes was specific, relatively simple for the public to grasp, and concerned a matter intimately in Ickes' field. Like Richardson and Ruckelshaus, there was not the

◇

slightest chance of Ickes' motives being self-interested, nor hint of personal gain.

That public-protest resignations be free of suspicion of ulterior motive is a key factor in their effectiveness. When James A. Farley resigned as Postmaster General from Roosevelt's cabinet,[32] and as chairman of the Democratic party, he let it be known that he opposed Roosevelt's seeking an "unprecedented" third term. Farley's opposition to Roosevelt before the nominating convention took the form of making himself available as an alternate candidate, and it was generally believed that some anti-Roosevelt elements in the party had "tempted him with suggestions of preferment."[33] This fatally undermined Farley's credibility when he argued that his sole object was to preserve the unwritten constitutional convention against a third term.

Richardson's and Ickes' public-protest resignations demonstrate that a senior member of the executive branch of government, through well-timed and well-executed public-protest resignation, can sometimes alter Presidential policy. But the importance and success of a public-protest resignation cannot be measured solely by the distance it causes a President to retreat. When a cabinet member or a White House adviser finds his conscience in profound and unbridgeable conflict either with a specific Presidential decision or with the general direction of government policy, he has the opportunity to become a major focus of public opposition to it. He can bring to that role the prestige, factual knowledge, the undefinable but vital "feel" for political reality gained in a stint of top-level government service. He has an opportunity to elevate the level of democratic discourse, to enliven and enlighten a process which depends on competent and informed challenges to government as much as on government itself. He can stimulate and concentrate the public consciousness while introducing new alternatives into the marketplace of ideas. Thus the system benefits, quite regardless of whether the protest resigner and his followers actually do succeed in changing a particular policy, or whether their policy is, indeed, better for the country.[34]

Webster Davis was one of those protest resigners whose cause may not endear him to posterity and who failed to reverse U.S. policy, but whose willingness to take a public stand on an issue of conscience drew the attention of the American people to an important but little-noticed foreign-policy issue, thereby taking it out of the discreet inner chambers of the bureaucracy and raising it to the level of informed public debate.

At the age of thirty-three, Davis had already won the mayoralty of Kansas City. When William McKinley ran for President, Davis campaigned for him, displaying an oratorical style compared to that of McKinley's opponent, William Jennings Bryan, whom he peculiarly resembled in appearance. McKinley rewarded Davis by appointing him Assistant Secretary of the Interior, then the number-two post in that key department. But by 1900 he had resigned and launched a national campaign that took him all over the country, out of the Republican and into the Democratic party, and to the brink of personal scandal.

Davis's breaking point appears to have been reached while on what he described as a "nerve mending" vacation[35] to South Africa. Even for someone subject to the rough political life of Washington, it seems odd to have chosen that country, then in the midst of the Boer War, to recuperate. In any event, what Davis saw persuaded him "to do everything in my power to arouse the American government and the American people to sympathize with the Boer patriots. . . ."[36]

The McKinley Administration was far from sympathetic to the Boers. Secretary of State John Hay was openly pursuing "the most friendly relations with England."[37] McKinley needed England's benign acquiescence in various U.S. initiatives: the Panama Canal, Cuba, Puerto Rico, the Philippines, against the European blockade of Venezuela and on China policy.[38] Undoubtedly there were also those, high in the Administration, who saw the Boers as racial bigots, obsessed with narrow Calvinism, people who had only recently been forced by the British to abandon slavery and were now fighting to restore, in Kruger's words, "proper relations between master and servant."[39] Although Davis's affection for the Boers seems to have been based on a mixture of support for the underdog and anti-imperialism, his enemies could hardly be faulted for discerning in his writings evidence that he had also swallowed Boer racism.[40]

Attacking the dominant pro-British views within the McKinley Administration, Davis battled to secure a change. "After learning the actual state of affairs" in Washington, he wrote, "I concluded to lay aside all political prospects and all personal ambitions and follow the dictates of . . . conscience. . . ." He resigned on April 3, 1900. "It became with me a matter of heart and conscience," he said, "and a perfect knowledge of being in the right."[41]

Immediately after resigning, on April 8, Davis addressed a rally at the Grand Opera House, then the largest auditorium in Washington. To an "immense" audience[42] which included seven senators and fourteen congressmen,[43] he painted a glowing picture of the Boer people and their struggle: "these men have the same spirit that prompted the farmers to face death at Lexington Green for liberty, that nerved the arms of Americans at Saratoga, Bunker Hill and Brandywine, that warmed hearts of Washington and his shivering patriots at Valley Forge, and at New Orleans where Jackson and his men taught old England that easier were it to hurl the rooted mountain from its base than to force the yoke of slavery upon men determined to be free."[44]

The passionate two-hour oration at Washington was followed the next day with an equal display of eloquence at the Academy of Music in Philadelphia. The public began to respond. A message of support signed by 30,000 Philadelphia schoolboys was presented to him for dispatch to Afrikaaner President Kruger.[45]

Davis's switch from the Republican to the Democratic party, in this Presidential election year, led to rumors that he had Vice-Presidential ambitions.[46] Of the Republicans he said: "When the party that I belong to has been too cowardly to take a stand for liberty . . . I leave it and leave it for good.''[47] While the Democratic party did not offer him their Vice-Presidential nomination, it did adopt a strongly pro-Boer plank.

At the convention, Davis made one of the key speeches nominating Bryan. He firmly hoisted the anti-imperialist colors, attacking the government not only for its South African but also for its expansionist Caribbean policies. America, he charged, instead of liberating Spanish territories, had proceeded to amass an empire of its own.[48] Throughout the campaign Davis developed his anti-imperialist theme, applying it with some courage even to the United States. "The Philippine war involves the colonial idea. . . . If the acts of the British in South Africa are wrong, then our acts at Manila are also wrong. The colonial tendency, which is the cause of both wars, must be checked.''[49] In this context, he continued to attack the Administration's "secret friendship" for Britain, the "whole Anglo-American humbug.''[50] The Hay-Pauncefote Treaty, he averred, "meant the surrender of American rights and interests" to imperial Britain.[51] In Omaha, on August 25, his personal crusade reached its climax when he shared the platform with Bryan in a spectacular oratorical twin bill to call for freedom not only for the Boers but also for Cuba, Puerto Rico, and the Philippines.

From the beginning of Davis's defection, he became fair game for attacks which eventually eroded his credibility. Even when he had first set out for South Africa, the press had already begun to report rumors that he would never resume his duties, that there had been serious friction and jealousies between him and Secretary Ethan A. Hitchcock as well as others in the Interior Department.[52] The government, it was reported, thought his visit to the Transvaal "might be misrepresented" and ought to be abandoned.[53]

Once Davis resigned and began to campaign, the game got rougher. On September 13, a former Interior employee, Gustave Thielkuhl, charged Davis with disloyalty and fraud. He reported that the Assistant Secretary, even before his trip to South Africa, had engaged him as "a mask" to recruit large numbers of "able-bodied men with military experience" to go from the U.S. to fight for the Boer republics, promising them shares of stock in the Kimberley Diamond Mines as compensation.

The Department had become suspicious of his recruiting activities, Thielkuhl reported, and for a while Davis, as his superior, covered up for him. When the scheme became so noticeable as to attract the attention of Secretary Hitchcock, Davis advised Thielkuhl to resign, promising to take care of him, but, he complained, "I have never received any compensation from Mr. Davis or any other person for my services. . . ."[54]

In October, President McKinley's close friend and supporter, Senator Mark Hanna, charged that Davis had received $125,000 in gold from the Boers to be their advocate in America. It is very unlikely that Hanna would have made the charge without McKinley's approval. Davis, in turn, called the Senator a "willful, malicious liar." It was not surprising, he added, that the McKinley Administration and its supporters would try to silence his attacks on the British. "I knew when I turned against . . . the present trust-owning, British-sympathizing American administration . . . that I would be accused of all manner of crimes."[55]

Davis did not succeed in electing Bryan or in turning United States policy to support of the Boers. In his mid-thirties, his promising public career came to an irrevocable end, the price of having chosen to resign and become a public crusader. Yet it was a conscious choice Davis had made, one not unmindful of the probable cost and certainly not without a splash of splendor, no matter the faults of the cause in which he chose to immerse himself. "How often in this life do we realize its brevity?" he wrote on returning from South Africa.

Money and power soon pass away. Fame is but the will-o'-the-wisp of an overheated imagination. The sweet lullaby heard by the baby boy upon his mother's knee is soon replaced by the solemn funeral dirge for the old white-haired man as he is laid to rest in the quiet cemetery. And in this world each fond ideal that gleams like a star on life's wave is soon wrecked on the shores of the real and soon sleeps like a dream in a grave. This being true, we have only time in this life to do something for our country's glory, and something, however small it may be, for the betterment of the conditions of our fellowmen.[56]

William Jennings Bryan was, in some ways, Webster Davis writ large. More significantly, Bryan is America's most dramatic instance of a public-protest resignation in the twentieth century, for, although he resigned from the Wilson cabinet sixty years ago, the issues he raised so eloquently remain central to our contemporary political life.

Bryan, more than any other U.S. public figure, illustrates the functions of the public-protest resignation:

—to expose an unconscionable government policy;

—to draw the public's attention to the importance of a hidden or insufficiently debated issue;

—to supply the public with the "inside" information necessary to an informed debate; and

—to obtain a reversal of the objectionable policy through legitimate political action.

Bryan succeeded dramatically in the first three, but, like Davis, did not attain the fourth objective. Nevertheless, the issues raised by Bryan concerning America's foreign-policy role, unlike those raised by Davis, are still unresolved and still on America's agenda. Bryan's views and insights remain highly relevant. While the Great Commoner did not succeed in keeping America out of World War I, it is too early to say that the alternative foreign policy he put before the public has been finally rejected.

For the first year of the Administration, Bryan, as Secretary of State, surprised even President Wilson with his cooperativeness.[57] As Wilson's subordinate, the three-time Presidential nominee, who had never worked for another man, demonstrated an unexpected ability to function in tandem.

The European war changed all this. The pacifist in Bryan and his passionate interest in mediation made him begin to appear pro-German against the background of a cabinet and White House of various hues of Anglophilia. His penchant for private peace schemes and initiatives seemed naïve to the hard-nosed professionals in his own department as well as to his colleagues in the cabinet. The sinking of the *Lusitania*, on May 7, inflated the issue. In this tragedy, 1153 noncombatants died, including 128 Americans. The *Lusitania* did carry munitions, it turned out. But the lawyers in the State Department argued that the Germans had nevertheless violated an obligation to stop, search, or at least warn the vessel and afford the passengers a reasonable chance to enter lifeboats.

In the struggle over how to respond to the *Lusitania* disaster, some, like Theodore Roosevelt, called for war. Robert Lansing, then Bryan's counselor at State, also took a strong line. He thought the Germans should be made to apologize and pay compensation. War Secretary Lindley M. Garrison was a hawk, Colonel Edward M. House, at the White House, an Anglophile. In the negotiations over the contents of the note, Bryan was almost wholly isolated by the group around Wilson. Still, he continued to urge that the U.S. do no more than propose arbitration. Briefly Wilson agreed, then changed his mind under pressure of other counsel.

The note which finally was dispatched to Germany was sent, as appropriate, in the name of the Secretary of State. But it was a message of which Bryan strongly disapproved. It asserted the right of U.S. citizens to travel on the vessels of belligerents and held the Germans to "strict accountability for any infringement of those rights, intentional or incidental."[58] Anguished, Bryan wrote Wilson: "Mr. President, I join in this document with a heavy heart."[59] But he went along with the group. His only other option would have been to resign, and this he was reluctant to do as long as there seemed a reasonable chance to influence Wilson toward peace from inside the cabinet.

The German response to the *Lusitania* note was a firm assertion of the right of self-defense. Berlin pointed out that the vessel had been a carrier of munitions and Canadian troops,[60] and added that its rapid sinking and heavy loss of life were due not to the torpedo but to the exploding of munitions being covertly carried on board. "Otherwise, in all human probability, the passengers of the *Lusitania* would have been saved."[61] There was no hint of compensation, no acknowledgment of guilt, no contrite promise of future good conduct.

During the next few days, Bryan continued to implore Wilson to promote conciliation and to draft a soft reply. But the President had made up his mind.[62] On June 4, the cabinet met once more and discussed what was, by now, the President's draft note. It contained Lansing's, rather than Bryan's, suggestions. After the meeting, Bryan informed the President that he would resign.

Wilson sent his son-in-law, William G. McAdoo, the Secretary of the Treasury, to try to convince Bryan to change his mind. He warned that Bryan's long career would end with this resignation. The Great Commoner remained unmoved by the pressure. "I believe you are right," he said. "I think this will destroy me; but whether it does or not, I must do my duty according to my conscience, and if I am destroyed, it is, after all, merely the sacrifice that one must not hesitate to make to serve his God and his country."[63] By liberating himself of the constraints of office, using his undoubted forensic skills, appealing once again to the people, Bryan believed he could change Wilson's assessment of what the public wanted.

The letter of resignation, dated June 8, 1915, made clear Bryan's desire to advocate pacifist policies that would place him in opposition to the government: " . . . you have prepared for transmission to the German Government," he wrote to Wilson, "a note in which I cannot join without violating what I deem to be an obligation to my country, and the issue involved is of such moment that to remain a member of the Cabinet would be as unfair to you as it would be to the cause which is nearest to my heart, namely the prevention of war." Wilson replied, expressing "deep regret" and "personal sorrow."[64]

That very evening, Bryan began his public campaign to vindicate himself and his antiwar views. Not for him the silent escape to a friend's hidden estate. Instead, he met the press at his leased home in Georgetown. "No man with the President's convictions could have done other than he has done," he told the reporters, "nor would I have done otherwise. A man can only do what he believes to be right. . . . Finally we agreed to disagree. . . . Our relations are still extremely cordial."[65]

The day after his resignation, Bryan issued a statement entitled "The Real Issue." This, its author asserted, was whether the United States should follow a system of international relations based on force or on persuasion. "Force represents the old system . . . persuasion represents the new. . . . The new system contemplates an universal brotherhood established through the uplifting power of example."[66] He emphasized the danger of being drawn into the old war system: "Already the jingoes of our own countries have caught the rabies from the dogs of war. . . ."[67]

On June 11, Bryan addressed a message to German-Americans. One of its features was a reasoned analysis of the responsibility of ethnic Americans in a crisis between their countries of origin and adoption. Though criticizing German submarine warfare and urging Berlin to agree to the U.S. note, the message also indicated that the Second Reich might be justified in asking for new rules of international transport which would bar neutral citizens from traveling on belligerent ships carrying war supplies.[68] Today, that opinion is wholly unexceptionable; then, many regarded it as treason.

Every day for a week after his resignation, Bryan produced a major essay on the issues facing the nation. In several he attacked the advocates of preparedness in terms that continue to have currency today. "Instead of preventing war, preparedness provokes war, because it is impossible to coerce the people into bearing the burdens incident to continuous and increasing preparation without cultivating hatred as if it were a national virtue. . . . Each step taken by one nation toward more complete preparedness excites the other nations to additional purchases and new levies, until all have exhausted their productive industries and menaced their moral progress."[69] Most newspapers vilified or tried to ignore

Bryan's arguments, but his messages continued to pour forth and to command national attention.

In a series of speeches around the country, beginning in Carnegie Hall, New York, on June 20, he took his crusade for peace to huge crowds. Madison Square Garden, three days later, was jammed to capacity and Madison Avenue was packed from curb to curb from Twenty-third to Twenty-seventh Streets with an enthusiastic overflow estimated at well over 100,000 persons. All that summer Bryan continued to address rallies: the Friends of Peace at the Medinah Temple in Chicago, 122,000 at the Panama Pacific Exposition in San Francisco, 40,000 at the National League Baseball Park in Boston. He attacked the loans being made by U.S. banks to the British government as violations of neutrality and "a gamble on the war."[70] Then on to rallies at Jacksonville, Atlanta, and tours of Texas, Tennessee, and Arkansas. Of Wilson, he continued to speak always as a man of peace.

From October on, Bryan devoted most of his attention to campaigning against proposals for massive rearmament and induction into the armed forces. "I have travelled over considerable part of the country," he said, "and I find that the taxpayers are not as badly scared as the people who manufacture munitions. . . ."[71] He called for a national referendum prior to any move toward war, and insisted that women, still disenfranchised, be included.[72] In New York, speaking before the National Educational Association, he attacked efforts to introduce military training in the schools.[73]

When Wilson outlined his preparedness program at the Manhattan Club, Bryan responded at once: "The spirit that makes the individual carry a revolver—and whoever carries a revolver except for defense?—leads him not only to use it on slight provocation, but to use language which provokes trouble."[74] He continued to profess allegiance to President Wilson,[75] but *The New York Times* thundered "flagrant disloyalty."[76] Why, Bryan demanded, should his loyalty as a Democrat and citizen be questioned on such an issue? But it certainly was. "Peace-at-any-price promoters headed by William J. Bryan" became the announced target of the American Defense Society, an Eastern Establishment group including ex-President Roosevelt and ex-secretaries of the Navy Truman H. Newberry and Charles J. Bonaparte.[77] Both Wilson and Roosevelt enlisted the prophet Ezekiel in the cause of preparedness, quoting his injunction that the watchman must sound the trumpet when he sees the sword come upon the land.

"I have read the quotation," Bryan growled in reply. "It is not surprising that Mr. Roosevelt should consult the Old Testament rather than the New, because he would class Jesus with the molly-coddles. But why should the President, a Presbyterian Elder, pass over the new Gospel, in which love is the chief cornerstone, and build his defense upon a passage on the Old Testament, written at a time when the Children of Israel were surrounded by enemies?" The United States is not surrounded. "What the world needs today is a Pentecost, not an Armageddon."[78]

By February 1916, Bryan was actively encouraging Congress to pass the McLemore resolution warning Americans not to travel on belligerents' ships and disclaiming U.S. responsibility for them if they persisted. Wilson strongly opposed the resolution as appeasement of Germany and, especially, as an invasion of the executive prerogative in foreign relations. "If Congress has the right to declare war," Bryan replied, "it certainly has the right to promote peace by restraining citizens from taking unnecessary risks."[79] It was only with greatest difficulty that Wilson was able to get the resolution tabled by the House.[80]

In April 1916, Bryan had his first chance to test the efficacy of his antipreparedness campaign with the voters. He fared badly. Running in the Nebraska primary, he failed, by 3300 votes, to secure one of the state's four places at the Democratic National Convention. Yet, the test was far from a clear-cut referendum on preparedness. While Bryan pressed this issue with the German voters of the state, the liquor interests weighed in heavily with attacks on his prohibitionist commitments. In the cities of Omaha and Lincoln, love of beer and schnapps appears to have outpolled any residual sentiment for the fatherland. Moreover, with Bryan now located primarily in Florida and campaigning all over the country, his Nebraska political fences had too long gone untended.

Whatever the reasons for the defeat, it would have devastated a less resilient man. Not so Bryan. He went to the convention anyway (on a press pass) and received repeated ovations from the floor. The bored delegates demanded to hear from their great orator. Despite evident reluctance, the convention managers could not but summon him from the press box to the platform.

The managers need not have been afraid of his loyalty. In what many thought was his finest speech, Bryan, with great political acumen, exuded admiration of Wilson and unity with the Democratic party. In so doing, he was able to set the theme for the convention and for the campaign: "I join the people in thanking God that we have a President who does not want the nation to fight."[81] Speaker after speaker followed Bryan to emphasize the peace theme. Wilson found himself, quite contrary to his personal inclination, running for re-election on a slogan engineered by Bryan: "He kept us out of war." It was a brilliant strategy of tactical cooperation.

Thereafter, Bryan campaigned for Wilson throughout the Middle West as if the President were the Apostle of Peace. The campaign took Bryan to nineteen states, and Wilson won in fourteen of them. Lest Wilson fail to appreciate the debt he owed his erstwhile critic, Bryan telegraphed the re-elected candidate: "I am proud of the West, including Nebraska. The states beyond the Missouri have rallied to your support and saved the day, and in doing so have honored themselves no less than you. They have been largely benefited by the great reforms secured under your leadership and they stand with you for peace, prosperity and progress."[82] In December, Wilson did, indeed, attempt the strategy of conciliation Bryan had so long recommended. Undoubtedly, he did so with less than total conviction, his doubts fed by strongly negative advice from the State Department. Still, Wilson felt he had to try. He asked the warring sides to outline the minimal terms on which they would be willing to end the fighting. Bryan was ecstatic. "You have rendered an invaluable service to a war-stricken world," he wired.[83]

But it was too late. German U-boat warfare had redoubled, sinking three unarmed U.S. merchantmen with the loss of thirty-six lives. Bryan continued to call for peaceful settlement, investigation, conciliation, arbitration. But the country's mood had changed. On April 6, 1916, Congress adopted the war resolution and Bryan's campaign ended.

◇

When an issue becomes "moot"—as does a campaign for neutrality once the country has gone to war—the official who resigned in order to press that issue is out of business. Even when his issue is still viable, however, it is a problem for the protester to keep it, and himself, before the public. A resignation is news, but what a resigner has to say six months after his resignation tends to be discounted by editors as the fulminations of a frustrated former officeholder. One way to avoid this premature obsolescence is for the resigner to legitimize his continued public campaign by creating a new role for himself within the system of party politics. This is why Bryan campaigned for Wilson and sought to retain his role in the Democratic National Convention. While not the only possible platform from which a resigned official can continue to address the nation, the political party or movement is more acceptable to the public and media, and a much more efficient way of handling the finances and logistics of a public crusade than, say, the presidency of a university.

All resigners who choose to carry their campaigns to the public, and to do so over a long haul, must calculate whether they can sustain their effort without the aid of an organized political party. It is not an easy thing, financially and operationally, to wage a lengthy campaign, alert the public, and reverse a national policy, without some such organizational backing. Webster Davis dealt with this problem by changing parties and becoming a leading spokesman of the institutionalized Opposition. William Jennings Bryan stayed in the party which formed the Administration from which he had resigned in protest; but he led a personal opposition from within its ranks. He concentrated on the party platform, on capturing control of the Presidential campaign—its spirit, if not its machinery. Neither man, after resigning, was primarily interested in party politics but each recognized the instrumental importance of the party to the task of getting his message across to the public and to policy-makers.

Henry A. Wallace, a one-time Republican, son of a Republican cabinet member and a convert to the Roosevelt New Deal, tried to resolve the resigner's problem of locating an institutional base by forming a new political party and running for President on its platform. Although he, too, failed to turn the country around or to reverse the cold-war policies of the Truman Administration, Wallace raised issues which became an important part of a continuing debate about American foreign policy, particularly in regard to the Soviet Union.

In one respect, Wallace does not belong in this discussion of public-protest resigners, for he did not, strictly, volunteer his resignation. Nevertheless, the distinction between the conduct of Wallace—who was fired by President Truman—and Ickes, who was allowed to resign, is more formal than real. Both chose to act as ethically autonomous men, to follow their consciences into a public confrontation with the will of the Chief of State and the policy of the Presidential team.

Truman had come to dislike Wallace, if possible, even more than Ickes.[84] This was practically inevitable since both men knew that Truman's selection as Roosevelt's running mate in 1944 had deprived Wallace of the Presidency he would otherwise have inherited a year later. But the disagreements were ideological as well as personal. Truman saw Wallace as a long-winded, confused, wishful thinker who believed that trouble with Russia in the immediate postwar years was preponderantly America's fault. Wallace, in turn, anticipated the revisionist historians of the 1970s in believing that the cold war was Truman's and Churchill's fault and that peace could be advanced by unilateral destruction of

America's nuclear stockpile. He advocated negotiating with the Russians from less strength and more flexibility.

In particular, Wallace opposed the Administration's policy of encircling the Soviets with U.S. military bases. Even while still in office, he began to speak up in opposition. When James F. Byrnes, the Secretary of State, was secretly negotiating for an American base in Iceland, Wallace's public denunciation blocked the agreement for a time.[85] Truman called it "sabotage."[86] In July 1946, Wallace sent Truman a twelve-page document in which he excoriated his Chief's foreign policy on nuclear testing, the negotiations for bases, and large expenditures for bombers. These, he said, made it appear that we were either preparing to win a war we regarded as inevitable or were trying to build up a "predominance of force to intimidate the rest of mankind."[87] Truman replied with ill-disguised sarcasm: "I appreciate your taking the time. . . . I have been giving this entire subject a great deal of thought and I shall continue to do so." In mid-September, Wallace reported that the memo had somehow fallen into the hands of Drew Pearson, and White House aide Charlie Ross then allowed himself to be panicked into authorizing its general release to newsmen. But it was the prevalent White House opinion that Wallace himself had deliberately leaked the memo to Pearson in the first place.[88]

Public protest or public maneuvers in opposition to Presidential policy cannot for long be undertaken by senior government officials without their being fired. This is generally understood, so that conduct like that of Wallace is really "departure behavior," regardless of whether the President, or his critic, is the one to cut the last tie. On September 10 the Secretary visited Truman and showed him the text of a speech he planned to give in New York two days later. The President skimmed it quickly, noted that it contained many criticisms of Russia, and seemed a balanced presentation. Wallace pointed to the key sentence: "I am neither anti-British nor pro-British—neither anti-Russian nor pro-Russian." Truman said he thought that was fine.

Two days later, Wallace released his text and reported Truman's approval. At the Presidential press conference that day, a reporter told Truman that in the middle of Wallace's speech were the words: "When President Truman read these words, he said that they represented the policy of this Administration."

"That is correct," Truman said.

The reporter persisted: "Does that apply just to that paragraph or to the whole speech?"

"I approved the whole speech," Truman replied.[89]

Whether Truman had made a mistake in not reading the speech more carefully, or whether, as the White House came to believe, Wallace double-crossed the President by changing the text substantially after it had been approved, the consequences were dire. Truman found himself on record endorsing what he too late realized was a "wildly pro-Russian" speech[90] from which the balancing criticisms of Stalin had largely been deleted. Senator Arthur H. Vandenberg, at the Paris Peace Conference with Secretary Byrnes, angrily told him that "the Republican party could only co-operate with one Secretary of State at a time."[91] Byrnes, too, was furious. Truman, deeply embarrassed, released a lame "clarification" that he had not approved the contents of the speech but merely Wallace's right to make it.[92]

The President interviewed Wallace on September 18, concluding that "the German-American Bund under Fritz Kuhn was not half so dangerous." He thought he had at least extracted a vow of silence from his Secretary for the duration of the Paris talks, but this new meeting, too, was fully reported in the press that afternoon.[93] Exasperated, Truman fired Wallace. "It has become clear," he told the press, "that between his views on foreign policy and those of the administration . . . there was a fundamental conflict."[94]

Thus released from formal inhibitions, Wallace became more voluble in his attacks on the bipartisan foreign policy of President Truman, Secretary of State Byrnes, and Senator Vandenberg. In due course, he became the fulcrum of a popular third-party movement and, in 1948, a candidate for President, forcefully putting his views to the public. Truman scornfully called it "the American Crackpots Association."[95]

Wallace, himself, had doubts about its efficacy as a vehicle for advancing his alternative foreign policy. Both before and after his resignation, he commented that a third party could not hope to succeed nationally but would, instead, drain off support from Democratic candidates.[96] Gradually, his position changed as he realized that, with a Presidential election coming in 1948, and with the Republican and Democratic parties welded into a tweedledum and tweedledee bipartisan foreign policy, only a third-party candidacy could hope to present the voters with a meaningful discussion of the crucial war-and-peace issues. By the end of December 1946, he had rallied around him the newly formed Progressive Citizens of America, a merger of liberal and radical groups with what were at first described as "third-party possibilities."[97] Exactly one year later, on December 30, 1947, he announced for the Presidency on a third-party ticket, a party "to fight [the] war-makers" and to show that the United States "is not behind the bipartisan reactionary war policy which is dividing the world into two armed camps and making inevitable the day when American soldiers will be lying in their Arctic suits in the Russian snow."[98]

Before and during his Progressive party candidacy, Wallace developed a coherent set of foreign-policy proposals. In the pages of the *New Republic,* whose editor he had become, and in countless mass rallies and radio speeches, he voiced his disagreement with Truman's and Byrnes's assessment of Soviet motives and objectives. Wallace argued for steps not to contain but to reassure the Kremlin. "The tougher we get, the tougher the Russians will get," he warned.[99] The Truman Doctrine, in giving "unconditional aid" to anti-Soviet governments like the Greek and Turkish regimes, would "unite the world against America and divide America against herself."[100] Instead, he urged that all foreign aid should be channeled through the United Nations.

Senator John L. McClellan charged that Wallace was "irrevocably aligning himself with the totalitarian forces of communistic aggression. . . . No living American has done a greater disservice to his country. . . ."[101] And there were calls in Congress for the revocation of Wallace's passport and for his prosecution under the Logan Act.[102] Nevertheless, he continued to insist that unilateral concessions to Russia alone would reverse the slide to war and evoke a favorable Russian response. "We ought to stop making atomic bombs," he insisted. "If we continue to make [them], Russia will naturally continue to throw every kind of obstacle in the way of efforts to reach agreement."[103] As for bases, "When we build airfields in northern Turkey, Russia may feel as we should feel if she built airfields in Mexico."[104] Domestically, he condemned the "war and anti-communism hysteria," insisting, "if there is a genuine emergency, the people have a right to an explanation" and, if not, then the prevalent war-mongering and communist-baiting "rates as the very lowest method of breeding fear."[105]

In the national election, Wallace secured no electoral votes but over a million people cast their ballots for him. Although the public did not flock to his standard, the 1948 election was the last, until 1972, in which the American people were offered a clear-cut choice between quite distinct and openly debated foreign policies.

◇

Davis, Bryan, and Wallace each represent a gutsy, scrappy Middle Western political style which differs from, and sometimes grates on the ears of, the more staid Eastern Establishmentarians. Each preached a populist anti-imperialism. Each struggled to stay in politics even while resigning office. Each displayed qualities of the successful lay preacher. Even so, none are typical Middle Westerners. Wallace was the son of a cabinet member; Davis, although identified with Kansas, was born in rural Pennsylvania and was educated at the University of Michigan; Bryan had achieved considerable affluence and maintained grand homes in Florida and Washington. Yet each had about him something of the soil, the Bible, and the town meeting. Above all, each had a faith in the ability of the common people to change the course of the republic once they had heard the truth. To all three, God and the people were their only jury. They believed in this jury, placed their destiny in its hands, and, with passionate conviction, gave the people every opportunity to hear all the evidence before deciding.

Somewhat in the same tradition was another Westerner: Lewis W. Douglas, who quit as Roosevelt's Director of the Bureau of the Budget in defense of the gold standard and against what he perceived to be the President's inflationary and fiscally unsound experiments with the dollar. Douglas, a pugnacious Arizona millionaire, spoke up repeatedly and at length after his resignation[106] and became the focus of continuing opposition, particularly among academic economists. In his old age, he continued to deplore the prevalence among Presidential advisers of men who "try not to give any serious offense" and who "never raise their voice except to chorus assent."[107] It is to this "faceless, conscienceless" breed that he later attributed the ethical pratfalls of the Nixon Administration, long before its failings were generally recognized.

At the other end of this geographical, stylistic, and ideological spectrum are Lindley Garrison, John L. Sullivan, and Kenneth N. Davis, Jr. They came out of a different culture and ethic, that of the Eastern lawyer: quiet, dignified, abhorring a raised voice, conscious that the real decisions get made in executive offices, board rooms, Senate committee chambers, and not at mass rallies at the Cow Palace. Not that they were soft, "effete Easterners." Both Garrison and Sullivan were tenacious, even passionate advocates. They resigned feeling as deeply outraged as did Bryan, Webster Davis, or Wallace. They cared enough not to stay on, not to leave quietly. But although they resigned in open protest, their style is that of men inhibited by a deep caring about what their friends at the Cosmos Club in Washington will say about them afterward, because it is here, rather than in the streets and fields of America, that they recognize their jury.

Lindley Garrison exemplifies the Eastern style of ethical autonomy. He had been appointed Secretary of War by Wilson sight unseen. The President knew him only by reputation but fell back in embarrassment on Joseph P. Tumulty's advice after his own choice for the job, A. Mitchell Palmer, had inconveniently turned out to be a Quaker pacifist.[108] He proved to be an industrious, articulate cabinet member, whose advice, even in areas outside his domain, was invariably based on extensive homework.

Garrison believed that national-defense expenditures were "the premium on a fire insurance policy. . . ."[109] He welcomed Bryan's resignation, having differed with him not only over preparedness and the German notes, but over U.S. "imperialism" in Mexico and the Philippines. A favorite of the Eastern Establishment and its press, Garrison did not hesitate to threaten the President with resignation whenever Wilson seemed to lean too close to Bryan's pacificism.[110]

Garrison's problems with the antipreparedness movement did not end with Bryan's resignation. The peace forces were strong in Congress, and their strength was augmented by congressmen who, for reasons not always related to pacificism, were opposed to the drastic program of military enlistment and rearmament favored by Garrison. The clashes between the Secretary and Congress soon began to embarrass Wilson. "Secretary Garrison has frankly torn off all disguise, disclosing the real purpose which is in his mind, that of placing the United States for the first time under complete military control," Congressman Warren Bailey exclaimed in horror after hearing Garrison testify for higher military expenditures.[111] Garrison's vice was an excess of virtue, of loyalty to and respect for the technical judgments of his military staff advisers, whose causes he championed not wisely but too well, without regard for the necessary art of political log-rolling.[112]

On January 6, 1916, Garrison appeared before the House Committee on Military Affairs, chaired by Congressman James Hay of Virginia, to testify for the Administration's proposals to fund a new Continental "citizens'" Army. However, he imprudently admitted that his scheme would lead to the eclipse of the states' militias.[113] This candor departed from the careful Wilson strategy of making the federal scheme appear to enhance the role of the states' National Guard. It also made inevitable the hostility of the Committee's majority and of Hay in particular. Writing to a not unsympathetic Wilson, Chairman Hay candidly reported that "[m]any southern members fear [the Continental Army plan] because they believe it will be the means of enlisting large numbers of negroes."[114]

The fears of the antimilitarists and the Southerners were further aroused when Garrison returned on January 8 for a second day of testimony.

"Is it not the opinion of military men that the continental scheme will be a failure, and that its failure will lead to compulsory military training?" asked Congressman John C. McKenzie of Illinois.

"Yes, if I may speak for what is in the minds of others," replied the guileless Garrison. He added that in his own opinion, the Continental Army plan was to be the final test for a volunteer force and that if it failed, some system of compulsory training would follow.[115] Tumulty ruefully noted that the President, in campaigning around the country for preparedness, had "never employed the term 'universal military service'" and carefully steered away from anything that would link the Administration's proposals to conscription. For that, he was convinced, the country was not ready.[116]

Pouncing on Garrison's admissions, Chairman Hay wrote Wilson that it was amply apparent, even to those in the War Department who were urging it, that the Administration's Continental Army plan was not feasible and was being advanced as the nose of the conscription camel.[117] As Garrison continued to fight for a Continental Army, burdening that fight with increasingly clear calls for conscription to ensure the desired 400,000 recruits, Wilson was quietly disengaging from the whole scheme and working out a private deal with Hay. "I feel we are under a sort of obligation to each other," Wilson wrote the Chairman, "to keep one another posted." He thereupon reported that he had informed Garrison that while he still favored creating a reserve force under federal control, "I did not consider myself irrevocably or dogmatically committed to any one plan. . . ."[118]

While Wilson was making his peace with the Committee, Garrison, at a meeting of the New York Bankers' Association, attacked the "sham" plan for federal support of states' militias being proposed as an alternative to his own. "Such a solution, of course, appeals to every pacifico, to every politico, and to all those who see therein an opportunity to divert Federal funds to local purposes." The advocates of this alternative "realize that if they can deceive the people into believing that these proposals provide a substantial response to the insistent demand for national defense, they will have accomplished what they set out to do, and in addition will have personally benefitted by the result." It was quite clear that the Secretary had Chairman Hay and like-minded congressmen in mind when he characterized these proposals as "forty-eight separate armies operating under forty-eight separate authorities" and "deceptive in the extreme."[119] The bankers rose and sang "For he's a jolly good fellow."

Even while continuing this public battle, Garrison was astute enough to realize that he was losing it. He surmised that secret negotiations were under way between the man who could defeat him, Chairman Hay, and the only person who could save the day, President Wilson. "I . . . am not advised as to the statements of intention made by Mr. Hay to you in the conversation had with you . . ." he wrote the President, but "it seems to me perfectly clear that, unless you interpose your position as leader of the country on this great subject, the result will be . . . lamentable."[120]

Tumulty alerted Wilson that the Secretary was plainly laying the groundwork for a resignation.[121] Soon Garrison wrote again, now demanding that the President declare himself "promptly, openly and unequivocally" for his original scheme, "or be charged properly with lack of sincerity and good faith."[122]

Wilson replied that he had, indeed, negotiated with Congressman Hay, that he rejected Garrison's negative assessment of the Congress, and that he refused to write off in advance the possibility of the House Committee producing legislation which, even if in a different way, would serve the purpose of creating a trained, viable army under federal control.[123] "I do not share your opinion that the members of the House who are charged with the duty of dealing with military affairs are ignorant of them, or of the military necessities of the nation. On the contrary, I have found them well informed, and actuated by a most intelligent appreciation of the grave responsibilities imposed upon them."[124]

In a further exchange of letters, Garrison asked the President to clear a speech he planned to give, criticizing Congressional initiatives involving both the Philippines and national defense. Wilson replied with a detailed itemization of the differences he had with his Secretary, adding icily: "I trust that you will feel no hesitation about expressing your personal views . . . but I hope that you will be kind enough to draw very carefully the distinction between your own individual views and the views of the Administration."[125] With that, it was all over. Garrison, on February 10, replied: "It is evident that we hopelessly disagree upon what I conceive to be fundamental principles. . . . I hereby tender my resignation. . . ."[126] Wilson, somewhat disingenuously, now confessed "to feeling a very great surprise. . . ."[127] The number-two man in the Department, Assistant Secretary Henry Breckinridge, wrote what Josephus Daniels, Secretary of the Navy, described as a "me too" letter.[128] I share without exception Garrison's conviction, he told Wilson.

The nation's newspapers of February 11, 1916, carried the whole of the correspondence between Garrison and Wilson from January 12 to the resignation. It had been released by the White House in accordance with the tradition prevalent in the first half of the century. Indeed, from the very beginning of this exchange of letters, both sides had acted on the assumption that they were building the public record of the Secretary's departure.

Garrison's reasons for resigning were thus communicated fully to the public via the resignation correspondence. Once that was done, he announced: "I shall not make myself vocal in any way."[129] He added that there was no pique and no politics in his decision; that he had no quarrel with the President, no desire to embarrass him, and no intention to remain in politics.[130] He slipped unnoticed out of Washington before the resignation was announced and hid from reporters in the Fifth Avenue apartment of a New York friend. His views on preparedness were well known, he told reporters when they found him, and he would not campaign further for them, nor would he consider running for President.

Daniels, no admirer of the War Secretary, wrote later that he set a good example of retiring with dignity and grace.[131] In only one subsequent speech did Garrison frontally attack the preparedness issue,[132] and, in general, he largely confined his rare public appearances to expounding broad generalities about cutting back big-government bureaucracy, in speeches delivered before appreciative Eastern associations of bankers and lawyers. In the manner of the Eastern public-protest resignation, he had expressed himself emphatically, once and for all, in his published resignation correspondence. It would not do to go on and on about it.

The resignation of Garrison's Assistant Secretary is counterpoint to this sedate Eastern theme. Chicago-born Kentucky lawyer Henry Breckinridge was diametrically the opposite of Garrison: young, excitable, Western in style. Unlike Garrison, whom he nevertheless admired with filial devotion, he was far from content to fade away into privacy after firing a single resignation blast. He became President of the Navy League and a vocal and controversial exponent of right-wing causes. In 1934, he campaigned for the Senate under the auspices of the Constitution party, created to oppose bureaucracy in Washington, and in 1936 he ran for the Presidency, this time flying the banner of the rabidly anti-New Deal Association for the Defense of the Constitution. His populist determination to take his case to the voters places Breckinridge more into a category with Bryan, Davis, and Wallace (although on a different part of the ideological spectrum) than with the austere Garrison.

John L. Sullivan is another example of the way the Easterner

with an unusual degree of ethical autonomy "goes public." Sullivan, a New Hampshire-bred lawyer with a long history of senior
government service and the founder of a moderate-sized Washington law firm, resigned on April 26, 1949, from the post of Secretary
of the Navy after his boss, Defense Secretary Louis A. Johnson,
had peremptorily canceled one of Sullivan's favorite projects, the
supercarrier *United States*. Sullivan feared that Johnson's fiat
meant that the Navy, under service unification, would be deprived
of its air arm. He further feared that this was only the first step of a
plan to take away the Navy's land capability by disbanding the
Marines.

"Are you determined to resign?" President Truman asked
him.

"Yes," Sullivan replied. "Johnson is going to abolish the
Marine Corps next. I have to take a public stand."

"Very well," Truman replied, "but do me a favor. Please fire
your public letter at Louis, not at me."

Truman knew that Sullivan's letter would be a scorcher, and
so it was.

The letter of resignation, published on the front pages of all
major U.S. newspapers, was full of detailed recrimination and
raised important policy issues. As recently as a week before,
Sullivan said, he had tried to discuss the carrier with Johnson, "but
before I had talked more than a minute you advised me that you
had another appointment."[133] It was an "unprecedented action"
to make so major a reversal of policy "without consultation" with
the service involved. Such procedures could have "far-reaching"
and "tragic consequences." In particular, Sullivan told Johnson,
he was "very deeply disturbed by your action, which so far as I
know, represents the first attempt ever made in this country to
prevent the development of a powerful weapon."[134] The letter
went on to say that professional Navy planners had repeatedly
placed the highest priority on the carrier's development and had
been led to sacrifice other expenditures to insure its completion.

After this mercurial public blast, however, Sullivan went back to his law firm and did not speak on the issue in public again. "I was swamped with invitations to lecture," he has said, "but I refused them all. I had made my point. Anything more would have seemed like carping. However, resigning did give me the opportunity to work quietly behind the scenes with the key Members of Congress. I knew them all, you know, their families and histories. That happens after a while, when you work your way up from an Assistant Secretaryship. And we did get the carrier eventually."[135]

More recently there was the case of Kenneth N. Davis, Jr., a promising young treasurer of International Business Machines recruited by the Nixon Administration to the post of Assistant Secretary of Commerce for Domestic and International Business. Davis, in June 1970, found himself in opposition to official tariff and trade policy. Contrary to the line being pursued by Henry Kissinger and Commerce Secretary Maurice Stans, he favored Congressional action to impose higher import levies and restrictions to counter what he saw as foreign, and especially Japanese, economic imperialism.

Davis's one shot was fired in a lecture to a management seminar at the Plaza Hotel in New York. A number of senior White House advisers, he felt, had given the President bad advice on trade policy. They were doing the President "a serious disservice," and had made it impossible for him to see Mr. Nixon. He told the surprised audience that it was through them that he was "trying to reach the President." Stressing unemployment and the deterioration of U.S. industry under the weight of foreign imports, he stated: "I am convinced now that the future economic strength of our great nation requires some form of limitation on the rate of growth of imports for a very few key domestic U.S. industries. . . ." He emphasized that voluntary quotas would not do the job.[136]

Commerce Secretary Stans, who was just about to negotiate voluntary quotas with the Japanese, noted that Mr. Davis had informed him of his desire to resign, and added gravely: "I agreed with his decision."[137]

Davis, in quitting, told John Ehrlichman, "I have no hard feelings, John, I wish you luck. You're going to need it. You're in trouble, John—worse trouble than you know—and I'm worried about the country more than I was before I came down here."[138]

Despite this apparent gift of prophecy, with only one minor exception,[139] Kenneth Davis ceased to make himself heard. A Massachusetts-born, Phillips Andover and M.I.T.-schooled Easterner is not prone to the public-crusading style.

Analysis of the way a man goes public in terms of his over-all life-style does not invariably work, however, thanks to the happy propensity of humans to surprise those who would categorize them. Elliot Richardson, the Eastern patrician, has not been noticeably more reticent than William Ruckelshaus of Indiana. Walter Hickel's public protest does not fit neatly into any of our categories. The life-style of this former Secretary of the Interior resembles that of the Middle Western frontier entrepreneur, but his courageous public protest was in the tradition of the Wall Street banker or lawyer. After firing off one passionate public bill of complaint to President Nixon[140] against the Cambodian incursion of May 1970, Hickel did not take to the hustings, to the college lecture circuit, or to anti-Vietnam war rallies. Rather, he faded from public view to a dignified five-year silence broken only by publication of a surprisingly muted book.[141] His cry from the heart came at a time— in the midst of the most serious internal turmoil—when it made a profound impression on the young and disaffected. But Hickel, like Garrison, Sullivan, and Kenneth Davis, seemed to have felt that one loud, clear sound of the trumpet was enough. Only four years later did he try again for public office—unsuccessfully—in the Alaskan gubernatorial primaries.

◇

Richardson, Ruckelshaus, Ickes, Webster Davis, Bryan, Douglas, Wallace, Garrison, Breckinridge, Sullivan, Kenneth Davis, and Hickel: the stories of these men pretty well summarize the significant victories of ethical autonomy over expediency and groupthink in the behavior, at the breaking point, of senior executive officials in the U.S. government during these traumatic first three quarters of the twentieth century. A few others did make equivocal or belated efforts to speak out. Some, like F.D.R.'s third Commerce Secretary, Jesse Jones, tried to transform the lowly affront of being fired by the President into an elevated confrontation on matters of high policy.[142]

A few others did engage in a relatively permissible form of public disagreement. This is the kind that proceeds not from ethical autonomy but merely reflects the position in business or law to which the resigner has returned. Russell Cornell Leffingwell resigned in 1920 after serving three years as Assistant Secretary of the Treasury under Wilson. He re-entered civilian life as a prominent Wall Street lawyer and, later, became head of the Morgan Bank in New York. After resigning, Leffingwell told the Academy of Political Science "that many of the departments of the Government were working at odds"[143] and proceeded to criticize extravagant public spending and excessive taxation of corporations. He sharpened these criticisms over the ensuing years. But he never suggested that he had resigned in protest or that his term in government had engendered a crisis of conscience. If Leffingwell, on resuming his private career, now seemed to criticize the colleagues he had left behind in Washington, it was because Wall Street and the banking profession as a whole were critical. As a leader of his profession, he was expected to give voice to its rather vague, self-interested fulminations against "Big Brother" and "overspending." This is really only a ritual form of petitioning or lobbying. It does not constitute a breach of team loyalty. A lawyer or banker who resigns from high office to return to his profession is permitted, even expected, to attack high public spending and corporate taxation, but not the war in Southeast Asia, or C.I.A. activities in Latin America.

In 1932, Walter E. Hope also resigned as Assistant Secretary of the Treasury, took up a banking career, and almost at once began to criticize government estate-tax policies. Similarly,

Roswell F. Magill, from the precincts of Columbia University to which he returned in 1938 after a stint as Under Secretary of the Treasury, called for an end to the tax exemption of municipal bonds[144] and warned that the country, with its unbalanced budget, was fiscally unprepared to enter an impending war.[145] And then there is John T. Connor, who, within ten months of leaving the Commerce Department in the Johnson Administration, proceeded to beat the drums for higher tariffs on man-made fibers even as his former colleagues were fighting for trade liberalization. But, then, Connor had become president of Allied Chemical.

Perhaps most interesting—and somewhat different—is the case of Abe Fortas. After resigning from the Truman Administration, he returned to a flourishing Washington legal practice. Soon he became an active fighter on behalf of eight clients who had been summarily dismissed from government service as security risks. This fight put him in public conflict with the loyalty and security procedures of the State Department under Secretary George C. Marshall, a battle not wholly confined to courthouse appearances.[146] Even so, his conduct did not violate the team rules which accommodate even such borderline activity on behalf of professional clients. *Autres temps, autres moeurs:* the rules of the club tolerate the modest public criticisms of those who, having returned quietly to private business or law, then find that their new professional responsibilities mandate a certain amount of disagreement with former government colleagues and the Administration in which they served. The system seems more willing to accept such protests "on retainer" than protests prompted solely by conscience. To this must be appended the caution that such public criticisms must never be directed at the President and must not draw on information to which the resigner is privy as a result of his government service.

In much the same way as the team rules bend to accommodate these "retainered" protesters, so, also, the team rules permit a limited form of going public on the part of senior officials of an

Administration who, having been co-opted from the opposite party, resign to return to the fold, usually just before an election. For these prodigal sons there is dispensation from the rule of silence, but only on the same strict terms as for the "retainered" protesters. They must strictly eschew attacks on the President, even if he is running for re-election against the candidate the resigner is backing, and they must abjure the partisan use of "inside" information. Beyond that, a Republican secretary in a Democratic Administration (or, more rarely, vice versa) may resign just before a Presidential election and campaign against his old boss. There may be some hard feelings on the latter's part, a tendency to say: "I made the sonofabitch what he is today, and now he's using it against me." But there is also a grudging recognition that, under the American team rules, if a player is borrowed from the other team he may be called back just before the big game. It is widely accepted that borrowing a player from the other side has its uses and its costs. It may make the Administration a little less open to attack and broadens the base of its support. This is especially the case when Democratic Presidents seek to reassure the skittish business community by appointing Republicans to Treasury or Commerce. Along with these potential advantages, a President must calculate and accept a higher risk of eventual public defection by the co-opted team member. Providing the defector stays within the clearly defined limits of propriety, he may publicly attack the Administration from which he has resigned without being put down as a bad team player.

In this century there have been at least four such "prodigals" who spoke up after leaving government: Crowell, Coolidge, Noble, and Hanes. Three played within the special team rules that apply to prodigals; one did not.

Benedict Crowell resigned in June 1920 from his post as Assistant Secretary of War in the Wilson Administration. His exchange of resignation letters with the President was innocuous and friendly.[147] In October of that election year, however, Crowell did break his silence—just once—to endorse the Republican candidate, Warren G. Harding. The statement carefully begins: "Now that President Wilson is retiring . . ." and utters no criticism of him or his policies, stressing, instead, the perceived qualities of the Republican candidate over his opponent. "Senator Harding's election will, I believe, insure more efficiency in the Government than the election of Governor [James M.] Cox because the latter would be saddled with holdovers from the previous Democratic administration that could contribute little to the strength of the next. . . ."[148] While this cannot particularly have delighted Crowell's colleagues in the former Administration, it carefully distinguishes between them and the retiring President. The statement is therefore permissible by the team rules. Crowell gets passing grades for discretion and team play, even if his expectations of high competence in the Harding Administration earn a failing grade for prescience.

T. Jefferson Coolidge was a Republican Under Secretary at the Treasury when that Department was headed by Henry Morgenthau. As a fiscal conservative, he frequently found himself at odds with Franklin Roosevelt's and Morgenthau's policies. The latter recorded a series of increasingly rancorous meetings in which Coolidge appeared "brooding" and "excited." In time, Morgenthau accused him petulantly of "throwing sand into the gears of our relationship."[149] Government silver-purchasing and pricing policies further exacerbated relations between the two men. On April 30, 1935, Coolidge "demanded" that the Secretary promise him that, as long as he remained Under Secretary, the silver price would not be raised to 75 cents. Morgenthau refused to make such a commitment, reminding his subordinate that the President had taken personal charge of the matter. He complained to his diary that Coolidge "was constantly upsetting him" and that he "simply could not stand it any longer."[150]

The next day, Coolidge returned to Morgenthau's office and said, "Henry, I don't know whether I can go along with you on account of silver."

"Jeff," Morgenthau replied, "please never say that to me

again. If you can't go along then resign. . . . I just can't stand somebody around me constantly threatening to resign."

Morgenthau recalled that Coolidge had tears in his eyes as he said, "Yes I will never threaten to resign again unless I am ready to go."[151]

Eight and a half months later, Coolidge was ready. The events that followed the final breach, however, are remarkable only for their gentility (in contrast to the raucous relations between Coolidge and the Administration throughout the preceding year). Nothing in the exchange of resignation letters even so much as hints at discord. It being an election year, Coolidge did, in August, issue an endorsement of his party's candidate, Governor Alfred M. Landon. But despite much urging—*The New York Times* in a lead editorial called on him to enter the campaign actively and "give to the public the benefit of his experience and observation"—he did not go beyond saying that he liked Landon and his ideas of economy: scarcely a ringing accolade and only the mildest kind of growl at Roosevelt's Administration.[152]

Indeed, so understated was Coolidge's role in the 1936 campaign that in September 1937, Morgenthau nominated him to represent the United States in the Finance Committee of the League of Nations. Other members of the Administration expressed some reservations about rewarding a Republican who had so recently endorsed F.D.R.'s rival, but Morgenthau, given their earlier fights, showed surprising tenacity in his preferment of Coolidge. To Jacob Viner, the Secretary explained, "[I]f a man acts like a gentleman and gets out, I think it's a very nice gesture to show that the administration can have somebody resign because they do have an honest difference of opinion and that the administration doesn't hold anything against them. . . . I mean Jeff never said a word."[153] Actually, he did say a word; but not enough to step outside the limits of the special indulgence for prodigals.

Edward J. Noble resigned in August 1940 as Under Secretary of Commerce. He had been an important and loyal member of the

Administration, often defending government trade policies on the Hill against attacks by his fellow Republicans. Because of his support for Commerce Secretary Harry Hopkins' decision to ask questions about income in the current census, he incurred the wrath of the Republican leader, Senator Charles Tobey. Yet Noble stood solidly with his chief. In his letter of resignation, however, he reaffirmed that "I have always been and continue to be a member of the Republican party." He assured Roosevelt that "I am especially anxious that the record show that political partisanship has had no part in either my entering or leaving government service,"[154] but, three days later, announced his support of Wendell Willkie. He did so, however, with only a modest pronouncement to the effect that a Willkie victory would promote "unification of the country" and that "[b]usinessmen are sore at heart at being held at half-speed"—a condition Willkie would remedy.[155] This very muted criticism, too, was still within the rules.

The resignation of John Wesley Hanes as Under Secretary of the Treasury at the end of 1939 and his subsequent support of Willkie presents the one clear instance of a breach of the rules governing the postresignation behavior of prodigals: an instance where public criticism of his former team exceeded the permissible limits. Hanes carried on an active campaign against the Administration during the elections of 1940, criticizing Roosevelt directly for wanting a third term and attacking the Democrats for soliciting campaign contributions from defense contractors. His resignation, not surprisingly, was soon described as a "bolt,"[156] and there was considerable nastiness on both sides. Roosevelt, commenting on Hanes's attacks, characterized his former associate as a young man whose "slant of mind ran more to dollars than humanity."[157] Morgenthau, speaking to Fiorello La Guardia almost three years later, still ruefully remembered of Hanes: " . . . while he was here he was all right, but then when he left here he went awfully sour on Roosevelt . . . nobody was more bitter during the campaign. . . ."[158] Needless to say, Hanes did not serve in Washington again. Both parties see themselves in "team" terms and neither a Republican nor a Democratic Administration is likely to take a chance on anyone who has proven not to be a team player.

The public criticism of government uttered by these "retainered" and "prodigal" resigners contributed very little to the quality of public debate on important issues, precisely because they stayed within the rules. They did, however, at least venture to make some use of the freedom which resignation gave them. Together with the outspoken public resigners like Bryan and Richardson, they form the tiny group of those who have quit and gone public. Virtually all of the rest of the nearly 2000 officials whose careers we studied stayed or left, but, in either case, proceeded without fuss, taking care not to upset their governmental colleagues, nor to stir up the sleeping dogs of public interest.

≷ 3 ≷

The Costs
of Candor

WHEN A SENIOR GOVERNMENT OFFICIAL reaches a crisis of conscience concerning the course of action being followed by the President, the executive branch, or his department, he has four choices:

—*he can stay on quietly, hoping for the best and, perhaps, trying to resist covertly from inside;*

—*he can leave quietly, physically severing his connection with "the team";*

—*he may leave with public protest, alerting the public to the egregiousness of the policy with which he disagrees; and*

—*he may try to have it all ways—first holding on for as long as possible, then exiting and walking a tightrope between discreet silence and public protest.*

The overwhelming majority of those who leave top positions in the U.S. federal executive branch locate themselves squarely in the second option: they leave silently, or "exit" without "voice" in the terms pioneered by Albert O. Hirschman.[1] This is true even among that smaller group whose circumstances of exit suggest a strong possibility of personal disagreement over matters of policy. The silent resignation of Robert S. McNamara in the twilight of the Johnson Administration exemplifies the norm. Although he had become disenchanted with the President's war policy, McNamara took care not to add the key element of "voice" to his "exit."

From mid-1966 on, while still Secretary of Defense, Mc-Namara began to have serious doubts about the war, especially its

◇

untimely escalation. He began to sense that it was not "cost effective"—that it could not be won with the speed, nor at the reasonable price, he had confidently predicted earlier. Biographies of the period are replete with tales of how, at night, the Secretary would confide dovish doubts to members of his old Kennedy crowd,[2] but then, in the morning, would return with visibly unperturbed confidence to the managerial tasks of pinpointing targets and authorizing call-ups of recruits.

This is not to say that McNamara had no views, or that he did not fight for them within the Administration. By 1967, he was in direct conflict with the recommendations of the Joint Chiefs of Staff on their request for 70,000 to 201,000 reinforcements and for stepped-up bombing of North Vietnam. But he preferred to fight in the inner councils of government and when he lost—as he did in 1967 on both troop reinforcement and air warfare—he loyally defended the new policies in public.

On only two occasions did McNamara appear to go public. One was the May 1966 Montreal speech, in which he almost seemed to be preaching for a call to the presidency of the World Bank. In it he said: "Neither conscience nor sanity itself suggests that the United States is, or could be, the global gendarme" and that it "has no mandate from on high to police the world . . . no charter to rescue floundering regimes, who have brought violence on themselves by refusing to meet the legitimate expectations of their citizenry."[3]

The other time McNamara doubted more or less in public was in testimony to a subcommittee of the Senate Armed Services Committee. Although the testimony was secret, even the partial text of his opening statement released to newsmen indicated disagreement with the Joint Chiefs' view that North Vietnam could be "bombed to the conference table"—this at a time when President Johnson had already decided in favor of escalating the bombing.[4] Technically, bombing escalation was still an open subject since the escalation had not yet been formally announced. But the Secretary knew the President would be furious, and so he was.[5]

Johnson was not about to enter the year of the Presidential election with his key aide wondering in public whether the war was worth it all or, even, whether it was being run properly. Although McNamara, around the time of the Montreal speech, had indicated an interest in the presidency of the World Bank (formally, the International Bank for Reconstruction and Development), that had been a year earlier. When Johnson decided his Secretary had "gone dove-ish"[6] he suddenly nominated him to the post without so much as a routine prior check to see whether he was still interested. The Secretary learned about his new job from outgoing World Bank President George D. Woods.

Unceremoniously shipped out, McNamara had a choice. Having just lost two very specific internal battles on escalation, there was no shortage of issues on which he could have gone public. No one else in Washington had his kind of access to data. He had authorized and already seen important parts of the retrospective study of the war which later came to light as the Pentagon Papers and was in an excellent position, now that he was released from office, to write and speak in public for a change in policy. With a national election coming up, McNamara could have played a key public role in changing the nation's carefully nurtured tolerance of the war and its belief in the importance and feasibility of winning it. Instead, he gratefully ducked into the shelter of the proffered foxhole. As president of a great international organization, he could maintain, correctly, that he had no right to speak out on political matters affecting a member state. But, after all, he hadn't been *compelled* to accept that post. There had been a choice, and he had made it in favor of silence.

He had also made it in favor of continued "effectiveness." The World Bank was an important vehicle for alleviating world poverty, and McNamara, not now less confident than in the past, believed it could become a major force for peace. If he turned it down, he might not be offered a similar chance. Worse, to have resigned and gone public would have meant, first of all, a public admission that his own calculations between 1963 and 1966 on the costs, consequences, and outcome of the war had been disastrously wrong. It would have meant admitting that his vaunted systems analysis was no more foolproof than any reasonably intelligent bureaucrat's hunch but that it could arm wrong conclusions with virtually unassailable statistical support. To have gone public in McNamara's case would have required the greatest ethical autonomy of all: the courage not only to leave his team and attack its policies, but to admit his own fallibility, to concede mistakes so enormous as to make it unlikely he would ever again be eligible for high office. The cost of dismantling one's own reputation for effectiveness is high. For McNamara, as for Shakespeare's Richard II, high responsibility is a fixed habit, and life's greatest "care is loss of care."

Concern about the loss of a painstakingly built and carefully projected image of eligibility for high office is a prime reason cited by men and women who have been at the ethical breaking point and who, like McNamara, decided to go out with neither a feud nor a fuss. Men of considerable personal courage, like W. Willard Wirtz, George W. Ball, and Bill Moyers, each, in different ways, repeatedly fought President Johnson and the Administration hawks over Vietnam policy. Each lost his battle inside the Administration. Wirtz, Secretary of Labor and once law partner of Adlai Stevenson, was known to harbor views highly critical of the war. "He was always going into Johnson's office and threatening to resign," a fellow cabinet member reports. Newspaper stories chronicled rumors of the disputes between the President and Wirtz.[7] Eventually Johnson demanded his resignation and Wirtz quit, furious but publicly disavowing all differences with the Chief. Bill Moyers, special assistant and press secretary to Johnson, also resigned in disagreement, but he, too, publicly maintained his silence.

It is a notorious shibboleth of government service that to resign and go public is to forfeit forever the opportunity of further service. If you resign, if, from the platform opened to you by Presidential grace, you criticize the President, his policy, or his

Administration, no future Administration—nor, for that matter, any other institutional team in the private sector—will welcome you into its ranks.

◇

So pervasive is the impression that public-protest resignation forfeits future public-career prospects that we decided to see whether this commonly held assumption and the accompanying fear is warranted by the facts. To do this, we formulated a question which could be answered statistically:

"Among senior political executives in government who resigned their posts as an act of personal volition, and who had reasonable prospects of returning to office, is there a difference in the rate of return of those who chose to go quietly and those who left and 'went public'?" In other words, are public-protest resignations penalized?

We identified almost all persons who had served in U.S. federal departments between 1900 and 1970 at the rank of assistant secretary or higher, or in senior White House posts (see Appendix A, p. 193). From this list we removed those who did not resign— that is, persons who served out a complete term or who were fired—as well as those persons who resigned but died within two years (on the statistical assumption that many of these had been forced to quit by ill health). Finally, we eliminated persons who were over sixty-two at the time they resigned on the assumption that they did not have reasonable expectation of future government appointment. This left us with a group of 389, made up of all those persons whose history suggested that they resigned as a matter of personal choice at a stage in their careers when they could have expected to have good future prospects.[8]

OF THIS GROUP OF 389 AMERICAN TOP OFFICIALS WHO RESIGNED OF THEIR FREE WILL AND IN THEIR PRIME BETWEEN 1900 AND 1970, 355 (91.3 PER CENT) LEFT GOVERNMENT WITHOUT ANY TRACE OF PUBLIC PROTEST. ONLY 34 (8.7 PER CENT) RESIGNED WITH PUBLIC PROTEST.

If we had included in this calculation *all* Americans who

served in the top echelons of federal administration during this period and who resigned routinely with the ending of a Presidency or who were forced out, rather than only the "prime" resigners, then the percentage of public protesters would have been even smaller, less than 2 per cent.

When we compare the future careers in public service of those who left docilely with that of the public protesters, the results leave no room for doubt about the different career implications of these two options.

OF THE 355 WHO LEFT QUIETLY, 73 OFFICIALS (20.6 PER CENT) WERE SUBSEQUENTLY APPOINTED TO FEDERAL GOVERNMENT POSITIONS AS SENIOR AS, OR MORE SENIOR THAN, THOSE FROM WHICH THEY HAD RESIGNED.[9] AMONG THE 34 WHO RESIGNED AND WENT PUBLIC, ONLY ONE (3 PER CENT) WAS SUBSEQUENTLY REAPPOINTED TO AN EQUIVALENT OR HIGHER POST.[10]

The quiet resigners also do much better than those who go public in receiving federal government appointments to prestigious *part-time* posts that are excellent symbols and repositories of influence and prestige.[11]

ALTOGETHER, ONLY 4 OF THE 34 (11.8 PER CENT) WHO RESIGNED AND SPOKE UP[12] WERE SUBSEQUENTLY READMITTED TO EITHER FULL-TIME OR PART-TIME POSITIONS IN THE FEDERAL GOVERNMENT, WHILE 127 OF THE 355 (35.8 PER CENT) WHO RESIGNED QUIETLY WERE LATER REWARDED WITH FULL- OR PART-TIME POSTS.[13]

While those who resign silently can reasonably expect a second chance to serve, those who choose instead to assert their ethical autonomy in public can expect no second chance. They cannot realistically expect to return either to full-time service in the upper echelons of the executive branch of government or in part-time diplomatic, policy-making, or advisory assignments. The commonly held belief about career costs of going public—and so widely cited as a reason for not doing it—turns out to be stark reality.

It is notable that, among those few Americans who resigned

and went public, exactly half (17 of 34) took issue with a foreign, defense, or national security policy. All but four of these had been in the State or Defense Department, or else responsible for an aspect of foreign policy or national security in the White House.[14] By far the second most protest-inducing issue is trade and monetary policy, which was the subject of nine public-protest resignations. All but one of these resigners were holding top-level positions in the Department of the Treasury (5) or Commerce (3). The sole exception is Raymond Moley, who was nominally in the Department of State but actually served as F. D. Roosevelt's White House adviser on monetary negotiations and economic affairs. The few other resignations with protest are scattered among internal or interdepartmental disputes (3), the McCarthy "reds in government" issue (1), farm subsidies (1), the Taft-Hartley Labor Act (1), enforcement of prohibition (1), and Roosevelt's decision to seek a third term (1). But the foreign policy and trade areas, together, accounts for 26 of 34 public expressions of dissent by U.S. resigners in this century.

This concentration, were it not on so minuscule a scale, would be appropriate and healthy for the system, since foreign affairs and international-trade policy are areas in which the Presidency enjoys particularly wide discretionary powers and where "exit" with "voice" can serve an especially useful checking function as well as helping to pierce the veil of secrecy which usually surrounds these subjects.

◇

The statistics do not fully convey the poignancy of the career costs of going public in America. It seems to matter not at all whether the exit with voice has served a useful social purpose, nor whether the public protester who warns of future dangers is proven right by subsequent events. Lindley Garrison and Henry Breckinridge, as Secretary and Assistant Secretary of War, warned first President Wilson and then, in a dramatic resignation in 1916, the American Congress and public that war was approaching and that the United States would need a trained federal army. They argued with foresight against a President and Congress more inclined to temporize that the ill-prepared state militias could not suffice to win if America entered the war. For this breaking of ranks, they were never forgiven by Wilson, even though—or, perhaps, more because—their judgment was confirmed by subsequent developments. Being right is no excuse for disloyalty to the team.

In the taut weeks of crisis immediately preceding U.S. entry into the war, Garrison and Breckinridge both telegraphed their support to President Wilson. "If I can be of any service," the former Secretary wired the President, "I shall be pleased to have you call on me."[15] The President's papers do not indicate receipt of these offers. The telegrams were destroyed. Nor was there any reply. Wilson's private papers do, however, preserve an article he had read in *Pearson's Magazine* entitled "Standing Back of the President." It cites Garrison's wire and exclaims: "What a silly, egotistical offer. . . . Of course Mr. Garrison would be pleased to have the President of the United States call on him for service. So should I. So would everybody. We all crave the honor of such distinction. But Mr. Garrison had his chance to serve; and, for reasons best known to himself, he refused to serve."[16] These, apparently, were sentiments endorsed by Mr. Wilson.

In a speech at Kenyon College, on January 31, 1918, Garrison seemed to be addressing the President personally when he said: "His mind must be open to counsel. He must welcome well-intentioned criticism. He must draw to his side the ablest aides the country affords."[17] But Wilson had not welcomed his former Secretary's criticisms and did not now choose to draw Garrison back to his side. Garrison had to be content with an honorary doctorate of laws from Brown University which cited him as a man "whose foresight discerned many things that have since come to pass, and to whose power of leadership America owes much of her strength today."[18]

In British politics, men like Anthony Eden who do what Garrison did—resign and protest publicly on a question of principle, especially one as crucial to national survival as defense preparedness—are quickly summoned back to high positions of leadership when subsequent events bear out their predictions. Events had largely vindicated Garrison's call to prepare for war. He had an undoubted reputation as a highly competent administrator who was profoundly trusted by the officers of the armed forces. His continued eclipse dramatically illustrates that in U.S. politics it is team-playing, not being right, that counts.

John L. Sullivan's resignation and public attack on the Truman Administration's decision to economize by discontinuing construction of large aircraft carriers was followed by a realization, in the late 1950s, that U.S. naval strength had been allowed to run down dangerously. The carriers were then built, but Sullivan received no credit when the doctrine of massive nuclear retaliation eventually gave way to one of flexible response in which carriers were again a crucial ingredient. Nor, when the Democrats came back, was he even considered for a post in the Kennedy Administration.

The day he resigned, in a loud and clear public protest that filled the front pages of the morning papers, Sullivan went to a Washington cocktail party. He was greeted near the door by Dean Acheson, who took his hand, patted him on the back, and said, "Welcome to the most exclusive club in America."

"What club is that?" Sullivan asked.

"The club," Acheson said benignly, "of men in public life who have resigned in a cause of conscience."

"Who are the other members of the club?" Sullivan wanted to know.

Acheson answered: "Just you and me and Lew Douglas."[19]

But, in fact, Acheson's commendation could not have been very sincerely meant. His own resignation in opposition to Roosevelt's 1933 devaluation was a model of public discretion and tact, leaving him, unlike the pugnacious Sullivan, eminently eligible for future calls to public service.

All "exits" with "voice" are unforgivable, but some are regarded as more heinous than others. Particularly unforgivable is the use, by a resigner, of confidential information gained in office to refute Administration policy. For the most part, this course has been assiduously avoided even by the handful of Americans who have bitten the bullet of public-protest resignation. As they tried to alert the nation to the dangers of a policy or course of action being pursued, they still tended to abide by the team's injunction against that most cardinal of all breaches of the rules: "telling tales out of school."

One who did not abide is Roger Hilsman. When he left—or, according to colleagues, was pushed out of—the State Department in 1964, Hilsman was not a dove. He called for less reliance on air power but a more determined U.S. effort on the land in the form of "really effective clear-and-hold operations" to "really impress Asians . . ." and urged giving "the Special Forces a much larger role in the delta of Vietnam as well as in the mountain regions." He accepted the logic of the domino theory, warning: "We can be sure that, if we do not succeed in meeting the Communists' skillful and highly ambiguous challenge in Southeast Asia, we will soon be facing it again somewhere else in the world."[20] This was hardly a public-protest resignation against the war as such.

Still, Hilsman's pen soon got him into trouble. A piece he did for *Look* magazine shortly after resigning told some of the inside story of the Cuba missile crisis. W. Averell Harriman, at State, was aroused not so much because of the strategic importance of the secrets disclosed but because he had promised another correspondent—American Broadcasting Company's John Scali, who, as a go-between in those dramatic events, had some proprietary interest in them—that when the whole story could be told, Scali would be the one to tell it.

Although it was three years after his resignation that Hilsman's book *To Move a Nation*[21] was published, it deepened the anger of the Establishment. The book came out at a time of crucial decisions about escalation. Thus it was embarrassing to have the former Intelligence Chief disclose that the North "would not have been successful in starting the insurrection if there had not been a substantial core of resistance already in existence among the people of South Vietnam and a framework of native Communist leadership there" and that "the personnel coming over the routes were not North Vietnamese, but still only the pro-Communist southerners who had gone north in 1954. . . ."[22] That was not the way Washington was selling the war to the media. And Hilsman backed up his assertions with the government's own intelligence statistics.

Not surprisingly, the book was widely perceived by the foreign-policy Establishment in New York and Washington as a serious breach of the team rules. "Roger," says the conventional wisdom of the Establishment, "has done himself in."

The more a resigner speaks up, the more he has been attacked by the men who govern, the press, and by ordinary citizens: not solely or primarily on the issues he is raising but on the propriety of his speaking up at all. In disarming a rebel the team always prefers to tackle his etiquette rather than his cause.

As suggested earlier, the most vociferous public-protest resignation in twentieth-century America is that of William Jennings Bryan, and it also provoked the most venomous counterattacks. As soon as he had resigned in 1915 and begun to speak up for peace and against preparedness, Bryan became the object of an unparalleled national campaign of vilification. Reacting to Bryan's resignation interview, *The New York Times* made a classic attack on behalf of the team and its rules:

> When a man quits the service of a private employer he is bound in honor not to disclose his employer's trade secrets. Such a breach of confidence would bring him into disrepute. Men would distrust him. His dishonorable behavior would be a serious bar to his obtaining a new place. Mr. Bryan has been Secretary of State. He has had the confidence of the Administration, he is the custodian of many secrets . . . yet . . . he does not hesitate to publish to all the world facts in respect to an important State paper of which he had knowledge only as a trusted adviser of the President, and which the President has not yet made public.[23]

The "State" paper to which the editors of *The New York Times* referred was the reply to Germany, which was dispatched on June 9, 1915, over the signature of Bryan's successor, Robert Lansing, but which had not yet been made public. After his second "message to the public," the New York *World* used "fanatical" and "treachery" in its comments.[24] The Atlanta *Constitution* stated that Bryan was "a public nuisance" and that they would publish no more of his statements, since they were embarrassing the President "in a most delicate situation."[25] *The New York Times* soon hinted at "a befuddled mind"[26] and commended Bryan's statement not to the public but to psychologists. "The Germans torpedoed one 'Nebraskan,'" the *Baltimore Sun* thundered, "oh, for a 'Busy Bertha' that could effectively dispose of the other."[27] Similar editorial views across the nation addressed Bryan as "cheaply commercial" (*New York Tribune*), "a preacher of disloyalty" (*Cleveland Plain Dealer*), a bearer of "treason" (*Louisville Courier-Journal*), "a menace" (*Chicago Herald*), a "pacifist temporarily bereft of reason" (*Seattle Post-Intelligencer*), and "a sorry misfit" (*New York Press*).[28]

The public attacks on Bryan took three lines, each prominently featured in the press: that Bryan was 1) disloyal, 2) running for President again, and 3) a psychotic oddball. The substance of his carefully reasoned essays and speeches got short shrift. *The New York Times* compared him to a bizarre Robinson Crusoe, off on his island with Friday and a goat, pursuing mystic fantasies out of all context of time and place.[29] Efforts were made to build up the so-called Dumba affair into a major scandal proving that Bryan, even while still Secretary, had surreptitiously communicated with the Germans and undermined Wilson.[30]

Throughout his campaign for neutrality and peace, Bryan refrained from attacking President Wilson and remained an active Democrat. Once war had broken out, Bryan ceased his campaign, stating that the discussion had ended and that the whole country must now stand behind their President.[31] In a telegram to Wilson he tried to mend the breach: "Please enroll me as a private whenever I am needed and assign me to any work that I can do."[32] Wilson thanked him graciously, but offered nothing, and Bryan spent the war years as a private citizen speaking at war-bond rallies. He also continued to campaign vigorously for women's suffrage and prohibition as he had for such other landmark measures as the income tax and direct popular election of senators. But he never returned to public office, and his reputation as an oddball became firmly fixed in the minds of much of the public. That reputation was reinforced by Bryan's tragic role in the antievolution campaign.[33] President Truman, who thought Bryan "a great one, one of the greatest . . . just too far ahead of his time," once remarked about Bryan's role in the Scopes trial: "What an old man said should not be held against him as long as his record was good when he had the power."[34]

The Scopes trial occurred when Bryan had already been intellectually debilitated by defeat. For those whose lives are directed toward public service, ostracism from the circle of power tends to have a profoundly unsettling effect. In such instances, lack of power can corrupt and absolute lack of power can corrupt absolutely. Given the generally perceived costs of speaking out, only persons with a remarkable degree of individuality, of inner voice— of what Socrates called his "prophetic guide"—are likely to expose themselves to sustained public hatred and scorn. For those who do, the experience of being made the group victim, together with the permanent deprivation of power, can transform them from strong individualists into comic-tragic oddballs. Adversity sometimes pushes persons with unusual qualities of ethical autonomy across the line that divides the virtue of integrity from the vice of obsessiveness and firm principles from the *idée fixe*. Comedy, and tragedy, are based on this dramatic formula. The comic tragedy of "being odd-balled" is a fate all persons in institutional life must risk if they choose to pursue their ethical autonomy to the point of going public.

A pioneering series of experiments made twenty years ago by Professor Solomon Asch have confirmed the extent to which group pressure weighs on the holdout individual and plays on his fear of appearing "odd." When persons were asked their opinion about an external reality (e.g., which of three lines on a screen was the longest) their adherence to the right answer was subject to extreme stress when the rest of the small group in the room, on instructions of the experimenter, unanimously insisted that another line was longer. Many of the individuals, faced with the pressure of the group's answer, abandoned their own judgment and either actually did "see it" the group's way or else simply suppressed their views in order to achieve group solidarity and approval. The few holdouts reported their intense discomfiture and assaults of self-doubt. "I felt disturbed, puzzled, separated, like an outcast from the rest," a typical case stated. "Every time I disagreed I was beginning to wonder if I wasn't beginning to look funny."[35] Only very few subjects had the independence to "assert the authentic value of [their] own experience" in the face of group pressure. The overwhelming tendency was to suppress that which within the self had failed to conform to the group expectation.[36] Only rarely did a subject face the group resolutely, in effect proclaiming like Luther, "Here I stand, I can do no other."[37] In a follow-up series of experiments by Richard Crutchfield, subjects who stubbornly continued to assert their reality against the group's felt themselves "to be queer or different. . . . With this went an arousal of considerable anxiety in most subjects; for some, manifest anxiety was acute."[38]

Mabel Willebrandt, an early leader in the battle for women's rights and prison reform, the first lady to reach what was then the top echelon in the subcabinet and the first female Assistant Attorney General of the United States, underwent a particularly comic-tragic oddballing after she resigned and "went public." Angered by corruption and laxity in the enforcement of the Volstead Act, the "Portia of Prohibition," as she had come to be known to her millions of admirers in women's clubs and church groups, quit in 1929 and campaigned with the zealous intemperance not infrequently characteristic of temperance enthusiasts.[39]

Within three months of leaving office, Mrs. Willebrandt had published twenty-seven syndicated newspaper columns[40] and addressed countless public meetings. After no more than six months, her fighting book, *The Inside of Prohibition*, was published.[41] In all, she waxed both eloquent and specific in her charges of lack of diligence, competence, and even integrity on the part of prohibition officials. The Chief Counsel and Head of the Law Division of the Bureau of Prohibition, Judge James J. Britt, felt so threatened that he flooded President Hoover with lengthy self-generated memoranda, minutely documented, that tried to refute her charges.[42] The agent of the prohibition unit in Missouri, Gus O. Nations, went further. He sued Mrs. Willebrandt for $200,000 for referring to him as "a friend of a felon"[43] who had accepted bribes.

The antitemperance forces, including many persons, particularly in government, who had always laughed at the idea of a woman Assistant Attorney General, did not content themselves with such comparatively above-board countermeasures. Soon, news items began to appear which cast doubt on her competence and, indeed, her sanity. It was reported that, while in office, she had in effect once done what would some years later come to be called a "Wrong-way Corrigan," inadvertently arguing in the Supreme Court for the acquittal of someone the Attorney General was supposed to convict. "Mr. Justice Pierce Butler," it was reported, "could scarcely believe his ears. . . . Mr. Mitchell [the Attorney General] was compelled to take the case away from Mrs. Willebrandt and to repudiate her position. . . ." The papers mock-gravely stated that "Mrs. Willebrandt's appearances before the Supreme Court were far from pleasant either for herself or the justices." What is said to have exasperated the justices more than anything else was her "irrelevant answers" to their questions. This her friends were said to attribute "to her deafness."[44] Not mentioned was the notorious lack of cordiality on the part of some Supreme Court justices toward lady attorneys. Also passed over was the admiration Justices Brandeis and Holmes had publicly expressed for her competence.[45]

Mrs. Willebrandt suddenly found herself the victim of numerous other allegations—some public, some in the form of hate mail—of participation in mad-hatter schemes. It was reported that she had placed wives of prohibition enforcement agents "into assignation houses" and used them "as decoys" in such a way that "decent women" were "reduced to common whores"—all "in connection with the enforcement of prohibition."[46] Tabloid news stories proclaimed that "Forty beautiful girls, experts in the art of amorous approach, unsealed the lips of hard-boiled agents of the mammoth rum trust . . . and lured them into the clutches of federal prohibition enforcement officials."[47] President Hoover received letters indicating that, on a specified Delaware and Hudson train from New York, "a naked harlot displaying credentials of the Government of the United States confiscated two bottles of brandy and entertained four men in her berth all of them naked."[48]

For a time, Mabel Willebrandt fearlessly continued her campaign, meanwhile serving as general counsel for the fledgling aviation industry.[49] A little more than a year later, however, she seems to have wearied of the fight. To the horror of her legion of followers, this fiery spearhead of the Anti-Saloon League and the Women's Christian Temperance Union suddenly agreed to take on a remunerative but incongruous new client: the California Grape Growers. These enterprising gentlemen had just begun to market a grape concentrate which could easily be fermented. The legality of the product—not to mention its morality—was doubtful at best.[50]

This affiliation with the grape industry terminated Mrs. Willebrandt's short but dramatic career as one of the century's most sensational public protesters among resigners of conscience. It ended amidst charges that the liquor interests had bought up her influence with the "drys," to whom she continued quite fervently, but less credibly, to pledge allegiance. It is unfortunate that one of the few genuine attempts in this century by an American subcabinet official to "go public," to rally public opinion in a clear-cut, name-naming, issue-pinpointing fashion, should thus have ended not with a bang but a snicker.

◇

Whatever her "true" reality, Mrs. Willebrandt was undoubtedly a woman of unusually strong self-definition, a person remarkably unsusceptible to the pressures of social conformity. It is this rare quality which makes a very few public officials fight for their ethical autonomy, but it is also a trait of character which, in our conformist culture, lends itself to being portrayed as eccentric. Subject to a sufficiently determined campaign of odd-balling, a real oddball may finally emerge from the complex matrix of fierce independence, unbending integrity, iron-willed determination, and indifference to costs. The group victim, when sufficiently subjected to group derision, may even assume the very role assigned to him which appears to justify that derision. "They've said I am an enemy of the people," says the doctor in Ibsen's play after being hounded for threatening to expose an embarrassing truth about the city's profitable medicinal baths, "well, then, I'll be an enemy of the people."[51]

Webster Davis, who resigned from the McKinley Administration where he had been a promising young second-in-command at the Commerce Department, was odd-balled when he launched a public campaign against the Administration's support of the British in the Boer War. The press reveled in the story that at the Democratic National Convention of 1900—after he had switched parties because Bryan was more favorably disposed to the Boer cause—Davis had culminated a passionate oration with a dramatic call for the election of "William J. Brennings."[52]

Stories, never proven but widely circulated, reported that Davis had been given large amounts of Transvaal gold bullion to recruit "volunteers" but had appropriated it to his own use. Much of the unprecedented $180,000 advance he got for his protest-resignation book, *John Bull's Crime,* was used up in litigation inspired by supporters of the President like Senator Mark Hanna and random crackpots.[53] Increasingly, his life became a battle to defend, in public, not his policies but his integrity and mental stability. In 1904, two Boer supporters, a General Samuel Pearson and Mr. C. W. Van der Hoogt, appeared at Davis's residence and tried to collect Boer funds they claimed Davis was hiding. The former Assistant Secretary had two detectives hide behind a set of curtains. Pearson, according to the gleeful *New York Times'* account, showed up (it was evening) inexplicably dressed "in full shooting costume" decked with a gold medal.[54] When the two interlocutors, according to another highly colored press account, "innocently touched upon the subject of the $250,000 . . . [t]his at once aroused Mr. Davis' ire. . . . [H]e sullenly summoned forth the minions of the law, and the two manhunters burst forth from their place of concealment and pounced upon their victims. . . ."[55] When Davis failed to prosecute, the "two victims" sued him for false arrest and continued to charge Davis with fraud. The seemingly endless saga kept the nation amused for years. Davis's serious and eloquent critiques of American support for British imperial policy, and of America's own imperialist tendencies in Latin America and Asia, were laughed off by many as the idle fantasies of a raving lunatic.

◇

The reluctance to speak out is getting worse. This lamentable fact emerges from a further examination of the 389 "prime" resigners. Among this group, the rate of going public has declined sharply during the past thirty years. The percentage of persons resigning and speaking out was 16 per cent of the officials surveyed in the decade 1910–19 (inclusive), 10.5 per cent between 1920 and 1929, and 21.7 per cent between 1930 and 1939. But in the decade 1940–49, only 10.7 per cent went public. In 1950–59 it was 5.1 per cent and in 1960–69, the era of the Vietnam war, only 6.3 per cent.[56]

This trend is examined more meaningfully in the context of the various Presidential administrations. Overall, during this century, the rate of going public has been slightly higher in the ranks of Democratic (9.9 per cent) than in Republican (6.8 per cent) administrations.[57] But the trend over the years within the two parties is sharply differentiated. Throughout the period, the Republican rate has held constant. It was 7.1 per cent during the McKinley, Theodore Roosevelt, and Taft administrations that governed between

1900 and 1913.[58] During the Harding, Coolidge, and Hoover stretch of Republican government between 1921 and 1933, the rate was 8.3 per cent. And during the Eisenhower and Nixon presidencies, from 1953 to 1961 and 1968 to 1970 (the end of the period statistically surveyed), the rate of public-protest resignations has been 6.0 per cent.[59] In the three Republican periods, therefore, the rate of going public has consistently hovered in the area of 6 to 8 per cent, a very low rate. By sharp contrast, the Democrats began the century with a tendency toward more such resignations of conscience. Public protesters constituted 17.9 per cent of those resigning during the Wilson era (1913–21), but declined to 11.3 per cent during the Roosevelt and Truman period (1933–52) and bottomed at 6.5 per cent during the Kennedy–Johnson years (1961–68).[60]

Thus, it appears that while members of Republican administrations have never favored breaking ranks to publicize differences among those in the upper echelons of their administrations, the Democrats[61] were at first substantially more inclined to resign in public protest. Now, however, members of Democratic administrations appear to refrain from going public exactly like their Republican counterparts. What makes this remarkable is that the sharp decline in public manifestation of ethical autonomy among members of Democratic administrations occurred against the backdrop of the Vietnam war, with its intensely argued strategic and moral issues.[62]

At no time during this century has there been anything like a flourishing of ethical autonomy among top officials in the U.S. federal government. The costs of ethical autonomy, in this society, are prohibitive and the rewards minimal. It is a disturbing but inevitable conclusion of the statistics and the case studies that, in America, it is both dangerous and costly for those best placed—the insiders—to speak out. One almost has to be a bit mad to resign in protest. Nice, sensible insiders keep quiet. And so the important arguments raised by the few who do go public can be—and usually are—brushed aside by *ad hominem* attacks on the personality of those making them. Conversely, the rewards for prudence are great. By the 1960s, discretion, not valor, had become both the measure and the rule of those who seek to serve the public weal.

◇

The high costs of going public influence the timid who decide to resign in silence and also those whose consciences (or wives, children, and friends) do not quite permit them to go in peace. These costs tend not only to reduce the frequency of open disaffection but also to lower the quality of protest among that hardy handful who do decide to "exit" with "voice." Very rare is the public protester who goes out with the clearly drawn issue, like William Jennings Bryan or like Elliot Richardson. Most of those few who feel they ought to speak up still cannot bring themselves to confront the issue openly. They tend to mumble, fudging whatever message they may have.

Perhaps the saddest thing about these "closet protesters" is that while they try to have it both ways—try to be perceived as critics by other critics but not by the Establishment—they tend to have it neither way. The case of Harry Woodring illustrates this.

Harry H. Woodring came out of Elk City, Kansas, and had been a banker and a one-term governor in his home state. After he lost his bid for re-election, Roosevelt appointed him Assistant Secretary of War under George H. Dern and, on the latter's death, the Secretaryship more or less devolved on him by default.[63]

Almost from the beginning, Woodring and Roosevelt went on separate paths, particularly as the European crisis unfolded. Woodring was a stickler for the neutrality laws, totally opposed to "the employment of armed force . . . to support . . . the British Empire."[64] F.D.R., on the contrary, was determined to help Britain and France rearm as America's first line of defense, even at the risk of circumventing the laws and leaving U.S. forces undersupplied. To do this, the President had to bypass Woodring, relying, instead, on Treasury Secretary Henry Morgenthau to expedite British and French weapons procurement and on Assistant War Secretary Louis Johnson as the effective head of the War Department. Politically, Woodring was dead but not gone.

◇

In many ways the strangest aspect of the Roosevelt–Woodring relationship was that it went on for so long. The President so hated to fire his Secretary that he put it off until Woodring's role became something of a scandal within the Administration. It is perhaps even more surprising that the Secretary would, for so many years, cling to a position in which he had been effectively stripped of all but vestigial power, limited solely to obstruction. For at least his last three years in Washington, Woodring presided over a Department of whose actions he strongly disapproved and remained part of an Administration whose defense policies he considered misguided, illegal, and immoral. His inability to assert his conscience, in these circumstances, is a telling commentary both on the man and on the system.

Technically, Woodring was allowed—i.e., forced—to resign. With some people, being fired wonderfully focuses the conscience and brings out a latent sense of ethical imperatives. If you are going to be forced out into the cold anyway, why not at least slam the door? The manner of Woodring's departure, however, is instructive, for he both wanted to protect his relation with Roosevelt in the hope of being summoned to some new appointment and yet could not quite suppress a need to ventilate his feelings. Woodring, thus, could not manage an unequivocal departure. Even in leaving Washington he still tried to have it both ways. He had become just another high official addicted to the paraphernalia of authority— the attentive reporters, the diffident headwaiters, the "inside" stories he could whisper to envious friends. So at first he clung to the office that entitled him to status, even after most real power had been taken from him. And when he was finally pushed out he, like McNamara, tried to protect his eligibility, his chance to stage a comeback.

On June 19, 1940, F.D.R. wrote Woodring: "I am asking that you let me have your resignation."[65] The Secretary's handwritten reply is a loud, clear attack on the President's policy: very specific and exactly within Woodring's sphere of departmental responsibility. In it he justified "my refusal of yesterday morning to agree to your request for the release of the flying fortress bombers to foreign nations . . . based upon my own belief, supported by the Gen'l. Staff, that it was not in the best interests of the defense of our own country." He wrote of being "fearful of a succession of events to which I could not subscribe" and spoke bitterly of "those who would provoke belligerency. . . ."[66]

At this time, in the customary course of events, letters of cabinet resignation were released to the public, and Woodring, in writing his indictment, could hardly have been oblivious of this practice. Yet attached to this message was the following note:

> Mr. President—
> I will not give out any statement, nor release my part of your letter or my reply—
> Inasmuch as I am packing my personal files I fear the situation may leak out over here—so I suggest that any announcement should not only come from the White House but perhaps immediately—
> H.H.W.[67]

In other words, publish this, if you dare.

Roosevelt replied at once, apparently abstractedly. "That is a mighty nice letter of yours and I greatly appreciate it," he began, adding lightly, "Don't worry about maintaining the non-intervention policy. We are most certainly going to do just that—barring, of course, an attack on the validity of the Monroe Doctrine."[68] In the official White House press release of that day, Woodring's resignation was merely announced—the resignation letter was not released—and the formal notification was accompanied only by an appreciative farewell note from F.D.R. to Woodring.

It did not take the media long to realize that something was amiss. Why was Woodring's letter being withheld? The White House could only suggest that Woodring's note was too "personal" to be made public. This merely fueled the press's speculation about the "mystery" of Woodring's "missing" letter, as Woodring must have known it would.

In one gambit, the Secretary had salved his need for ethical autonomy by resigning and putting on the docket his protest against the President's policies, had signaled the media and the public, but had yet retained the form of a totally silent resignation accompanied by a ritual display of team loyalty to the Chief: "I will not give out any statement. . . ."

On June 22, the Kansas City *Star* carried a full story—none of it attributed to Woodring but phrased as "speculation" about the missing letter—in which the Administration is made to appear to want "to turn over to the British the country's No. 1 defense secret, the Sperry bombsight."[69] On the floor of Congress, Senator Gerald P. Nye charged that the Secretary had been fired because he refused to allow the transfer of equipment which was needed by our own military establishment. Woodring said nothing. By keeping silent, he was adhering to the rules of the team player, while effectively fanning the speculation of the opposition.

By June 25, the public controversy engendered by Woodring's "closet protest" compelled F.D.R. to reassess his earlier judgment of that "mighty nice letter." He sent his former subordinate a stiff three-page message for the record denying Woodring's earlier allegations. At the same time he tried to head off any temptation on Woodring's part to ally himself even more publicly with the isolationist elements in Congress, who were threatening a full-scale investigation of Roosevelt's arms sales policy. "Doubtless many efforts of mere partisanship in these days, when we should be thinking about the country first, will be directed to having you appear before Committees in order to stir up controversy," he warned, and counseled the ex-Secretary to resist these efforts.[70]

Woodring, still anxious to be perceived as a team player by the coach, took the warning to heart. On January 15, 1941, he wrote Roosevelt that "I have many wires, letters, phone calls, etc., to testify before the Foreign Relations Committees . . . but you may understand, as I know you do without my saying so, that I shall never do anything to embarrass your program. I may not always agree 100% but I am always loyal."[71] Woodring wanted F.D.R. to know that, although benched, he was still a team player, still eligible to play in the big leagues. And, indeed, he did withhold his support from the Congressional isolationists, where it might have been effectively deployed.

"Of course, I need no pledge of your loyalty," the President purred in reply. "I always assume it as a matter of course. I am delighted to have your assurance of confidence."[72]

But Woodring's loyalty, having been less than the obligatory 100 per cent, was never rewarded. With the outbreak of war, he wired, then wrote the President offering his services. "If you ever are in search of a couple of enthusiastic, loyal, good-neighbor policy advocates of Latin American friendship—Ambassador to Mexico—better look over Harry and Helen—it might be smart Middle-West strategy."[73] Roosevelt replied at once. The "suggestion" was "interesting and well worth considering."[74] But nothing happened. Woodring continued to write F.D.R. about being "happily tied down here in this delightful city of Topeka" while eagerly thrusting himself forward for new assignments.[75] To the very end, the President continued to promise to give these suggestions earnest consideration. The last letters have Roosevelt pledging he would "take up with the State Department" Woodring's offer to campaign for a strong postwar International Peace Union. In pencil, the office copy simply notes: "did not write to State."[76]

Woodring's case illustrates the difficulty of being perceived to be *almost* wholly loyal in a system of team play that demands total suppression of any public signs of disenchantment and complete loyalty to the President. It also illustrates the way leaders play on the reluctance of men like Woodring to burn their bridges, to be transferred from the White House's "Christmas Card" to its "Enemies" list.

Yet for all the difference it would have made to his career, Woodring might as well have given in to his conscience and testified against the Administration before the Congressional Committee. He could not have set back his public career more had he campaigned for neutrality like William Jennings Bryan. Roosevelt purchased his silence cheaply, without ever paying off with any real reward. Woodring should have known: where assertions of an autonomous conscience are concerned, the system does not reward anything less than total abstinence. By trying to have it both ways, he had sacrificed his own ethical autonomy, and yet also failed to remain eligible for further Presidential favors.

Faced with the internal struggle for ethical autonomy and the external pressure to conform, good, honest men bend themselves into pretzel-like configurations to stay on speaking terms both with their consciences and the power Establishment. One common contortion is verbalized as follows: "I am strongly opposed to a government policy but no one in particular is responsible for it, so there is no justifiable target. We are all guilty. So no one is guilty." This, for a time, was Richard N. Goodwin's public position after he resigned. In *The New Yorker,* Goodwin tried to dissociate himself from Johnson's Vietnam policy without attacking his former boss—for whom he continued to be a free-lance speech writer.[77] If Vietnam were to turn into the apocalypse, he wrote, "[t]here will be no act of madness, no single villain on whom to discharge guilt; just the flow of history."[78]

It is relatively safe to attack "the flow of history," which neither has temper tantrums nor tries to destroy your academic career by telephone calls to the Ford Foundation. The result of trying to dissociate without offending, however, as Hans Morgenthau pointed out in his *New York Review of Books* critique of Goodwin, "is bound to be psychologically revealing but politically calamitous."[79] The effect tends to be neither dissociation nor avoidance of offense.

Another compromise made by those whose consciences demand that they must say something but who don't want to get into a brawl is to seek, and fix blame on, "root causes." These, like "the flow of history," also don't bite back. Charles Frankel of Columbia University, when he resigned in November 1967 as Assistant Secretary of State, was bitterly disillusioned with Vietnam policy and its effects on his educational and cultural affairs programs. But he largely confined his public criticism[80] to attacks on institutional and bureaucratic inflexibility, rather than spotlighting identifiable, disastrous policies and the very specific men who were still making them. His public-protest book, *High on Foggy Bottom,* vividly portrays the frustrations of governing, the bureaucratic diffusion of power and of responsibility. "It is poets and military conquerors," Frankel tells us, "who have a simple conception of power as the successful exercise of one's will. That is what writing a poem or knocking down the walls of Jericho is like. But in a political or bureaucratic context a man works through others . . . your policies . . . become collective products."[81]

In Frankel's too benevolent world, there are no villains, only a faceless bureaucratic network creating "a kind of rolling commitment to policy." Decisions and disasters tend to accrue like silt at the mouth of a river. At each stage along the line of command, a vague policy, not necessarily believed in by anybody, is embroidered and passed along the bureaucratic busy-work grid.[82] The product of this network is something quite unintended by the participants: like the game in which a dozen players are each, in sequence, asked to draw one small part of a human figure, then fold the paper over, and pass it on to the next player. Such an explanation, however, excuses bad policies as the sum total of everyone's minor inadvertences. It does not account for those policies, like the Vietnam escalations, that are the direct results of deliberate decisions by misguided but dynamic leaders, willingly carried out by loyal team players, under cover of deliberate lies and subterfuge.

Frankel was clearly appalled by the folly of Vietnam policy and did not mind saying so in public once he had left Washington. This, in itself, marks him as an unusually brave man in this era of silence. After he had submitted his letter of resignation, he had repeated calls—one from a Presidential aide at three in the morning announcing he was speaking "from the Oval Office"—urging him to keep silent. At first the calls were condescending: "You've established an excellent record. Now don't spoil everything by shooting your mouth off." Then abusive: "We'll see to it you never get another job in Washington." Finally, there were threats:

"The President will be so angry he'll kill off the very cultural affairs programs you've worked so hard to build up."

Despite all this, Frankel spoke up. But his way of speaking out was a bit like a liberal theologian's effort to explain evil without recourse to the devil. Thus, it is primitive to incarnate what is really an aspect of us all. But while this may be valid theology, it is bad politics. It seems to accept the insidious kind of argument later used by President Nixon in connection with Watergate: I'm only the President. I can't be responsible for what goes on around here. In a democracy, power *must* remain firmly linked to accountability. And it is no kindness to the cause of systemic reform to overlook the very concrete, intentional decisions of identifiable men—not least the President, his foreign-policy advisers, and the Secretary of State—who brought the U.S. into a massive land war in Asia. In politics without a concept of fault there can be no reform.

John W. Gardner is an example of the man of Great Intellect, who is so rigorous in his analysis of events that he comes to concern himself solely with the search for Root-Causes, for Fundamental-Institutional-Restructuring and Goal-Reorientation, so as to bring about Basic-Social-Transformation. In the quest after these transcendent objectives the practical question of means tends to be overlooked.

When John Gardner resigned as Secretary of Health, Education, and Welfare in January 1968, it was widely believed and reported by friends that he had become disillusioned with the shift in Presidential priorities away from the social war on poverty and urban blight to the military war in Vietnam.[83] Privately, he let it be known that the Administration was providing an inadequate response to the crisis in the cities.[84] Publicly, however, he went out of his way to assert that the "war was not a factor"[85] in his decision to quit. His letter of resignation reached beyond formal courtesy, commending the President "for the great programs which you have initiated" during "a period of so much progress— in education, health and all the other programs to which you are deeply committed.''[86] The Secretary also prepared a memorandum for Johnson summarizing "our progress" in domestic programs to dispel the suspicion that his resignation implied dissatisfaction.[87]

Thereafter, for the next two years, only in vague hints did Gardner connect the need to end the war with his campaign for a better society. "A great many people seem to believe that the war will be brought to an end . . ." he said. But then he quickly changed the subject, proceeding in broad, statesmanlike brush strokes to call for "Justice, liberty, the worth of the individual, equality of opportunity, individual responsibility, brotherhood. . . ."[88] And "excellence." Gardner appears to have taken to heart Socrates' admonition that "no greater good can happen to a man than to discuss human excellence every day. . . ."[89]

It took the Cambodian "incursion" for Gardner to find a clear and present issue: two and a half years and a Presidential election later. A speech was to have been given to the Illinois Constitutional Convention on May 13, 1970, but was canceled when the advance text was read by the officers. Writing of the Cambodian invasion, Gardner criticized the "suddenness of the decision, the lack of consultation with key leaders, the evidence of internal differences," and noted that these "brought to a climax the growing crisis of confidence in our leadership."[90] Nevertheless, in chronicling the charges being leveled at President Nixon in that hour of massive domestic agitation, the former Secretary carefully stood aside from alignment: "A great many informed Americans believe, justly or not, that the President is isolated . . . justly or not that he has not offered the level of moral leadership which we so need . . . justly or not that he has given undue sanction to members of his administration who seem committed to divisive courses of action. . . ."[91] *Justly or not:* still the litany of semi-non-involvement in the critical issue of the day. And with that, Gardner returned to his familiar theme of the need for reconciliation and constitutional reform. "I am not interested in indicting the President," he proclaimed, "all of us have failed in our duty as Americans."[92] Again, no one is responsible.

◇

Gardner's failure to indict the war system and its managers in his effort to rally the nation to a concerted attack on domestic decay may not have been due to a failure of personal courage but merely an inability to make the connection between the war and the downgrading of domestic priorities. His closest colleagues, however, say that he did appreciate the connection, even though he chose not to make it publicly. This was too bad. After the silent departures of McGeorge Bundy, Bill Moyers, George Ball, and Robert McNamara—the last one of these on the same day as Gardner—a substantial portion of the American public yearned desperately for one man to walk out and become the antiwar spokesman, one experienced, ethically and politically responsible leader to articulate, sharply and specifically, the case against the hard-nosed security managers with their "inside" information and operational wisdom who were still bent on enlarging the war, squandering American lives and funds, and dissipating the nation's moral leadership abroad. Gardner, a man of evident compassion in an Administration of war hawks, realists, and systems analysts, was something of a hero to the nation's poor, to students, and to intellectuals. Perhaps the doves and the poor, confusing their hopes with political reality, invested Gardner's resignation with a symbolic significance that, objectively, it did not have.

At Health, Education, and Welfare, on the day the Secretary resigned, employees lined the halls in an emotional tribute. A letter signed by more than a hundred of them deplored their chief's sudden resignation: "Mr. Secretary," it said, "those of us who stay will miss you. They will miss your leadership, your emotional commitment. . . . Under your guidance H.E.W. blossomed" but, they feared "an unfavorable climate now exists." Referring unmistakably to the war, they went on: "Priorities have changed . . . we know, as you do, Mr. Secretary, that all casualties of war do not occur on battlefields. We abhor the direct loss of life as well as the loss of opportunity to wage a battle against poverty and disease in this country."[93]

It was this passionate sentiment the H.E.W. employees

thought they heard in John Gardner's resignation, but it was they, not he, who had articulated it. Yet how could the Secretary have imagined it possible to lead a people's crusade against poverty, blight, and civic unrest in 1968 without taking a stand on the war?

The irony of Gardner's postresignation strategy is that, in seeking to accomplish too much, in taking the high road and in avoiding attacks on specific persons and policies, he dissipated the opportunity which any important resignation offers. That limited opportunity, at most, is to focus public concern on a specific, immediate issue—whether it be President Wilson's warlike diplomatic note to Germany, Truman's failure to build the supercarriers, or President Nixon's firing of a special prosecutor investigating White House activities. A public-protest resignation that aims squarely at a decision to raise the level of U.S. troop commitments in Vietnam and to cut back funds from domestic programs is more likely to be effective than general fulminations, however perceptive, against the institutional shortcomings of American democracy. The road to general institutional reform leads through the specific public denunciation of abuses of power by those in a position to know and with the ethical autonomy to tell.

A resigner may summon the people to a higher level of analysis in pointing the way to reform, but he is unlikely to find many followers unless the intellectual journey upward begins at a plain, earthy point of practical departure, and unless he puts himself on the front line. Words of protest by a resigning public official which are not pointed to a limited, specific disagreement with real persons and their concrete decisions tend to represent a retreat from the opportunity offered by resignation.[94] So do attacks against disembodied entities like "history" or "institutional intransigence." Eugene McCarthy, in running against President Johnson in the New Hampshire primaries and focusing attention on the President's personal responsibility for the war and its consequences, did more to remedy urban blight than all the sociological and institutional analyses of the systemic defects of American society made by critics who begin with the assumption that "we are all guilty" and that no one in particular is at fault.

The effect, perhaps the unconscious intent, of these ineffective tactics of protest resignation is similar to that achieved by the driver who paints the left side of his car green and the right side red in order to confuse the witnesses at his next accident. The impossible mission, deliberately assumed or not, of those who fudge their protest resignations is both not to offend "the team," to appear loyal to the President and the inner circle, and yet to be perceived as a courageous critic of national policy in Congress, the media, and the universities.

Not that vaunting ambition solely or, in many instances, even primarily, explains the ambiguous conduct of men with the ethical awareness of a John Gardner. The reality is more complex. Like so many U.S. cabinet members, Gardner was not a politician when he entered government. He had no taste for public dispute, no desire to lead a crusade. President Johnson had taken him from the dignified obscurity of the foundation world and placed him in a position of responsibility. The Chief had trusted him, had taken him on rambling excursions into the inner recesses of his psyche. In Gardner's world, a decent man in whom the President of the United States has chosen to confide, doesn't turn around and kick him in the shins. The only trouble with these sentiments is that they perceive the government of the country as a network of personal relations between a President and his staff, rather than as part of a public process in which the central role is assigned to the people. Thus, to a public official with a taste for service but none for politics, maintaining a civilized standard of personal decency to the President tends to loom larger than any abstract duty to "the public" or "the system."

Another way of fudging a protest resignation, of copping out of effective public dissent while still seeming to be possessed of heroic ethical autonomy, is to delay going public just long enough for the issue to become—that deadly word!—academic. Washington, today, is as full of lately self-confessed opponents of the Vietnam war as postwar Berlin was of Germans claiming Jewish grandmothers. If all the top State, White House, and Pentagon officials whose recently published memoirs place them squarely in the camp of the doves had indeed been doves, Presidents Kennedy, Johnson, and Nixon must have conceived, organized, administered and almost fought the war alone.

The chroniclers of former administrations are particularly adept at walking the tightrope between publishing too early—in which case the Establishment will thereafter exclude them—or too late, in which event their royalties suffer. The loyalty and royalty issues do, indeed, get carefully weighed in deciding exactly when to go public.

Spruille Braden, to take an extreme case of loyalty over royalty, resigned on May 29, 1947, in opposition to the U.S. policy of arming Latin America, and Argentina in particular, said nothing publicly, and waited twenty-four years, until 1971, to publish his side of the story.[95] The issues, the Peronistas, and the venerable Ambassador Braden himself do remain with us. But Braden's public disclosure cannot now receive the attention it might had the book appeared in the 1940s. But, then, Braden had striven to remain, essentially, a team player. Many of his friends, Braden writes, wondered that he did not "go public" on so key an issue. They "marvelled that I refrained from making a scandal. . . . But I had departed with dignity as far as the public was concerned, and I was content to leave it at that."[96]

Robert Lansing resigned as Woodrow Wilson's Secretary of State on February 12, 1920, finally snapping the long, frayed tether that had tied him to President Wilson. A period of intense infighting, rancorous recrimination, and profound policy differences between them had developed at the Versailles Peace Conference. They disagreed with each other as much as with any foreign country: over the defensive alliance with France, over whether to cede the Chinese province of Shantung to the Japanese, over the terms of the League Covenant, and over linking that instrument with the Peace Treaty. Lansing considered the cession of Shantung a sellout, the enforcement provisions of the League Covenant as a device to "legalize the mastery of might."[97] Yet he kept putting off resigning and going public, even when an impetuous junior member of the U.S. Versailles delegation, William C. Bullitt, angrily quit and testified before the Senate Foreign Relations Committee that Lansing had privately described the Peace Treaty as "thoroughly bad," the League as "useless," and had opined that Congress, if fully informed, would unquestionably defeat both.

When Lansing finally did resign under duress, the break came not over a pointed policy issue like Shantung or the League but in an acrimonious muddle about the Secretary having summoned the cabinet during Wilson's incapacity.[98] Only this dispute was made public. It was not until after the battle over Senate ratification of the League—and Wilson's Presidential term—had ended that Lansing finally let the voters in on that important but now dead policy issue.[99] "There have been obvious reasons of propriety for my silence until now . . ." he wrote, in a remark that calls to mind G.B. Shaw's admonition that "Decency Is Indecency's Conspiracy of Silence."[100] But the time had come "when a frank account of our differences can be given publicity without a charge being made of disloyalty to the Administration in power."[101]

Yet the team rules continued to haunt him. In publishing his book, Lansing admitted that he knew that there would be those who would accuse him of deceitful conduct. His public revelation, he wrote, " . . . may be characterized in certain quarters as disloyal to a superior and as violative of the seal of silence which is considered generally to apply to the intercourse and communications between the President and his official advisers."[102] In self-defense, he protested that he was merely following a principle that silence is waived when the resigning official's honor is impugned by his Chief. He declared: "Certainly no American official is in honor bound to remain silent under such an imputation which approaches a charge of faithlessness and of secret, if not open, avoidance of duty." He had "the right to present the case to the American people in order that they may decide. . . ."[103]

"Was I justified then? Am I justified now?"[104] the harried author asks the reader. As Lansing correctly surmised, there were those who thought not. Lansing had merely proven Wilson's charge of insubordination, Josephus Daniels sniffed. "'O that mine adversary had written a book,'" he confided to his diary, noting that he "preferred that an enemy should destroy himself with his own pen than to be compelled to use the sword."[105]

More serious criticism was made by William Bullitt, who accused Lansing of saying too little, rather than too much, and, particularly, of waiting too long. Undoubtedly embittered by Lansing's expression of contempt for his own earlier, more courageous breach of confidence,[106] Bullitt, in an open letter to Lansing, declared:

> The real difference between us is this: You now publicly urge that the American people were and are entitled to know the truth. You have taken them into your confidence after they have given judgment upon the treaty, when it is too late for the facts you reveal to help them. I acted when the issue was still doubtful, and it seemed certain that the treaty would be passed.[107]

Lansing's lengthy but "decent" delay in going public robbed his protest resignation of its relevance and effectiveness in enriching the public dialogue when it counted, without sparing him much of the opprobrium of open dissent.

The problem of when to publish and how much to say also faced Raymond Moley, a key member of Roosevelt's brain trust[108]—who resigned in disagreement with the government after the failure of the London Economic Conference of June 1933. The initial cause of the break was a telegram Moley sent Roosevelt from the London home of his "good friend" Ambassador Robert W. Bingham, corrosively blaming Secretary of State Cordell Hull for the failure of the Conference and questioning his "adequacy." Bingham thoughtfully passed the telegram to Hull.

This was the muddle-age of American Depression diplomacy. Roosevelt had twice, during the Conference, seemed to disown his own delegates publicly. Courses already set and strategies already worked out kept disintegrating. Amid the ruins, Hull at once sent his own dispatch to Roosevelt, asserting that Moley had almost singlehandedly produced the London debacle, had set a woman from his office to spying on the Secretary, and had secretly and disastrously negotiated behind the delegation's back with British Prime Minister James Ramsay MacDonald.[109]

On his return to the U.S., Moley was first shifted from State, then resigned. He denied for the record that there had been any conflict with Roosevelt or Hull,[110] "although," he said later, "I had plenty to growl about. . . ."[111] He did, however, openly attack Hull as an "old-fashioned Democrat" who adhered to "international views" which were "out of harmony with the rational economy of the New Deal."[112]

Until 1936, Moley and Roosevelt maintained a love-hate relationship which the former prized for its prestige and the latter for old times' sake and because Moley could still ghostwrite excellent speeches, even when he disagreed. Their ties closely resembled those between President Johnson and Richard Goodwin for the first year after the latter had quit. By 1937, however, Moley's combative views as a journalist and lecturer had brought the relationship to an end. Yet it was not until 1939 that Moley finally published his version of some of the events leading up to his resignation.

Appropriately entitled *After Seven Years*,[113] Moley's book was treated as a breach of the club rules against public resignation, both by the President and even by F.D.R.'s opponents, despite the time that had elapsed between Moley's resigning and speaking up. Writing to Owen D. Young, Roosevelt spoke of "the false innuendos and complete misstatement of fact" which appear all through the Moley "writings" and regretted that "people of the Moley type are wholly willing to write history with the mere objective of getting *Saturday Evening Post* prices."[114] The book was reviewed, prominently but venomously, by Nicholas Roosevelt, a distant relative but ordinarily a political foe of the President. It "is an exposure of much information of a highly confidential nature about the Roosevelt administration," he grumbled. "At the same time, the writing of it displays unpleasant evidences of a lack of that common loyalty which is the basis of close personal relationships."[115] Never mind whether the issues were important, whether their publication conduced to an informed public. Among members of the club, even ones who are political adversaries like the two Roosevelts, the public's so-called right to know is an utterly invalid excuse for breaking the rules against public disclosure. These rules apply to gentlemen at the time of resigning and continue to bind them for as long as they care to be known as gentlemen.

To Moley, the issue appeared quite differently. "If I wrote another bland memoir, the reflection would be on the book. For the sake of history, I preferred the reflection to be on me. To pussyfoot would have been to have the book condemned by historians. To speak up was to invite condemnation by my former colleagues, to bring opprobrium on myself. I preferred to write the book and take the rap."[116]

The merest handful of Americans have been willing to take the rap. Almost all have preferred, when in disagreement, to soldier on, to resign quietly, or to fudge their public protest.

In general, debate on crucial issues affecting the public's lives and well-being is impoverished by this practice of nonparticipation by those whose experience inside government ought to equip them to be the most effective critics.

Of those who have defected, most have chosen to disclose their disaffection in obscure words, abstract images, and muted tones. Dissent, such as it is, has been typified by John Gardner rather than by William Jennings Bryan; by vague mumblings, the issuing of dignified and inoffensive reports under cover of Establishment "study groups"; by an occasional book published too late to have political, as distinguished from historical, value.

There are dramatic, but also dramatically few, instances of persons who openly attack policy. Even more rare is the resigner who points the finger at the Chief Executive or at specific former colleagues. Elliot Richardson, William Ruckelshaus, Webster Davis, William Jennings Bryan, Lindley Garrison, Henry Breckinridge, John Sullivan, James Farley, Henry Wallace, Harold Ickes, and Kenneth Davis stand out like lonely stooks of wheat on a flat prairie. That this is so should be of deep concern to those who care about the ethical condition of American government and politics.

This is not to say that whenever a senior official encounters a crisis of ethical autonomy, resignation followed by public protest must invariably be the only moral option. Under certain circumstances, the tactics of asserting one's ethical autonomy may actually lead one to stay on the job, and staying on thus need not invariably bespeak a deaf ear to ethical imperatives. Conversational syndrome number one among persons at an ethical breaking point in top-echelon government is: "I'm only staying on the job because, if I don't, someone else will do it worse."

What this means, and its ethical implication, varies enormously according to who says it and under what circumstances. A "good functionary" who is basically supportive of his leader's policy—Adolph Eichmann, for example—would argue, to himself and perhaps to a few intimates, that, were he not doing his job, someone else would be dispatching 8 million persons, instead of only 6, to the gas ovens. But the same kind of rationale for staying on quietly can be used under quite different circumstances. The Nobel Prize-winning German chemist Otto Hahn, who codiscovered uranium fission in 1938, covertly arranged the escape from Germany of his Jewish collaborator, Lisa Meitner; then, knowing the military potential of his discovery, he stayed on as head of the wartime German nuclear-research program in a clandestine, and successful, effort to impede development of Hitler's atomic bomb.

Most men who choose to stay on cannot realistically hope to be so effective in subverting the policy they find ethically repugnant. This may be a matter of the degree of dedication to the covert purpose. Pierre Laval was less of a force for moderating the Nazi occupation of France than Henri Philippe Pétain, for example. And the man who stays on must weigh not only the gains to be had by staying and opposing from inside but also the opportunities missed by not being able to oppose publicly. Even Pétain, the heroic symbol of World War I triumphs, might have been of more use to France in London than in Vichy. History and the populations most directly concerned seem to feel that Queen Wilhelmina did better work by leaving the occupied Netherlands than did King Leopold of Belgium by remaining on the job. Still, there is the temptation to "see it through"—to tell oneself that by going along one can perhaps steer events, modify the way policy is applied, or see that the worst aspects of the policy get waylaid in the bureaucratic thicket.[117]

This proclivity to stay on can be further reinforced by invoking widely used moral tranquilizers: "All policy options are essentially choices between evils"; or, "Since the policy is set, I'd be wasting my small hoard of effectiveness if I try to hold out"; or, "It's not my responsibility since the decision rests with someone else"; or, "You can't win 'em all." Then there is the popular adage—good folk wisdom but also ideal for ducking an ethical confrontation— "He that . . . runs away, may live to fight another day."[118] Hubert Humphrey, during the height of the Vietnam war, used the "if-I-don't-do-it-someone-else-will-do-it-worse" argument with liberal friends who urged him to resign the Vice-Presidency. He reminded them that, if he did, Speaker of the House John McCormack, an old relic of the Boston boss politics era, would be only a heartbeat removed from the Presidency.[119]

Aleksandr I. Solzhenitsyn has written in *The Gulag Archipelago:* "Every man always has at hand a dozen glib little reasons why he is right, why he does not sacrifice himself."[120]

Robert McNamara, after 1966, sometimes confided to friends that he was only staying on in order to prevent the Vietnam escalation from getting worse. Townsend Hoopes, half admiringly, half critically, notes the Defense Secretary's genius for "managing" difficult decisions without confronting the basic ethical and policy issues. After the January 1968 Tet offensive, he recalls, General William Westmoreland asked President Johnson to send a further 100,000 U.S. troops immediately, with a further 100,000 by the end of the year. It would be difficult to find a more specific issue on which to resign and go public. Instead, "[e]ven in the advanced state of disenchantment which had overtaken him by late February, McNamara's instinctive reaction on receiving the new military request was to 'manage the problem,' whittle down the numbers, muffle the differences, and thereby avoid a bruising confrontation within the Administration. . . ." Hoopes concludes: "It was a technique which exemplified McNamara's mastery of, and strong instinct for, managed decision-making: by holding control within very narrow channels, developing an advance position, and moving fast, he finessed serious debate on basic issues. . . . It had worked smoothly, but it had also resulted in a twenty-five-fold increase in the military manpower commitment to Vietnam—from 21,000 to 510,000—over a three-year period."[121] Those who stay on may think they are using their position to change policy only to find, too late, that their position has used them to reinforce the *status quo*.

Also staying on, Charles Frankel wrote in his diary in 1966, "unless Vietnam policy changes radically, I won't stay past the end of 1967 at the latest. . . . But as of now, dim though the prospect looks, I've still got a fighting chance to help accomplish some important and lasting things. They certainly won't be accomplished if I leave. . . ."[122]

A senior official may, therefore, choose not to resign and go public, but rather to stick it out, for reasons that are themselves manifestations of his ethical autonomy. His decision may be tactically wise or foolish, and his ethical reasoning may be sound, faulty or even bogus, self-deluding or self-justifying. But in some instances, not to resign could be a moral act. What is much more difficult to justify is the decision to resign, but not to speak one's mind. To resolve an ethical dilemma by leaving quietly or with a compromised, ambiguous public protest is to give up whatever opportunity may exist for effecting change from within the government, without using the freedom that comes with being released from public office. Moreover, to resign and to deny any differences with the government, if such differences do exist, is an attempt to delude the public which, in time, encourages the most profound cynicism about the ethics of those who govern.

Yet ambitious men and women, possessed of red-blooded political aspirations, cannot be entirely to blame for heeding a lively sense of self-preservation; at least as blameworthy is the political system that prices ethical autonomy so high. Why does it so penalize persons who merely wish, for a time, to dissociate themselves from government on a question of policy and who openly seek to argue public issues in the democratic arena? Why have the social graces of loyalty and discretion taken such callous priority over the political virtues of candor, high principle, and being one's own person?

Resignation
British Style

ALTHOUGH THE BRITISH are notorious for what Thomas Carlyle described as "le grand talent pour le silence,"[1] the historic behavior of their cabinet and subcabinet ministers evinces a long and firm political habit of ethical autonomy, manifested through the time- and custom-honored tradition of public-protest resignation.

It is said, in defense of the contrary American tradition of overriding group loyalty which submerges ethical autonomy beneath the greater good of team play, that a democracy cannot function without cooperative social behavior—without everyone "going along." If individual cabinet members were to set their subjective judgments against the collective will of "the government," the resulting erosion of executive cohesiveness would quickly lead to paralysis of the will and of the ability to rule. The British experience, despite the significant differences in constitutional structure of the two countries,[2] shows that this fear is exaggerated. It indicates that when there is a reasonable degree of ethical autonomy on the part of those in top government positions, far from paralyzing the political system, a tradition of public-protest resignation develops, with its own etiquette, and that this enriches and protects the nation's public life. It is democratically enriching to have Parliament and the voters "in" on the more important differences of judgment among the decision-makers. Similarly, the open vying of ethical constructs and counterposing of policy options protects the nation from rule by whim or fiat.

To an American, the British practice is astounding: in the

◇

willingness of public men and women to resign on issues of conscience, in the explicitness and voluble intensity of their protests, and in the tolerance of the British system for such public demonstration of ethical autonomy. When, for example, Lord Robert Cecil resigned in 1918 as Under Secretary in the Foreign Office over the disestablishment of the Church of Wales, that voice of the Establishment *The Times* of London, while differing on the issue, remarked approvingly, "no one is entitled to question the dictates of another's conscience when they are so palpably sincere."[3] Not only did Cecil's conduct seem honorable even to those who disagreed with him but within five years he was back in the cabinet as Lord Privy Seal, a munificent promotion.

This is the heart of the contrast. In interviewing dozens of American former White House and cabinet officials, it became dramatically clear that the successful men who build their lives and careers around IBM, Wall Street, or Washington law firms very much need to be perceived, and to perceive themselves, as prospective secretaries of the Treasury, or White House special counsels. It is of extraordinary importance always to be part of that Establishment pool from which future cabinets and White House staff are drawn. Part-time work for the White House or a department, as head of a task force or study group, for example, is welcome reassurance that one is still in the pool. But again and again in interviews we were told by these Americans: "You don't resign in public protest against your own team if you ever hope to be invited back into the game."

In sharp contrast, our British interviews yielded the opposite answer: "Speaking up did me no harm. On balance, I think it rather helped my career in politics." The resigner may be counterattacked by those whose judgments he impugns, and, of course, there are risks. But the probability is that, after a period out of office, the resigner will be able to stage a comeback.

This perception of the difference in career costs is borne out by statistics. We surveyed all British Cabinet Secretaries, Under Secretaries, Ministers in Cabinet, and Junior Ministers in the

period 1900–70—a group consisting of roughly the same top echelons as those studied in the American survey[4]—and, after eliminating
those categories whose resignations were probably not voluntary
and who had no reasonable future career prospects,[5] found 78
"prime" resigners.[6]

OF THE 78 BRITISH RESIGNERS, 42 (53.8 PER CENT), OR MORE
THAN HALF, LEFT OFFICE IN A PUBLIC DECLARATION OF PROTEST
AGAINST A GOVERNMENT POLICY. THUS, WHILE PUBLIC-PROTEST
RESIGNATION IS AN EXTREMELY RARE PHENOMENON IN TWEN-
TIETH-CENTURY U.S. POLITICS (8.7 PER CENT), IT IS A RATHER
COMMON OCCURRENCE IN BRITAIN. MOREOVER, THE CAREER COSTS
OF "GOING PUBLIC" IN BRITAIN ARE STATISTICALLY INSIGNIF-
ICANT. OF THOSE WHO RESIGNED IN PUBLIC PROTEST, 45.2 PER
CENT SUBSEQUENTLY RETURNED TO OTHER EQUIVALENT OR
HIGHER FULL-TIME GOVERNMENT POSTS (19 OF 42), WHILE OF
THOSE WHO RESIGNED SILENTLY, ONLY 41.7 PER CENT (15 OF 36)
RETURNED. THUS, IN TERMS OF SUBSEQUENT CAREER, THOSE WHO
RESIGNED IN PUBLIC PROTEST DID MARGINALLY BETTER—BUT IN
ANY EVENT NO WORSE—THAN THEIR MORE COMPLAISANT COL-
LEAGUES.

Where lesser part-time patronage appointments are concerned, however, those who went public did considerably less well
than those who did not: 14.3 per cent as against 30.5 per cent
subsequently received such "plums" as the Prime Minister is able
to dispense to persons no longer making a career in the House of
Commons. Taking the two categories of "return to public office"—full time and part time—together, 25 of the 42 who went
public returned (59.5 per cent) as against 26 of the 36 (69.4 per cent)
who left silently. This statistic is much less significant, however,
than that showing equal opportunity of return to full-time senior
political office in the government. The comparatively strong statistical showing of the silent resigners in securing part-time patronage
appointments is primarily due to the fact that, during this century,
seven of them were given peerages, a part-time plum entitling them
to sit in the House of Lords, while only three of those who spoke up

went to the Upper House. This is not necessarily because of career discrimination against those who go public but, rather, because most protesters wished to stay in active politics in the House of Commons, while more of the quiet resigners were happy to "retire" to the Lords.

It may thus be inferred that while in America the general perception about career costs and the actual high cost of speaking up are mutually reinforcing mechanisms insuring conformity and public silence among top officials at the ethical breaking point, in Britain the situation is just the opposite. There, the relative lack of actual career costs, together with a popular expectation that going public does not forfeit future ministerial prospects, makes for ethically autonomous behavior at the breaking point.

◇

That Americans who speak up are so heavily penalized while the British are not is particularly remarkable because, as we have seen, most Americans who do go public tend to fudge their protest, while the British, overwhelmingly, let out long, loud, clear, and repeated blasts. The public-protest style of a William Jennings Bryan is exceptional, even unique, in the annals of U.S. resignation behavior, while in Britain it is more nearly the rule.[7] Not only do British protest resignations tend toward boldness in style but also in substance. Few issues are out of bounds.

Even in wartime, public-protest resignation is permissible. Sir John Simon resigned as Prime Minister Herbert Asquith's Home Secretary at the height of World War I, in vehement opposition to conscription. In the Commons he openly fought the Military Service Act, speaking frequently and with intense conviction, offering amendments and pleading for wide exemption for conscientious objectors. "I should call myself a coward," he said, "if . . . I refused to put before the House . . . the convictions which I hold." He insisted that "it is right and proper, even in the very crisis of war, for an honest opinion to be honestly and moderately stated. . . ."[8] Although there were some criticisms of Simon for undermining the war effort, his public resignation and opposition clearly did not destroy his political career, even though he reports having for a time suffered "an hour of great personal unpopularity" and that his resignation was "a long setback in my political career."[9] This view seems excessively dour. Asquith seemed to feel no resentment against him, saying only: "Poor Simon, I am so sorry for him in his self-righteousness."[10] And, indeed, Simon returned as Foreign Secretary, serving from 1931–35, and, thereafter he held numerous prominent government posts, including another as Lord Chancellor in the cabinet formed by Churchill during World War II. Were he an American, Simon would never have been recalled, particularly in so parallel a situation. "Simon?" one could hear the President say. "Don't you remember what he did the *last* time?"

Simon's public protest in wartime is by no means unique. Sir Edward Carson resigned as Attorney General in October 1915, speaking up in unvarnished protest over the conduct of the war. He attacked the inefficiency and drift of the unwieldy Asquith cabinet, calling them, to their faces in Parliament, "twenty-three blind mice" and comparing the Prime Minister to "a Vicar chairing a Vestry meeting."[11] Dissatisfied with events at Gallipoli, his resignation was finally provoked by the government's decision to abandon "our gallant little ally," Serbia.[12] He did not hesitate to reveal what had gone on in the cabinet. "At the last War Committee that I attended," Carson said, the majority had decided "upon the advice of our military advisers, that it was too late to assist Serbia." If so, he reported telling the Cabinet Committee, "Serbia ought to be told . . . in order that the little nation might take . . . steps . . . to preserve herself from absolute destruction."[13] Nor did Carson shrink from public ventilation of war plans. To "send an Army to Egypt to await action which may or which may not be possible," he thundered, "seems the most futile and hesitating decision that could be come to, and one calculated merely to lead to a further dissipation of our forces."[14] As for a systematic campaign strategy, up to the time of resignation "I could find no trace of any such existing."[15] Consistently, the government had failed to keep itself, let alone the public, informed of real conditions, which had rapidly deteriorated. "I think it is a great public scandal that three months have elapsed since the [Gallipoli] landing . . . and that, except a telegram or two, we have never heard one word of those operations"[16] even while the government had known that its troops could not hold out.[17] Could one conceive of a disenchanted Robert McNamara or Maxwell Taylor speaking out like this after the Tet offensive?

Carson reinforced these charges by reference to a cabinet memorandum circulated by his party's leader in the House of Commons, Bonar Law. This skates on thin ice, not because it raised militarily sensitive issues in wartime but because it came close to quoting a cabinet document, which is frowned upon. Nevertheless, Carson was not reprimanded, much less prosecuted under the Official Secrets Act. On the contrary, his public protest helped banish Winston Churchill (who was assigned responsibility for the Gallipoli fiasco) from the government. Carson, moreover, was back as First Lord of the Admiralty in just over a year and, in 1917, even rose to membership of the inner War Cabinet.

David Lloyd George, in resigning from the same wartime cabinet, did even better for himself. In a long, discursive letter of resignation he informed the Prime Minister that he was exiting "in order to inform the people of the real condition of affairs," including "delay, hesitation, lack of forethought and vision."[18] This was quickly followed by the fall of Prime Minister Asquith and Lloyd George's own recall to form a new government.

During the 1956 Suez invasion by Britain and France, two junior ministers of the government resigned in protest: Anthony Nutting from the Foreign Office and Sir Edward Boyle from Treasury. Boyle in his public letter of resignation said: "I do not honestly feel that I can defend, as a Minister, the recent policy of the Government, and I feel bound to associate myself with that body of opinion which deeply deplores what has been done."[19] In a speech shortly afterward, he even congratulated the United States for refusing Britain the fuel and economic support necessary to continue the Middle East intervention.[20] Despite these outspoken criticisms, Boyle was back in government in just over two months as a Parliamentary Secretary, and Minister at the Treasury in a little less than three years. He went on to become Minister of Education in 1962 and Minister of State for Education and Technology in 1964.

Nutting, on the other hand, although he could not bring himself to remain in a government that was engaged in an action he believed unconscionable, at first played down his opposition. He had been asked by Eden to delay publicizing his resignation until after the opening of the military campaign, and he was then further dissuaded from making a Parliamentary statement of his reasons for resigning by the Chancellor of the Exchequer, Harold Macmillan. Nutting says he was told by the man who was to succeed Eden as Prime Minister: "Why say anything at all? You have already been proved right and we have been proved wrong. You have also done the right thing by resigning and, if you keep silent now, you will be revered and rewarded. You will lead the Party one day."[21] Nutting was won over, at least briefly, by these blandishments. But he was probably ill-advised not to insist on his customary right to speak up. In the end, it earned him no credit with the Tory Establishment and prevented him from becoming an effective leader of more radical forces. Paradoxically, Nutting, a promising young leader in 1956, is one of the few British protest resigners to have done his career serious damage. But this may have been, in part, because he said too little rather than too much at the moment when it really mattered.

Issues involving national security and defense do not arise only in wartime. Anthony Eden, Lord Salisbury (then Lord Cranborne),[22] and A. Duff Cooper each resigned from cabinet in public protest against aspects of Neville Chamberlain's prewar policy of appeasement, and, in the process, opened up public debate on matters of the greatest diplomatic sensitivity. Eden quit as Foreign Secretary over the Prime Minister's decision to negotiate with Mussolini about Italy's Ethiopian invasion, the intervention in the

Spanish Civil War, and other matters. Chamberlain's decision to open negotiations was taken without informing Eden. "I did not show my letter [to Mussolini] to the Foreign Secretary," Chamberlain wrote in his diary, "for I had the feeling that he would object to it."[23] Sir Horace Wilson, confidant of Chamberlain at the Treasury, warned Eden's Parliamentary Private Secretary that if Eden went public, "he would use the full power of the Government machine in an attack upon A.E.'s [Anthony Eden's] past record with regard to the dictators and the shameful obstruction by the F.O. [Foreign Office] of the P.M.'s [Prime Minister's] attempts to save the peace of the world."[24]

This did not deter Eden. He proceeded to tell Parliament "that there has been too keen a desire on our part to make terms with others rather than that others should make terms with us."[25] He complained that "we yield to constant pressure"[26] and hinted that Italy had given Chamberlain a "now or never" ultimatum.[27] Salisbury added that "for His Majesty's Government to enter on official conversation would be regarded not as a contribution to peace, but as a surrender to blackmail."[28]

The dissenters' protests continued to gather intensity. When others were celebrating the Munich settlements, Eden warned that "Surely . . . foreign affairs cannot indefinitely be continued on the basis of [the hold-up demand] 'stand and deliver!' Successive surrenders bring only successive humiliation, and they, in their turn, more humiliating demands."[29] He went about the country calling for a government of national unity, full-speed mobilization, and warning against faith in Hitler's promises. "I am convinced," he cried, "that if the present methods in Europe are to be allowed to continue unchecked, we are heading straight for anarchy, for a universal tragedy which is going to involve us all."[30]

Salisbury echoed Eden. "Peace with *honour?*" he thundered after Munich. "I have looked and looked and I cannot see it. . . . The peace of Europe has in fact been saved . . . only by throwing to the wolves a little country. . . ."[31] Agreement of this sort "is not to cure the distemper from which the world is suffering, but merely to conceal from the patient the ravages of disease until it is too late to cure him at all."[32]

Of these men who resigned from the Chamberlain government to condemn appeasement and call for preparedness, the most vociferous was First Lord of the Admiralty Duff Cooper, who quit in the autumn of 1938. "The Prime Minister," Duff Cooper told Parliament, "has believed in addressing Herr Hitler through the language of sweet reasonableness. I have believed that he was more open to the language of the mailed fist." Speaking of Hitler's "terms," he said that when, as a cabinet member, he first saw them, "I said to myself 'If these are accepted it will be the end of all decency in the conduct of public affairs in the world.'"[33] He revealed a record of differences within the cabinet, over rearmament and over policy toward the Axis. Then, he continued with extraordinary poignance to speak a resigner's creed:

> I have given up an office that I loved, work in which I was deeply interested and a staff of which any man might be proud. I have given up associating in that work with my colleagues with whom I have maintained for many years the most harmonious relations, not only as colleagues but as friends. I have given up the privilege of serving as lieutenant to a leader whom I still regard with the deepest admiration and affection. I have ruined, perhaps, my political career. But that is a little matter; I have retained something which is to me of great value—I can still walk about the world with my head erect.[34]

The resignations of Eden, Salisbury, and Duff Cooper from Chamberlain's government no doubt caused the Prime Minister severe discomfiture, but the phenomenon, so firmly established in British life, was not one with which he could have been unfamiliar. Chamberlain had, himself, resigned in protest twenty-one years earlier from the wartime government of Lloyd George, charging that the cabinet's military recruitment policies were not, in his opinion, "an effective method of organizing recruiting."[35]

Even among militant pacifist leaders in Parliament, the sincerity of the three "hawks"[36] earned them the respect to which a resignation and cry of conscience is entitled in Britain. Speaking after Duff Cooper's address to the Commons, Labour-pacifist leader George Lansbury said: "As one who disagrees with him very much, I would congratulate him on the manner in which he stated his case and on his courage in taking the decision he did. It is a very good thing that the right hon. Gentleman should be prepared to sacrifice office and power because of his convictions and I would like to express my admiration of him for that."[37] In the event, the sacrifice was temporary. Eden, Salisbury, and Duff Cooper were all soon back in the cabinet of the new Prime Minister, Winston Churchill.

The process of British government vastly benefits from this recuperative mechanism which insures that once a sharp change of policy becomes necessary, there will be experienced officials ready to step back into office, tempered like steel by the fire of their own courage, and respected both for having been ahead of their time and willing to stand by their principles when it seemed disadvantageous to do so. It is revealing, however, to contrast the treatment accorded Eden, Salisbury, and Duff Cooper with that meted out to Lindley Garrison and Henry Breckinridge in America. These two, like Eden, Salisbury, and Duff Cooper, had been apostles of preparedness in a period just before a war. They, too, had resigned in an act of principled self-assertion and had taken their case to the people. When events proved them right, however, they were treated not to higher office but to cold rejection.

The national-security issue also arises in Britain, as in the United States, in variations on the "guns versus butter" theme. Some of the bitterest, most provocative public debates about defense policy have been generated by disputes between ministers responsible for such things as housing, health, and, more recently, foreign aid to developing countries, whose programs have been cut by the defense Establishment's seemingly insatiable demands on the treasury. What makes the "guns versus butter" debate different in Britain from that in America is that, in the United States, those whose public welfare programs are being cut either bear it quietly or else leave, like John Gardner from H.E.W., stanchly denying that the "guns versus butter" issue caused their resignation.

The British behave quite differently. Dr. Christopher Addison, a Minister of Munitions in World War I, had been asked by Lloyd George's government specifically to take charge of post-World War I housing programs. He drew up and initiated an extensive plan for slum clearance. After the program's initial acceptance, it began to run into difficulties and opposition. By April 1921, he was shifted out of the ministry (Health) responsible for housing and, three months later, resigned from the cabinet when the building program was further cut back for reasons of economy. In his letter of resignation, which Addison read to the House of Commons, he said: "I cannot think that Government can safely rest on a shifting opportunism to the neglect of conviction."[38] He complained of "a breach of faith on the part of the Government . . . a betrayal of our solemn pledges to the people."[39] If money was tight, programs other than housing should have been reduced. "We have poured out and are proposing to pour out in this year's Estimates 26,000,-000 pounds on Palestine and Mesopotamia, roughly 8 pounds per head of the population. I object to scattering this money on the population from Dan to Beersheba while at the same time stopping housing. If one or other of these expenditures has to stop, let the expenditure on Mesopotamia stop first. We have nothing much to show for it all!" Later, he added, "For your ten million pounds subsidy on housing you will at least see houses. You can see them on every high road now. I feel there is nothing to be ashamed of about it. You will not see much for your twenty-six million pounds in Mesopotamia."[40]

In expressing his anger at the priorities which curtail programs of social reform at home in order to sustain imperial commitments abroad, Addison previews by fifty years the feelings of John Gardner and Charles Frankel at the robbing of cultural and health programs in the United States to pay for the Vietnam war. But neither Gardner nor Frankel on resigning from office produced anything comparable to Addison's clear public delineation of the issues. "I object to stopping expenditure on housing," Addison argued, "while you are continuing it in the desert."[41] Accused of being a British isolationist, he replied, "I do not pose—I never did and never shall—as a little Englander, or anything of that sort. Let us discharge our obligations, wherever they are. But after all is said and done, the British Empire depends first and last upon the vitality, character and stamina of the people of these islands."[42]

The Mesopotamian parallels to Vietnam, incidentally, are remarkable. The Prime Minister, in defending the rises in expenditure on British overseas commitments by something very like the Vietnam theories of Presidents Johnson and Nixon, replied: "It is not easy, once you get into a country, to get out. . . . We had destroyed the Government. . . . We might have cleared out bag and baggage, helter skelter, but that would have left the whole country in absolute confusion. . . ."[43]

Addison's resignation blast carried him right out of the Liberal and into the Labour party. It was widely mooted that he was politically finished. Yet Addison was more wounding than wounded. In Lord Beaverbrook's view, his resignation speech had dealt Lloyd George "a damaging defeat" and "humiliation."[44] Addison, however, was back in the government within eight years. In 1930, with the election of a Labour government, he returned to the cabinet as Minister of Agriculture and Fisheries. In the 1945–51 Labour government, as Viscount Addison, he held five different cabinet appointments and became Leader of the House of Lords and the first Socialist Knight of the Garter.

The resignation in 1951 of Aneurin Bevan, one of the great orators of the century, resembles that of Dr. Addison. He, too, argued eloquently that the priorities of the government were shifting from social needs at home to the demands of imperial and global interests. Like Addison, he had just been moved out of the ministry in which he had initiated a large new scheme of social services. As in Addison's case, those services were then cut back. His letter, addressed to Prime Minister Clement Attlee while the latter was in hospital, despite its solicitous wishes for his good health, could not have helped Attlee's recovery from a duodenal ulcer. At their narrowest, Bevan's objections focused on the government's plan to begin charging the public for eyeglasses and lower dentures under the hitherto free medical scheme for which he had been responsible. Like an inverted pyramid, the argument rests on a small, very specific point on which is balanced a broad expanse of policy difference. At its broadest, Bevan's attack was directed at the entire tax philosophy and the system of priorities of Attlee's government: "The budget, in my view, is wrongly conceived in that it fails to apportion fairly the burdens of expenditure as between different social classes. It is wrong because it is based upon a scale of military expenditure in the coming year which is physically unattainable without grave extravagance in its spending."[45]

In his Parliamentary explanation, Bevan thundered, rather like Bryan, that "the Western world has embarked upon a campaign of arms production upon a scale, so quickly, and of such an extent that the foundations of political liberty and Parliamentary democracy will not be able to sustain the shock."[46] He begged his colleagues to "think before it is too late," and not to sacrifice social for military services. "It has always been clear that the weapons of the totalitarian States are, first, social and economic, and only next military. . . ."[47] England should not allow itself to be "dragged too far behind the wheels of American diplomacy"[48] toward the cold war arms race, but should set a third course of its own, one emphasizing "social reconstruction."[49] Attacking the Chancellor of the Exchequer, Hugh Gaitskell, who had prepared the budget, Bevan said: "If he finds it necessary to mutilate, or begin to mutilate, the Health Services for 13 million pounds out of 4,000 million pounds, what will he do next year? Or are you next year going to take your stand on the upper denture? The lower half apparently does not matter but the top half is sacrosanct."[50] Then, invoking his Welsh origins, he added: "Those who live their lives in mountainous and rugged countries are always afraid of avalanches, and they know that avalanches start with the movement of a very small stone."[51]

Thereafter, Bevan continued a lively public campaign, speaking to his constituency, writing in the *Tribune,* and participating in broadcasts and Parliamentary debates. He died before he could return to office in the next (Wilson) Labour government, as he otherwise certainly would have done.[52]

Bevan's dramatic resignation overshadowed the other minister who resigned with him. *The Times* noted at the time that "this second resignation appears to be treated by the Government and the Labour Party as a matter of no great consequence." He was discounted because he "was the youngest member of the cabinet"[53] and was in his first Parliamentary term. Perhaps so, but history has questioned that verdict. The "other Minister," then President of the Board of Trade, whose defection seems to have done him no harm either, was Harold Wilson.[54]

Others in Britain who, during this century, have resigned and protested against the decimation of projects to which they had a commitment and for which they had taken political responsibility in cabinet include Sir Charles Trevelyan, Sir Oswald Mosley, and Reginald Prentice. Trevelyan, a lifelong educational reformer and, like Dr. Addison, a former Liberal turned Socialist, vigorously castigated the minority Labour government in 1931 for failing to act with sufficient Socialist zeal, in particular for not pushing his bill raising the school-leaving age. Sir Oswald Mosley resigned and spoke up because a cabinet committee headed by the Chancellor of the Exchequer had for reasons of economy rejected his scheme for the relief of unemployment.[55] Reginald Prentice resigned and complained publicly, after being relieved of responsibility for foreign-assistance programs. He argued vigorously that help to overseas development should be increased rather than diminished.[56]

Naturally, British public-protest resignations do not focus exclusively on sensitive war, defense, and foreign-policy issues. Labor matters[57] and trade policy have been recurrent grounds for resignations of conscience accompanied by public airing of the issues.[58] Not untypical of the heat generated by trade policy is the public letter of resignation, protesting against the policy of imperial trade preferences, sent by Viscount Snowden, the Lord Privy Seal in the cabinet of Ramsay MacDonald, to the Prime Minister. "I can no longer," it begins, "without all loss of self-respect remain a member of a Government which is pursuing a policy which, I believe, is disastrous to the welfare of the country. . . ."[59]

Whatever the issues—be it disestablishment of the Welsh Church or the most transcendent questions of national destiny— the British public has benefited from having them delineated clearly in public by the resigners. It is significant to the quality of British political life that the public-protest resignation is not only permitted and practiced but that it receives institutional sanction from the Parliamentary "club," where those who resign on a matter of principle are encouraged to explain their actions publicly. In particular, the practice has served to keep able and ethically autonomous men and women in politics without forcing them inevitably to jettison either their political careers or their convictions.

The point should not be overstressed, for there are certainly careerist considerations ranged against resigning and going public—even in Britain. Yet, there is in Britain always a reservoir of persons who, having served in government and disagreed with one of its policies, remain within the political mainstream even while they oppose, and who are ready to resume the leadership of the country when circumstances warrant. The reconciliatory and recuperative. value of this system becomes the more evident when set against the absence of such mechanism in the United States.

◇

Despite the vehemence and frequency of the public-protest resignations, going public in British politics is not an anarchic free-for-all but a "time-honored courtesy" both circumscribed and legitimated by ritual and rules. These, on one hand, prevent expressions of ethical autonomy by key officials from paralyzing the process of government or turning it into a public brawl. On the other hand, the rituals and rules legitimate public protest while insuring that those who go "by the book" will not be unduly penalized for manifesting their integrity.

◇

The customary first step in a British ministerial resignation is to set out the decision to resign and reasons for the resignation in a private letter to the Prime Minister. This should be done before making a public announcement. The resignation correspondence will then be released by the Prime Minister. This courtesy permits the head of government time to think out his response, or even to attempt to persuade the resigner to withdraw his resignation.[60] Lord Morley, resigning over British entry into World War I, wrote Asquith on August 3 tendering his resignation. This letter was private, as was Asquith's urgent reply dated "Midnight, 3 Aug. 1914." In it, the Prime Minister says: "to lose you in the stress of a great crisis, is a calamity which I shudder to contemplate, and which (if it should become a reality) I shall never cease to deplore." Asquith continues: "I, therefore, beg you, with all my heart, to think twice and thrice, and as many times more as arithmetic can number, before you take a step which impoverishes the Government, and leaves me stranded and almost alone."[61]

The practice also insures that, initially, both sides of a dispute will be heard simultaneously by the public. This British ritual, sanctioned by the national preoccupation with "fair play," is very rarely violated even by the angriest resigner and violations are not forgiven. Lord Randolph Churchill ignored it to his cost. In the heat of a quarrel with the Prime Minister, Lord Salisbury, he wrote a furious letter of resignation which he dispatched to the Salisburys' ancestral home, Hatfield House, by special messenger. It arrived in the early hours of the morning, in the midst of a ball that Lord Randolph's mother, the Duchess of Marlborough, happened to be attending. Salisbury read the letter and stolidly retired. Meanwhile, however, Churchill had shown a copy of the letter to Buckle, editor of *The Times,* in the hope of winning favorable editorial treatment. Lord Salisbury was awakened the next morning by his Lady, who reminded him of his duty, as host, to see the Duchess of Marlborough off. "Send for *The Times* first," was the Prime Minister's sleepy response. "Randolph resigned in the middle of the night, and if I know my man, it will be in *The Times* this morning." It was; and so the Duchess of Marlborough, to her intense indignation, had to make her way from Hatfield alone, without either her host or hostess attempting to see her off.[62]

Churchill's conduct was unprofitable in other ways. Despite being handed this "scoop," *The Times* did not support him. And he was never permitted back into the government either by Salisbury or by Salisbury's successor (and nephew), Arthur Balfour, who continued to bear his uncle's grudge. When Randolph's son, Winston, resigned in 1915, he studiously avoided his father's mistake, taking care to follow the customary procedure in this regard.

It is a ritual of more recent origin for the resigner also to go before the party organization in his constituency to extend them the courtesy of a full and frank explanation of his decision to resign and speak out. Since most ministerial appointments, by far, are made from among the Members of the House of Commons, a British politician's future rests, at its base, on the continued support of the organization which nominates the candidate for election. While a resigning Member who loses the support for his constituency may, in time, find himself adopted by another, ridings do not grow on trees. Therefore, since the advent of universal franchise and the resultant mass political party, a resigner must concern himself not only with making his explanations to Parliament but also with satisfying his own local organization.

In most instances he is able to do so, but it is not to be taken for granted. The constituency organization, having had its Member "in the Government," may resent the loss of influence and prestige entailed in their Member's decision to resign. The constituents may feel that the resignation will make it more difficult for their needs to receive favorable attention at Westminster. Then, too, the organization's members, having worked for the party's victory in the previous election, might be distressed at what may be perceived as the "splitting" tendencies of their M.P. In the case of the two resignations in protest against the Suez campaign of 1956, the importance of reconciling the constituency party organization emerges clearly. Sir Edward Boyle, although the more vociferous

in speaking up, was able to carry his local Conservative organization along.[63] They disagreed with his decision but voted to recognize "the right of a Conservative Member to act in accordance with
his sincere convictions."[64] Nutting was less fortunate. Having
decided to resign but to postpone speaking up at the urging of the
Prime Minister, he had to forgo the opportunity of an explanation
to his constituency organization. The Melton Conservatives
quickly authorized a telegram to the Prime Minister assuring him of
their "loyal support and complete approval of Government action
in the Middle East."[65] With that, Nutting had no choice but to
resign the seat.[66] He was thirty-six years old and a strong future
contender for the Prime Ministership. But he was never again able
to get himself adopted as a candidate for Parliament by a constituency Conservative organization in any district in which the
Tories have had a reasonable chance to win.[67]

The British ritual of protest resignation is usually—but not
invariably—climaxed by the resigner's statement in Parliament,
during which he explains his reasons for quitting. Aneurin Bevan
referred to this as "one of the immemorial courtesies."[68] By
custom, also, the resignation speech is made from the second
bench below the Ministerial Gangway if, as is now usually the case,
the resigner is a member of the House of Commons. Not only does
the British system provide the resigning minister with an important
public forum—Parliament—in which to speak but that forum even
has a special, time-honored place from which the speech is made to
an attentive House, press, and public. Whereas Americans who go
public are made to walk the gangplank, their British counterparts
walk the Ministerial Gangway.

This solemn ritual is not to be lightly invoked: in the United
States, the rules insist that the resignation statement must trivialize
the reasons for leaving; but in Britain the rules require that the
reasons must be significant ones. A trivial resignation is *de rigueur*
in America but inexcusable in Britain. "No Member," Aneurin
Bevan said, "ought to accept office in a Government without a full
consciousness that he ought not to resign it for frivolous rea-

sons."[69] Parliament does not forgive a Member who resigns high office, except when he does so for weighty reasons of principle. Thus, whereas the American cabinet member will deliberately overlook policy differences in stating that his resignation is for personal reasons, the British cabinet member will tend to overlook the personal aspects of a resignation to stress policy differences. Neville Chamberlain reluctantly decided to resign from Lloyd George's World War I government, in which he had been Director of the National Service Department, primarily because, having lost the friendship and confidence of the Prime Minister, his office lacked clout to deal with competing departments in jurisdictional disputes.[70] But, instead of just quitting, he waited for the "right" issue to come along. "With all the Departments against me," he wrote, "and a Chief who won't help, I see no chance of success, and if so it would be folly to let slip an opportunity of getting out on a principle. . . ."[71] Realizing he could not just quit, he had to await the right "opportunity" to leave on an issue of principle.

One final act in the ritual of resignation is a formal public assurance by the resigner—unless he changes parties—that he intends to continue to support the government in all matters except the one which has caused his resignation. No matter how vigorous and profound his expressions of difference with the government on a specific issue, the resigner must stipulate that his opposition in one particular instance is not to be interpreted as a break with party solidarity in all other respects. If he cannot give that assurance, then his only honorable course is to "cross the floor" as Major General John E. Seely did in 1919 and, later, Addison, to join the Opposition.

Joseph Chamberlain went even further in pledging loyalty to Prime Minister Balfour. Even as he resigned and mounted his national campaign for Imperial Preferences, he warned: "Understand that in no conceivable circumstances will I allow myself to be put in any sort of competition, direct or indirect, with my friend and leader, whom I mean to follow."[72] The Marquess of Salisbury, after resigning in vehement protest over the release from detention of Cypriot Archbishop Makarios, said publicly to Harold Macmillan: "May I, however, assure you that, in general, I remain a strong supporter of the Government and of you personally as Prime Minister."[73] Enoch Powell promised, on resigning: "It will be my endeavour by word and deed and, perhaps more important, wherever possible by silence, to give my utmost support to the Government, despite all that has passed. . . ."[74] —a promise he has not been wholly able to keep.

Even Aneurin Bevan, whose resignation has been widely interpreted as being at least in part motivated by ambition to replace Clement Attlee as party leader, went through the formal protestation of loyalty but directed it specifically at the party, rather than to the Prime Minister, telling Attlee only that "my adherence to the cause of Labour and Socialism is stronger than ever. . . ."[75] John Freeman, leaving with Bevan, wrote: "It is unthinkable to me that a Tory Government could have any effect other than that of aggravating our difficulties, and I do not, therefore, intend, having left office, to use my vote in any way which could contribute to the fall of the Government."[76] This rather grudging formulation only barely satisfied the requirement.[77]

Once these ritual acts have been seen to, the resigner is relatively free to say what he wishes in defense of his decision to quit and by way of attack on the policies of his former colleagues in the cabinet. The Parliamentary statement of a resigner, since it is expected to deal with serious differences rather than trivial generalities, usually involves, and is expected to involve, some disclosure of hitherto secret information. This can be an important source of information for Members of Parliament, press, and public, enabling them better to evaluate the issues raised and to participate in the democratic process. If, as is often the case, cabinet secrets—memos, positions taken by the resigner and other ministers, written or oral communications among ministers or with foreign governments, or cabinet minutes—are a part of the explanation, the resigner is expected to request the Crown,[78] through the Prime Minister, to permit their being made public. Except for a few extraordinary circumstances, this is always given, although it is an oft-violated principle that cabinet memoranda should not be quoted even if the resigner must refer to their contents, and that if secret discussions held in cabinet must be adumbrated, the resigner should at least refrain from attributing views to specific ministers.

Except for these caveats, a resigner should be allowed to say whatever his taste and discretion allows. Despite the tradition that permission must be given, however, Lord Salisbury, in 1886, for reasons already noted, refused permission to Lord Randolph Churchill to make any statement at all.[79] During the Suez crisis of 1956, as we have seen, Anthony Nutting was strongly urged by the Prime Minister not to disclose what he knew about Israeli, French, and British collusion. Ordinarily, however, permission is always given as a matter of course, and this applies even to statements that reveal matters embarrassing either to national security or to the government in office.

Perhaps the most remarkable exposure of secrets came in the previously discussed resignation by Sir Edward Carson in 1915 over government strategy toward Serbia and in Gallipoli.[80] Similarly, Winston Churchill, resigning the same year, was characteristically underawed by the need for diffidence. He defended himself against the many critics of his policies among fellow cabinet members in a very detailed discussion of wartime strategy, revealing confidential ministerial advice he had received from First Sea Lord John Arbuthnot Fisher, the staff of the Admiralty, plans before the War Council, War Office State Papers, private discussions with the Prime Minister, with Lord Kitchener, with the French Minister of the Navy, and with the French General Staff. He paraphrased telegrams to and from the naval commanders at the Dardanelles front. The most reproof he received from the Prime Minister, however, was a mild comment to the effect that Churchill "has said one or two things which I tell him frankly I had rather he had not said . . ."[81] If British resigners are on a leash, it is a very long one.[82]

What traditional constraints may exist in practice on the disclosure of cabinet and ministerial secrets are wholly lifted if the resigning minister's initial explanation to Parliament is counterattacked by the Prime Minister or members of his cabinet.

When Viscount Cecil resigned as British minister in charge of post-World War I disarmament negotiations, he chose to do so with a public statement that rather generally delineated his differences with the majority of the cabinet. Prime Minister Stanley Baldwin, in his reply, said: "You exaggerate any differences that have arisen . . ." adding, "you . . . practically drafted your own [negotiating] instructions."[83] With that, Cecil really opened fire, for he passionately believed that "the difference between myself and my colleagues was fundamental. . . ."[84] In a statement to the House of Lords he told an extremely detailed "insider's" story of how the British objectives, policy, and instructions to the delegation had been hammered out in interdepartmental committees and in cabinet. Cecil disclosed antidisarmament positions taken in cabinet by the Chancellor of the Exchequer and in confidence by Admiralty officials. He produced evidence of his disagreement with key British negotiating positions, as well as with specific tactics. At one point, he said, he had been "preemptorily" ordered to have the conference adjourned and to return home.

Cecil, appalled that the negotiations were stalemated by what he regarded as cabinet obduracy over trivial matters, in effect went over their heads to Parliament and the public, which had not known why the negotiations were stalled. He revealed that, on resumption of negotiations, the U.S. wanted cruisers with eight-inch guns while the majority of the British cabinet wanted them with six-inch guns. Thus "the question arose how many six-inch cruisers go to one eight-inch cruiser."[85] The Americans wanted cruiser parity regardless of the bore-size of its armaments; the British thought their smaller guns entitled them to have more ships.[86] He agreed with his colleagues' preference but "it also seemed to me madness to allow the negotiations to break down on such a point."[87] He had suggested from Geneva a seven-inch compromise which the cabinet rejected. A further compromise, which would have left the matter for future decision, was also rejected by cabinet.

When Cecil had finished his speech in Parliament on November 16, 1927, no Englishman need any longer have been in doubt about the issues. Even by British standards, he had gone rather far in revealing so many cabinet secrets, including detailed positions taken by individual members, and in attacking the very negotiating posture he had been charged to defend. He did virtually everything possible to alert the people to those forces whose policy, he believed, "bangs, bolts and bars the door against any hope" of an arms control agreement.[88] Cecil's performance makes an eloquent contrast to a comparable American resignation: that of Harold Stassen, in 1958. Stassen, President Dwight Eisenhower's disarmament negotiator, became fed up with what he regarded as Secretary of State John Foster Dulles's nit-picking approach to a nuclear test-ban treaty. He finally quit—or was pushed out—over these differences, but so generalized his subsequent criticisms of Dulles's policies that only a trained political seismologist could have detected any disturbance.

The Eden-Salisbury resignation over Prime Minister Chamberlain's decision to negotiate with Mussolini exemplifies the enlargement of the resigner's discretion to reveal secrets at the rebuttal stage, if the government chooses to impugn his first set of disclosures. Chief among Eden's reasons for opposing Chamberlain's decision to negotiate with Mussolini over Abyssinia was the Foreign Minister's view that on no account must anything take priority over the British-American alliance. President Roosevelt had secretly proposed to the British government the convening of a world peace conference to deal with the Abyssinian war in the context of a world-wide settlement of disputes and easing of tensions. Chamberlain thought the American idea useless while Eden wanted the British-Italian conversations called off lest they offend the United States. When Chamberlain refused to retreat, Eden suggested that he would step down, only to be informed by the Prime Minister that, if he did so, he would not be allowed to reveal the real differences between them because "Roosevelt has enjoined complete secrecy upon us."[89] When Eden did resign, his respect for this injunction made it difficult for him to justify his decision to the satisfaction of Parliament and the public.

Then, however, Prime Minister Chamberlain ill-advisedly chose to minimize the seriousness of Eden's cause, suggesting that the timing of talks with Italy, to which he and Salisbury had taken public exception, was a mere matter of detail not sufficient to warrant a protest resignation. In response, Eden revealed that the secret Italian invitation had actually contained a "now or never" ultimatum,[90] that the Prime Minister was, in reality, proposing to lead from weakness. Even so, the Roosevelt initiative was not made public, although Eden did threaten to make further revelations if the Prime Minister continued to cast aspersions on the importance of his motives in resigning.

Eden's revelations were just sufficiently indiscreet to confirm that he was a man of principle resigning over a serious policy issue, yet not so egregious as to brand him an adventurer. Sir John Simon, though a stout supporter of appeasement in the Chamberlain government, could still write gracefully: "Eden's withdrawal was a grievous blow to us all, but the manner of it and his whole conduct afterwards showed the quality of the man."[91]

◇

The ability of the British political system to accommodate public-protest resignations even when they involve disclosure of secret "inside" information is all the more remarkable for having evolved in the face of the express prohibitions in the Official Secrets Act of 1911. These forbid any person communicating "to any person other than a person to whom he is authorized to communicate it" any information whatsoever "which has been entrusted in confidence to him by any person holding office under Her Majesty" or which he has obtained "owing to his position as a person who holds or has held office under Her Majesty. . . ."[92]

This Draconian law,[93] which has recently come under fire in Britain,[94] has never once been invoked against any resigning minister. The public-protest resignation is so important a part of British political tradition that it is treated as a total, if unwritten, exception to the criminal law.[95]

In the United States the legal position is the reverse of the British. Only the revealing of information to enemies of the United States is made a criminal offense under the Espionage Statutes.[96] Beyond that, the Constitution precludes laws making it a crime to reveal secret information.[97] Indeed, until the government tried, but failed, to prevent *The New York Times* from publishing the Pentagon Papers[98] there had been no effort to use the courts to inhibit the dissemination of information merely on grounds of its secrecy, or because the information was embarrassing to the national interest.

Yet, although American law permits the revealing of the kind of secrets which British law prohibits, American top officials, even at their ethical breaking point, tend to maintain a tomblike silence while their British counterparts speak up. This paradox is interesting for what it tells us about the role of law in society. American law is wholly permissive toward going public; still, top federal executives do not speak up. British law makes "going public," insofar as it is necessarily based on revelation of official information, a serious crime. Still, resigning British ministers regularly speak up, reveal secrets, and do so with impunity. This paradox suggests that, at the top echelons, social sanctions are usually more important than legal strictures. In Britain, the club tolerates, even at times encourages, resignations for reasons of conscience while protecting the resigner against enforcement of specific legal provisions that are applied to everyone else. In America, the social sanctions of the team militate so strongly against going public— and the career costs are so high—that top government officials do not dare take advantage of that right to free speech which is so firmly protected by the Constitution.

In contrast to the United States, the incidence of public-protest resignations in Britain has not been diminishing.[99] In this century, it has been highest during the most recent decade, 1960–

69, when a remarkable 81.8 per cent of all resigners in the prime group studied actually went public. This is in part attributable to the prevalence of Labour party government during the period. The propensity of resigning Labour ministers for public disclosure of their differences with the government[100] is statistically far higher than that of the Conservative or Liberal parties: 70 per cent, as compared to 40 per cent and 33.3 per cent respectively. Only coalition governments in Britain have generated almost as high a ratio of ministerial public-protest resignations (60 per cent of all coalition resignations studied) as Labour. If one divides the number of public-protest resignations by the number of years each party has been in government, the Labour governments and coalitions each averaged one protest resignation per year in this century, while the Liberals had only one in ten years and the Conservatives averaged approximately one every 2.5 years in government.[101] Unlike the Democrats in the United States, moreover, the Labour party ministers have continued to adhere to their tradition of ethical autonomy and public-protest resigning right through their most recent term of office.

It may be that the intensity, sweep, and passion of British resignation speeches have subsided a little, in keeping with the somewhat smaller scale of the issues facing Britain after the demise of Empire. But even today, and in both major political parties, the practice of resigning and going public remains an important feature of British democracy. The gesture may or may not attract the attention and support necessary to effect a change of policy; in the majority of cases it probably does not. But British politics recognizes both the symbolic and practical utility of the practice. It is accepted, in the words of Anouilh's *Antigone,* that "what a person can do, a person ought to do."

A Cabinet
of Yea-Sayers

IN Bertolt Brecht's *Galileo,* when the great scientist refuses to bow to prevailing dogma, a young colleague exults: "A man has stood up and said 'no.'" In twentieth-century Washington, as in the Vatican of Galileo's time, "no" is not a word heard often enough at the seat of power. In the modern United States, it is not only home on the range where seldom is heard a discouraging word. The failure of American politics to generate a substantial ethics-driven exodus of senior cabinet and White House officials during policy crises may be convenient for the Chief Executive, but it is bad for the country.

When British ministers resign and speak up, they may embarrass their Prime Minister, but they also precipitate public participation in important policy debates. While British, like American, cabinet and subcabinet members are appointed to their posts by the head of the government, they do not enter into a Faustian pact with him that binds their souls.

In America, by stark contrast, every political appointee who joins the executive branch by fiat of the President is expected to remember that he owes his leader total public loyalty. He must constantly bear in mind that his power is the President's revocable gift. Therefore, while U.S. top officials may occasionally oppose a particular Presidential initiative, they rarely do so vehemently, rarely in public, and rarely as part of the act of resigning.

In the exceptions to this American rule of conduct, when a dissenter did make his views public, he has invariably been consigned to the political scrap heap. Further prospects of service in the executive branch are out of the question. Appointments to the judiciary, insofar as these are within Presidential discretion, are unlikely to be proffered. Election to Congress is virtually precluded. Even the resigner's professional life is likely to be irrevocably discounted. As an outcast, in deep disfavor with the Washington Establishment, he is unlikely to be an asset to his law firm's larger clients, or to his bank, business, or industry, which may depend heavily on being in the benign graces of regulatory agencies, departmental assistant secretaries, and White House aides. He should expect to spend weary days with Internal Revenue Service auditors.

But, beyond that, the public-protest resigner tends to become the object of a generally successful effort—on the part of the Presidency, its agencies, and allies—to destroy his reputation and credibility. He finds himself being vilified as an oddball, a self-seeking egomaniac; there are broad hints that his public-policy differences with the President are intended to distract attention from his incompetence, perhaps even dishonesty, in office. Above all, he stands, self-accused, of disloyalty, of breaking his compact of faith with the President, and, by extension, with the American way of team-playing.

That Americans in high government posts who go public should be so harshly rewarded is more than a minor political artifact, more than just one of those ways "we are different from the British." How a society treats the resigner who goes public reflects how it deals with dissent and reveals the role that diversity and ethical imperatives play in its politics. Thus, in focusing on the relatively narrow phenomenon of public-protest resignation, we are really examining the most basic component of the democratic process, its checks and balances, its protection against the over-concentration of power.

Unanimity is the natural state of no society; no real politics are free of tension. Dissent, therefore, is inevitable: inside and outside government, at the top, middle, and bottom of the ladder, and in the streets, wherever men are free, some are likely to object to whatever the government happens to be doing. Some societies institutionalize this dissent, others put dissenters in institutions.

The British system encourages independent-minded persons with alert political consciences to rise even as high as the cabinet. The Nazis and Stalinists sent their dissenters to death in concentration camps. The Soviet writer Alexander Galech has described the impact:

> Where today are the shouters and gripers?
> They have vanished before they grew old—
> But the silent ones now are the bosses,
> And the reason is—silence is gold.[1]

America does not lock its dissidents up, but it does lock them out of the inner core of politics: the upper echelons of the executive branch. There is currently no place in the cabinet, subcabinet, or White House staff for public officials who believe in speaking their minds openly, in putting their own consciences and personal responsibilities to the public ahead of getting ahead. Presidents of the United States deliberately exclude from the executive branch the kind who resign and go public or, indeed, anyone who is likely to stand up, particularly in public, against Presidential will.

The authors of the United States Constitution visualized Congress and the courts as the principal balance to Presidential power. This power was to be checked by institutions *outside* the Presidency. That the President's executive power might need checking and balancing from *within* the executive branch was not a notion to which they gave credence. Oddly, the Founders did provide for balances *inside* both of the other two branches. Open, public dissent is institutionalized within Congress and within the federal judiciary—but not within the executive branch. Members of Congress can, and do, effectively oppose legislation favored by Congressional leaders, even to the point of delaying and sometimes defeating the will of the majority of their colleagues. The federal courts, specifically at the Circuit and Supreme Court levels, create every opportunity for the minority view to be expressed and published. Not infrequently these judicial dissents are so prestigious and persuasive that they are adopted by the majority in a subsequent case. Only in the executive branch does the Constitution locate all power, all discretion, in one person—the President—without providing an opportunity for public dissent on the part of those within the executive who oppose a particular Presidential initiative.

This omission stemmed from a constitutional miscalculation by the Founding Fathers. In his Federalist essay on the system of checks and balances, Madison assumes that "In republican government, the legislative authority necessarily predominates." Therefore, he explained, it would be necessary to meet the dangers of what he called the "inconveniency" of too much power in one place by dividing the legislature into different houses, and so, "to render them, by different modes of election and different principles of action, as little connected with each other as the nature of their common functions and their common dependence on the society will admit."[2] But no such internal division was deemed necessary or desirable in the executive branch. This is because its growth at the expense of the other branches was not anticipated. Madison calls the Presidency "the weaker department" and, although no champion of Hamilton's ideas for a strong Chief Executive, was more than a little concerned about whether the Constitution would adequately protect against the legislature capitalizing on the "weakness of the executive."[3]

What Madison could not foresee was the extraordinary growth of Presidential power in the last two thirds of the twentieth century. Control over foreign relations, growing particularly out of the constitutional role of the President as Commander-in-Chief, has concentrated in the executive branch enormous powers over war, peace, defense, and national (including internal) security.[4] The geometric growth of the government's role in the life of American citizens during this century has redounded primarily to the executive, not the legislative, branch. The power of the Senate to share in the making of treaties and of war has been eroded, in practice, by the growing tendency of the President, acting alone, to enter into executive agreements and dispatch troops for defensive police actions that are undeclared wars. Yet as late as 1879, the young Woodrow Wilson was still able to write: "The most important, most powerful man in the government of the United States in time of peace is the Speaker of the House of Representatives."[5]

In more recent years, the Congress, too cumbersome and too limited in supporting staff and services, has had to confine itself to general authorization and occasional review of programs. Nowadays, it is a burgeoning bureaucracy—responsible and responsive almost exclusively to the President and to his senior political appointees in the departments—which actually defines and implements the Congressionally authorized programs and administers their operation. And it is this process of defining, implementing, and administering which is the cutting edge of power. If Madison could not have foreseen this development, neither could he have envisioned an eight-year military struggle, in which were committed half a million American troops and $100 billion, all without a Congressional declaration of war.

Were he to reconsider the matter today, Madison would almost certainly, if sadly, conclude that it is the executive, not the legislative, branch which, in this republic, "necessarily predominates." Only the executive has the legions of administrators, investigators, fact-gatherers, evaluators, and the technological hardware necessary to respond effectively to the pressing and complex urban, energy, environmental, racial, and foreign crises that tumble over themselves in their demands for immediate attention. If there is now a branch of the government that Madison would perceive to be in need of internal as well as external checks to guard the nation against the "inconveniency" of disproportionate power aggregation, it would surely be the Presidency.

It is important to understand Madison's distinction between internal checks *within* a branch of government and those balances which derive from the separation of powers *among* the branches. While it is still useful, it is no longer sufficient that public opposition to Presidential policies should, from time to time, be led by powerful senators, as it was by J. William Fulbright during the latter part of the Vietnam war. Such checking and balancing, to be effective, must be reinforced by the voice of dissent raised by some of those who have been at the real core of power, in the executive branch. A Presidency unchecked from within is too able to "fly now, pay later," too prone to credit-card policy-making.

In the crunch, Presidents performing in the vast arena of their executive discretion can only be checked by those on the spot and in the know at the crucial moments in policy-making. This, effectively, means the President's immediate circle of advisers and heads of departments.

But the top federal executives around the President can be expected to act as a check on his discretion only if they—or at least some of them—are recruited from among persons with a capacity for ethical autonomy, with the will to defend their judgment in the Oval Office if possible and in public if necessary. And the checking and balancing of Presidential discretion by his advisers can be effective only if those advisers have political clout, if they can exert pressure on the President. An effective "gadfly"—as Socrates pointed out in his self-defense before the Athenian jury—is essential but hard to find.

In Britain, members of the cabinet have this kind of "gadfly" power because they are politicians, with a public following of their own that gives them leverage. Every Prime Minister knows that a sufficiently angered member of his government may resign and go public and that this can hurt him.

Even in recent years, when their power has supposedly increased, Prime Ministers of Britain have still generally had to submit most policy initiatives to the cabinet, or at least to a committee of the cabinet, for full discussion. To proceed with a policy without such opportunity for revision, and, ultimately, without cabinet approval, is to court cabinet resignations and an open split in the Parliamentary party. Eden's failure to consult the full cabinet before joining in secret agreement with France and Israel in preparation for the Suez crisis of 1956 was considered highly irregular and contributed to the defection of three important members of the government (Walter Monckton, who resigned as Minister of Defense, and two junior ministers: Sir Edward Boyle and Anthony Nutting).[6] George Brown, resigning from Harold Wilson's cabinet in 1968, spoke up, specifically, about "the way this Government is run and the manner in which we reach our decisions."[7] Two years earlier, Wilson had been forced to set up a special, representative Cabinet Committee on Economic Policy by the collective representation of several ministers that "too much was being settled by too small a number of senior Ministers."[8]

Patrick Gordon Walker, the former Foreign Minister, recalls a substantial number of instances when Prime Ministers have been overruled by their cabinets. One was the blocking by a negative cabinet vote of Mr. Wilson's and his Foreign Secretary's desire to send naval ships through the Gulf of Aqaba in 1967 to forestall the Six-Day War. Another of Wilson's initiatives—to impose criminal sanctions on "wildcat" strikers—was considered by an "almost evenly divided" cabinet. The proposal was dropped.[9] On about six other occasions in this century, cabinet revolts have forced Prime Ministers from office or hastened their resignations.[10]

The Prime Minister must not only go through the motions of consulting, but he must allow most ministers to express themselves on most issues. He must "carry them along" or else subtly shift direction. He can sometimes act on his own but he cannot do so all the time, particularly in matters in which there is a deep difference of opinion among his colleagues. In Gordon Walker's opinion, a "Prime Minister who habitually ignored the Cabinet . . . could rapidly come to grief."[11]

As in most British constitutional matters, so in the balance of power between ministers and Prime Ministers there is little written or "hard" law. The conventions of the constitution are helpful historically evolved guidelines. But underpinning the unwritten limitation on Prime Ministerial power is the threat of ministerial resignation, with the implied additional sanction of a public statement of grievances. It is this latent threat which insures that Prime Ministers, although not compelled by law or invariable convention, will usually consult, and even go along with, the wishes of colleagues. It is this, too, which strengthens those colleagues in presenting and pressing independent points of view in cabinet committee and in meetings of the full cabinet, even when those views are opposed by the Prime Minister. This is not to say that the regular meetings of the cabinet resemble free-for-all pub brawls; but by comparison to the infrequent and perfunctory meetings of the U.S. cabinet, the British government is a relatively open forum for the formulation of policy in which men and women, all with some political standing, and some with a great deal of it, negotiate from different political and departmental perspectives toward a broadly agreed policy consensus. The comparatively stronger and more independent position of the British minister vis-à-vis his Prime Minister is thus protected by the latter's knowledge that his colleagues might, if unduly subordinated, resign and "go public"; the minister's right to resign and air his differences with the Prime Minister is, conversely, reinforced by the relatively more independent position he enjoys vis-à-vis the Prime Minister.

American Presidents, on the other hand, are balanced by no comparable counterweight. They take care to recruit individuals unlikely to want to make serious trouble. They appoint men and women who, for the most part, have no political base of their own and so could make little trouble even if they felt the urge. Moreover, Presidents are further insulated from having to worry about disaffected advisers by the strong historic tradition against public-protest resignations.

◇

The cabinet and White House staff are a "team" of which the unchallengeable captain is the President. He is not a *primus inter pares*—a first among equals—like the Prime Minister of Britain. The U.S. President stands alone, awesome, commanding the respect and obedience of his cabinet, not, like a British Prime Minister, consulting, compromising, and, ultimately, dependent on his associates' willingness to be brought along. If the President consults and compromises, it is because he wants to, not because he must.

This difference, at its base, is grounded in the Constitution. Unlike the British Prime Minister, the President is the only member of his Administration to hold an elective mandate from the people. *His* person, *his* policies, *his* wisdom are put to the public for approval. His Administration is therefore an extension of his personal mandate from, and his sole accountability to, the nation. His cabinet is not an institution known to the law. The Constitution does not breathe the word. If the cabinet meets at all, it is to transact formal business, hear reports, and adjourn as quietly as possible. It does not argue about policy or decide controversial issues. No one in it raises embarrassing questions or criticizes the Chief. Whereas the British cabinet resembles a coalition of individuals, each with his own direct ties to, and endorsement from, segments of the public, the Presidency is a solitary affair (fictionally dualized by the Vice-Presidency) in which none of the top officials of the federal government shares except by derivation. Hence, these officials, in relation to the President, are players on a team, perceiving themselves as the instruments of play. The President, at once coach and captain, conceives the play and directs all major aspects of its execution.

The vocabulary of Presidents and their principal aides is replete with "team-talk" which palpably conjures up the locker room. Warren Harding looked for men who would "associate with each other in effective teamwork . . . fit together, work together, and respect each other's work."[12] His principal adviser, Harry M. Daugherty, asserted as his guiding principle, "I just play ball with the fellows on my team."[13] Eisenhower compared his cabinet and staff to his military aides: "The teams and staff through which the modern commander absorbs the information and exercises his authority must be beautifully interlocked, smooth-working mecha-

nism. Ideally, the whole should be practically a single mind."[14]
Theodore C. Sorensen entitles the chapter of his White House
memoirs that deals with appointment process: "The Kennedy
Team."[15] Charles Frankel, speaking of his tenure in the Johnson
Administration, reports that: "after a few months . . . I had
become a member of a team, and was concerned about its goals
and requirements."[16] Bill Moyers, too, speaks of the "sense of
teamwork that must pervade a White House staff. . . ."[17] Irving
L. Janis, examining the case histories of executive task forces,
concludes: "In a sense, members consider loyalty to the group the
highest form of morality."[18] He adds that the "more amiability and
esprit de corps among the members of a policy-making in-group,
the greater is the danger that independent critical thinking will be
replaced by groupthink, which is likely to result in irrational and
dehumanizing actions directed against out-groups."[19]

The team, of course, has its rules that are a bulwark against
dissent, against negative thinking, against bouts of doubt. They
militate strongly not only against resigning in protest and speaking
out but also against any ethically autonomous behavior which
might be a prelude to such a public show of dissent.

The first and overriding rule of the team is absolute loyalty to
the President. During the Senate Watergate hearings, the cardinal
importance of team loyalty was frequently contrasted to an individual's obligation to his own moral sense and to the society. Replying
to Senator Howard H. Baker's question, Herbert Porter of the
Committee to Re-Elect the President said that he had not spoken
up against his bosses' wrongdoings "probably because of the fear
of group pressure that would ensue, of not being a team player."
He went on to explain that loyalty to the President and his team
had taken precedence over loyalty to principles or to country.[20]

Later in the hearings, the Senate Select Committee discussed
the same issue with former Chief of the White House Staff H. R.
Haldeman.

"Mr. Haldeman," Senator Daniel K. Inouye asked, "was

loyalty the name of the game at the White House and was loyalty much more important than the truth?''

"I would not say that either of those was the case," Haldeman replied. "I would say that loyalty was important. I would say that the truth is overridingly important."

But this reply was not persuasive. The dialogue between Inouye and Haldeman arose in connection with a staff memorandum from Alexander P. Butterfield, then also of the White House, who had written Haldeman in 1970 concerning A. Ernest Fitzgerald, a Defense Department cost analyst dismissed from his job after revealing publicly a $2-billion cost overrun on the C-5A transport plane. Butterfield's memo stated: "Fitzgerald is no doubt a top-notch cost expert but he must be given very low marks in loyalty, and after all, loyalty is the name of the game."[21]

Loyalty to the Chief is not, of course, a quality to be deplored. Indeed, it is an appropriate, universally shared, and internalized ethic of key personnel in any functioning enterprise and, particularly, of governments. However, the extraordinary extent to which, among top federal executives, loyalty to the President has become the overriding ethic, taking precedence over all other considerations, is reported by many recent officials. And this has rightly become a matter of deep concern to the American public. According to Pierre Salinger, "Our commitment to the President . . . was total" and, again, "[o]ur faith in him and in what he was trying to do was absolute."[22] Who, then, was testing, rebutting, and nay-saying? The scary answer: "nobody."[23]

Sorensen, too, reports that in selecting his "team" Kennedy looked for persons whose "qualities largely mirrored his own . . . for the most part men who thought his thoughts, spoke his language" and who "believed implicitly in him."[24] He even notes Kennedy's fondness for quoting to his aides King Henry V's Saint Crispin's Day battle speech:

> From this day to the ending of the world,
> . . . we in it shall be remembered;

> We few, we happy few, we band of brothers;
> For he to-day that sheds his blood with me
> Shall be my brother; . . .
> And gentlemen in England now a-bed
> Shall think themselves accursed they
>   were not here. . . .[25]

What Sorensen does not stress in quoting this panegyric to team play is that the story casts Kennedy in the role of a feudal monarch exhorting his warrior serfs. (Neither does he note the odd coincidence of Henry's call to "shed blood with me" being occasioned by the arrival on the battlefield of "my cousin Westmoreland.")

◇

Such loyalty tends to overwhelm doubt and hesitation. When the Bay of Pigs plans were reviewed by the President's advisers, according to Sorensen, "No strong voice of opposition was raised in any of the key meetings. . . ."[26] Arthur Schlesinger, Jr., observed that "Our meetings took place in a curious atmosphere of assumed consensus."[27] Those who wanted to speak felt unable to do so. Or if they did, a key member of the group would see them privately and urge that they "don't push it any further."[28]

The pressures to be loyal—and to be perceived by the President and the public to be wholly loyal—are so great that men of principle, like McNamara, and even seasoned politicians who have given up their political base, like Hubert Humphrey, were willing to destroy their credibility in vigorous public defense of positions with which they privately disagreed and which they knew to be publicly untenable. According to one White House staffer, Vice-President Humphrey's way of resolving his personal doubts about the war and the urgings of his liberal constituency that he dissociate himself from it "was to talk more, and not only to defend but to over-defend." Even in the inner circles, he did not play much of a role in criticizing the conduct of the war for fear a leak might place him in a posture of public dissent. Instead, "he increasingly resolved all his impulses by a language and stance of super loyalty to the President, expressed over and over again in word and deed."

◇
——— ———
132

Throughout, his overriding objective was to "stay in the good graces of his boss as the way to greater power in the Administration and perhaps a real chance at the Presidency."[29]

Another instance of this debilitating ethic of unreserved loyalty is Nicholas deB. Katzenbach's stint as public defender of the war. Katzenbach had earned a national reputation as a protégé of Robert F. Kennedy and as the cool, unafraid Deputy Attorney General who, with great inner force and dignity, had led the battles of the early 1960s for desegregation in the Southern states. Later, he served President Johnson as Attorney General and Under Secretary of the Department of State. Despite—or in Eric Goldman's view,[30] perhaps because of—his close association with Robert Kennedy, the doves, liberals, and intellectuals, he became one of the unhappier spokesmen for President Johnson's right to wage and escalate the Vietnam war even without Congressional authorization. Before the Senate Foreign Relations Committee, in 1967, he argued that declarations of war were outmoded,[31] implying that, in foreign affairs, the President is pretty much free to do what he pleases especially in view of the Tonkin Gulf resolution.

Shouldering this unpopular role seemed natural to Katzenbach's concept of cabinet loyalty. The former Attorney General has observed that a cabinet member's status and prerogatives are a trust bestowed by the President and must only be used to help the Chief Executive. Thus, whenever possible, a member of the team, regardless of his private views or preferences, should deliberately take and defend public positions which represent Administration policy but which he knows to be unpopular, thereby drawing fire away from the President and increasing the Chief's room for maneuver.[32]

It is not only White House staff and the cabinet who owe their positions uniquely to the President and are thus bound to him in these close ties of nearly feudal fealty. Deputy Secretaries, Under Secretaries, Assistant Secretaries, Departmental General Counsel, Deputy Assistant Secretaries, Directors of Agencies and Bureaus, and even some officials at lower levels also populated by civil servants, are appointed directly by the Chief Executive. Their selection is often a Presidential decision that bypasses the head of the department, as when Chester Bowles was selected by Kennedy for the Under Secretaryship of State even before the appointment of Dean Rusk.[33] The ties of loyalty thus tend to run directly from the President not only to the top echelon of his advisers, but to several echelons down the chain.

President Johnson's press secretary, George Reedy, warns that this pervasive atmosphere of diffidence, self-effacement, and single-minded loyalty, emanating from cabinet, subcabinet, and staff, cuts the American Chief of State off from the crosscurrents of dissent and reality. Herbert G. Klein, Nixon's one-time director of communications, attributes his former boss's fall to the President's self-imposed isolation from dissident advice. Doors became closed to all but the sycophants. "He denied himself the opportunity for a cross-fertilization of ideas which any successful executive needs."[34] This creates a malady familiar to students of authoritarian regimes that tend to suffer from a congenital disorder of their information and idea flow. Their leaders tend to hear what loyal stooges, dependent on their favor, think they want to hear, rather than the dissonant clash of data and ideas from which truth is more likely to emerge. Separated from passionate and powerful dissent, authoritarian leaders are prone to act on incomplete information and set out on insufficiently test-flown hunches. They may make decisions which are the right answers to the wrong problems. Reedy, too, speaks of loyalty souring into sycophancy. "From the moment he enters the halls [of the White House, the President] is made aware that he has become enshrined in a pantheon of semidivine mortals who have shaken the world. . . ."[35] There is among those who are his human environment, according to various Presidential aides, a prevalent belief that "[o]nly a churl will 'blow the whistle' on a man who's racked with the agony of facing daily the apocalyptic decisions of life and death. . . ."[36] Thus discourse becomes almost supernaturally "soft spoken"[37] even if such diffident "tone of voice . . . seems inappropriate to the desperateness of the issue being discussed."[38] Yet such self-effacement can be a terrible disservice to the man, the institution and to the nation. "Some of us," Reedy recalls, "should have stood up earlier and screamed some four-letter words."[39]

But the men Presidents select for their cabinet and staff are rarely the sort given to cussing out their superiors. According to Emmet John Hughes, one of Eisenhower's principal White House aides, the General liked to surround himself with "colleagues of whom rather few held profound convictions, while those who did possess them, perhaps more sensible and sensitive than his own, either fought for them only sporadically or lacked talents to make them persuasive."[40] John Kennedy, according to Sorensen, preferred men with "an outlook more practical than theoretical and more logical than ideological"—a dichotomy which is eloquent in itself. He sought "able administrators, loyal to his philosophy"[41] rather than men moved by philosophies of their own. Walter Heller, the Chairman of the Council of Economic Advisers, worked out just fine "[o]nce he learned to adjust to Kennedy's . . . emphasis on the possible"—the implication being that Professor Heller's theoretical bent inclined him, at first, to futile pursuit of the impossible.[42] Johnson particularly valued Edwin Martin "Pa" Watson because, according to Harry McPherson, "he did not press his ideological views on the President."[43] His sole commitment was service to the Chief.

Charles Frankel, at State, felt the pressure. "Is long-term policy created by abstract theorizing about future goals?" he asked himself.[44] The professional's guiding principle is "to endure." He "lives in an arena where causes and principles collide"[45] and he knows enough to hedge his bets and keep his head down, relying on bargaining and compromise to see him around the shoals of other people's principles and ideologies. The game, Frankel learned, belongs to "team players, to bargainers, to the gregarious, to men who like to get together with other people more than they like to see ideas clean and neat."[46]

So the "art" of executive politics is one of "seduction"[47] rather than the clash of ideas. Professor Theodore Lowi has commented on this "end of ideology" in American government. "Ideology is the embrace of a whole future state of affairs. Ideology is moralizing on a grand scale."[48] The American political man is essentially a manager, not an ideologue. His loyalty is to getting things done—if he is in the White House or cabinet, to getting things done for the President and the department. "He worships at the shrine of process, and he counts his treasures in large numbers of small units."[49] It is his constant aim to accept the general direction of events—if there is one and it can be perceived—but not to think about it. Rather, he emphasizes the immediate situation "and the small departures that can be made from it without disrupting or deranging the position of all the participants."[50] He has "a narrow goal because he believes narrowness is the right way"[51] and minimizes conflicts, shunning the questioning of fundamental assumptions or underlying goals. To Presidents harassed by foreign enemies, Congressional opponents, the hostile media, and kids in the streets, it is a token of loyalty and kindness to avoid needlessly questioning "goals" or "priorities." The inner circle at the White House knows that the best way to bench a member of the team is to post him to the wilderness of "long-range planning."

Chester Bowles, when Under Secretary of State, knew that he was being eased out when he began to see newspaper reports quoting "highly placed White House spokesmen" to the effect that he was only at home with "big thoughts."[52] At the time, Bowles noted in his diary that the Kennedy Administration lacked a "genuine conviction" of right and wrong, as the Bay of Pigs incident had revealed. An Administration not actively engaged in thinking about its moral values must inevitably face each crisis concerned only with the immediate pluses and minuses. "The Cuban fiasco demonstrates how far astray a man as brilliant and well intentioned as President Kennedy can go who lacks a basic moral reference point."[53]

Presidents do not expect their cabinet to help them develop a "moral reference point." The Administration was glad to see

Chester Bowles off to India, where, presumably, the pursuit of life's deeper ethical meaning is encouraged. What Presidents do want is men whose imaginations, in Macaulay's phrase, should "like the wings of an ostrich enable them to run but not to soar."[54]

The rule against ruffling Presidential feathers is virtually absolute. "There is no such thing as adversary discussion in a cabinet meeting," Reedy reports. "Men do not pound the table, contradict each other, challenge contrary opinions. Whatever fire may have been in their bellies when they entered the White House gate has been carefully quenched by the time they reach the Cabinet Room doorsill. What follows is a gentlemanly discourse conducted on an extremely 'high' level, and enveloped in the maximum dullness conceivable."[55]

This contrasts with the British cabinet, which not only engages in table-pounding and discusses issues with intensity but also overrules the Prime Minister. Cabinet revolts have driven heads of government like Gladstone, Asquith, Lloyd George, MacDonald, and Neville Chamberlain from power. "[S]ometimes passion and even anger can enter in," former Foreign Minister Gordon Walker reports, and ministers have been known to walk out in fury over issues of policy.[56]

Lord Lytton has ruefully observed that there is "no man so friendless but what he can find a friend sincere enough to tell him disagreeable truths."[57] The significant exception appears to be the President of the United States. That "modern-day monarch"— according to Reedy—cannot, like Peter the Great, have the bearer of bad tidings strangled. Still, fear, and the sense of diffidence toward all that incorporeal power, discourages the members of the team from bringing him bad news or rude evidence that he is wrong.

During the worst days of the Tet offensive, President Johnson continued to be reassured by key members of his team both at home and in Saigon that disaster was, in fact, victory; that Hanoi had decided to go for broke only because it was tired and discouraged. Various senior cabinet officials and White House staffers have remarked that W. W. Rostow's effectiveness with Johnson was enhanced by his dogged optimism[58] and that pessimistic reports were usually ambushed by Rostow before they could reach the President's desk. When McNamara began to feed the President his own pessimistic doubts, Johnson was alienated and came to rely increasingly on his team optimists: Dean Rusk, W. W. Rostow, Earle Wheeler, and Maxwell Taylor. These were "can-do guys" and, at least until the end of March 1968, that was clearly the thing to be.

In the United States, "[t]he aura of reverence that surrounds the president when he is in the Mansion is so universal that the slightest hint of criticism automatically labels a man as a colossal lout."[59] Another result of this lack of intense challenge from his own advisers is that the President is misled about the intensity of feeling there may be about an issue among the general public. He is surprised by rioters who throw themselves in front of his automobile or chant obscenities from the streets, and he tends to think them aberrations. In this delusion, he wanders at dawn out of the White House toward an encampment of antiwar protesters and tries to engage them in talk about football. He lives in an environment that shelters him from the higher and lower decibel levels of grief and rage. This is not only bad for the country but also a false kindness to the Chief Executive. Like a deaf man with his back to a buzz saw, the President, sheltered from the sounds of danger and anger, cannot make the judgments necessary to his own and his policies' survival.

◇

The unwillingness of top federal executives to take vigorous issue with the President inside the White House, let alone in public, is abetted by an atomistic bureaucratic concept of "areas of responsibility." The Secretary of Health, Education, and Welfare is able to avoid confronting his conscience over the Administration's Vietnam policy because it is not in his area of responsibility—even though defense expenditures are bleeding major domestic programs. An utterly disillusioned Deputy Assistant Secretary of

State, Robert W. Barnett, agonizing about how to resign in opposition to the 1970 Cambodian campaign, decided, at last, that he could not go public because Vietnam was not within his bureau's jurisdiction. Not that his area was far off. His responsibilities included China and other parts of the Far East, but not Vietnam. Yet, in Washington, these distinctions matter. George W. Ball said, recently, "Why *should* I have resigned in protest over Vietnam policy just because I disagreed with it? My main responsibility and my principal interest was Western Europe. Perhaps five per cent of my time was spent on Vietnam. It simply wasn't my responsibility."[60] After all, he added, "it wasn't as if I were the Honduras desk officer being put in the position of having to approve a U.S. military action in Honduras." For team players, responsibility runs directly and solely from each player to the coach. Unlike British ministers, they are not responsible for or to each other.

Thus it has been possible for Presidents to enlist and keep in their cabinets men and women with specific responsibilities for one subject who were content enough to do their jobs, although consistently out of sympathy with almost all the Administration's major initiatives. Roosevelt's first Secretary of State, Cordell Hull, was a conservative ex-senator from Tennessee who, when he thought about domestic affairs, was almost wholly opposed to the New Deal.[61] He neither wanted to be consulted on, nor to accept responsibility for, "the 'liberal' game" being played at the White House.[62]

Cabinet meetings in the United States, despite occasional efforts to make them into significant decision-making occasions, have, at least in this century, been characterized as vapid nonevents in which there has been a deliberate nonexchange of noninformation as a part of a process of mutual nonconsultation. Votes are not taken. Collective decisions are not made. Formal records are not kept, and no cabinet minutes exist for any Administration prior to Eisenhower's. Papers for cabinet discussion were prepared during Eisenhower's tenure, but rarely before or since. Typically,

cabinet agendas call for secretaries to make reports on the state of
their departments. These are carefully edited to avoid controversy
and are rarely discussed by the members.

Eisenhower, of recent Presidents, was most interested in making the U.S. cabinet work as an institution. Sometimes he "would
stop a cabinet officer in the middle of a private presentation in his
office to tell him he did not like to spend time twice on a subject
which could be resolved in one meeting. He would point out that
the item under discussion was the type of thing he wanted presented to him before his cabinet colleagues and would order it
placed on the agenda." The results were, however, disappointing.
"Cabinet officers," Eisenhower's secretary to the cabinet reports,

> if the choice were theirs, generally would prefer to present their
> recommendations to the President in private, without special-
> ists in other fields looking over their shoulder. While each
> appreciated his opportunities to be informed about and contrib-
> ute to the plans of others, it was only natural he would hesitate
> to put his brain child on the table for all to attack. One cabinet
> officer spoke for many when he once told me, "Putting a pet
> project on the cabinet agenda is a good way to get it nibbled to
> death by ducks." As a consequence, Eisenhower's desire to
> have major nonsecurity proposals masticated by the cabinet
> machinery would have fallen apart without a continuous assist
> from his firm hand.[63]

President Kennedy had none of Eisenhower's patience with,
or interest in, the cabinet. During his Administration, neither the
cabinet nor the White House staff received any encouragement to
regard themselves as a collective institution. Each member of the
Administration, instead, was to regard himself in a one-to-one
relationship to the President. "Not one staff meeting was ever
held, with or without the President,"[64] Sorensen states. Salinger
adds that Kennedy "held to the belief that the productivity of all
meetings is in direct inverse ratio to the number of participants. He
had given each of us precise duties to carry out. . . . If we had
something to tell him or ask him, the door to his office was always

open. We were not to waste his time, and ours, with formal meetings."[65] As for the cabinet, Kennedy held meetings as rarely as possible and "these meetings bored him."[66] He thought "general Cabinet meetings . . . to be unnecessary and involve a waste of time. . . ." According to Sorensen, Kennedy "had little interest in the views of Cabinet members on matters outside their jurisdiction. He summoned former Under Secretary of State [C. Douglas] Dillon to most major meetings on foreign policy and former Ford President McNamara to advise on the steel price dispute. But he did not want McNamara's advice on debt management or Dillon's advice on Nike-Zeus."[67]

President Johnson did try to revitalize the cabinet as an institution, holding regular meetings with agendas and prepared memos. But these sessions, too, amounted to nonevents, with officials reading each other statements prepared for later release to the press. Individual cabinet officials had their responsibilities, and some—McNamara, Rusk, Udall—at times had great influence with Johnson. But such influence did not adhere to the cabinet as an institution. Reedy notes that "[a]s a collective body, they are about as useful as the vermiform appendix. . . ."[68]

In Britain, all important matters of policy become the collective decision of the cabinet and every cabinet and subcabinet member must keep in mind that each of them accepts full responsibility for the policies of every one else's department.[69] Resignation in genuine matters of conscience thus becomes a duty, whether the issue is one directly concerning a minister's own department or not. A British cabinet member is directly responsible to Parliament and to the people, in his own right as an elected political figure, for all government policy. Since the very act of remaining in the cabinet fixes him with this constructive responsibility, he *must* dissociate himself by resignation if his conscience or political sense does not allow him to assent. Key cabinet defections in public protest against foreign policy have thus been ventured by an Attorney General (Sir John Simon), a Solicitor General (Dingle Foot), and by numerous others (Sir Edward Boyle, Duff Cooper,

Sir Edward Carson) whose own ministerial jurisdictions were purely domestic.

Only in the most extraordinary circumstances may a British minister stay on and yet escape personal responsibility. Viscount Monckton, Minister of Defence in the Eden government, was opposed to the 1956 agreement to join with France and Israel in the occupation of the Suez Canal. He decided he could not remain in the Defence Ministry while the campaign was being planned, but allowed himself to be persuaded to dissociate himself without "giving the show away" by taking a brief, nominal appointment in the government as Paymaster General.[70] Even this makeshift compromise was of questionable propriety. In general, in Britain, you must agree or go.

But the practical, as opposed to the constitutional,[71] reason British ministers resign and go public over issues which, strictly, are outside their area of responsibilities is that, as practicing politicians, they see policy as a seamless web. They are not, as in the U.S., men borrowed from the management of various divisions of General Motors or Union Carbide. In large corporations, a division head learns to keep out of the hair of managers of other divisions, both as a matter of reciprocal courtesy and because he knows that his abilities, powers, and responsibilities stop at his own door. A chairman of the English department at a university does not try to affect economies in the department of economics. Corporate lawyers stay away from the work of the litigation department in their firm. Commerce Secretary Jesse Jones's pungent statement is illustrative: "I made no suggestions to other Cabinet members about their departments and asked none from them."[72] Politeness as between cabinet members means minding one's own business. "I don't care a damn about the Navy and you don't care a damn about the Army. You run your machine and I'll run mine," Secretary of War Lindley Garrison admonished Secretary of the Navy Josephus Daniels. Charles Frankel, more recently, told himself that it would be improper to resign over policy in Vietnam when his responsibility at the State Department was confined to cultural affairs. No such "scruples" affect the British. Frank Cousins was Minister of Technology, but as a dedicated trade unionist he did not hesitate, when he saw his government impose an incomes policy of wage restraints, to resign over its inequities to the workingman.[73]

If the U.S. cabinet were more politicized, a Secretary of Health, Education, and Welfare would assert himself on defense or treasury policies, even without a formal doctrine of collective responsibility, because he would know that what happened in those departments must intimately, if indirectly, affect the prospects of his own department's plans and commitments. If he were an elected politician, he would also know that the voters back home would not absolve him of responsibility for government policies in which he acquiesced, even though they were not directly in his area of responsibility. But the U.S. cabinet and subcabinet are not political, and they cannot be politicized without radical surgery.

◇

The key executive posts in the federal government are now locked into a recruitment process that insures a population of yea-sayers, of men who speak softly and carry big, as well as small, secrets; who define themselves in terms of membership in a select "club" of eligibles; men who can be trusted by a President never to respond to higher loyalties to themselves or to the public, loyalties that might conflict with their service to the Chief Executive. This style is not that of the politician who made a career in elective office but of the successful corporate lawyer and business executive. Its essence is an upper-class in-group exclusivity, low-keyed confidentiality, and personal loyalty to one's employer, client, or fellow member of the club, be he President of the United States or only of General Motors. Incompatible with the style is independence, individuality, a passionate conviction, a delicate conscience, or a tendency to articulate issues in the public forum.

With the core of executive power in America thus open only to self-disciplined insiders, it becomes obvious and necessary that

◇

those with executive ambitions should model their life-and-career styles, as early and as completely as possible, on that of the team player. The ambitious should begin by finding themselves a powerful insider and building a confidant/sponsor relationship, modeling their career-style on that of the sponsor. The young man determined to join the inner circle must learn to play the game by the team rules and to internalize its ethics. Above all, he must not waver. Personal role-ambiguity can be disastrous, as it was for William Jennings Bryan when the Great Commoner tried to be a cabinet insider in the Wilson Administration. A future American cabinet member should never, as in Britain, be a brilliant public debater. He should not try to be a candidate for elective office, nor should he cultivate his own political following. Both alarm Presidential talent hunters, for they bespeak a high degree of ethical and political autonomy, of self-directedness, of ambition to cultivate public support. The would-be recruit must not, as he would in Britain, become active in public causes, a literate public crusader for reform, or an ideological theoretician. He should not, as in Britain, write controversial books, edit newspapers, appear frequently on television, lead demonstrations, nor achieve visibility as head of militant trade unions or iconoclastic student movements. He should not strive to illumine public dialogue or enroll the public in influencing policy. The American self-styled insider, to be eligible for service in cabinet or White House, should rather strive to be, and to remain, virtually unknown to the American public, equally on leaving, as on taking, office. He will not, however, be unknown to fellow bankers and to the presidents of large corporations. His repute in these circles will be that of a fellow who can keep a secret; an expediter who knows exactly the right, equally "unknown," people; who has clout in the board rooms; who runs a tight ship; and, above all, who functions most effectively behind the scenes.

A British cabinet recruit, on the other hand, is the product of a rather different—a highly political—career strategy. Whether he climbs up the steps of a university debating union, leadership of the

Young Conservative movement, as an executive of one of the trade unions, or via professional activism at the bar, the route lies through the espousal of public causes and participation in public politics. The young man or woman who achieves sufficient eminence to be adopted as a candidate for Parliament is expected to provoke public discussion on the hustings, and, if elected, is most likely to attract the attention of party leaders by some first-rate contributions to its public debates or to "question time" in the House of Commons.

Out of this process, despite the exceptions, emerges a British pattern of leadership recruitment that is based on the individual's lifelong, full-time involvement in public, Parliamentary politics. There are, of course, the clubs, the board rooms, the protégés, the old boy and nepotistic networks; but alongside is an obligatory participation in a public political dialogue in which serious issues are openly debated before colleagues, the media, and the voters. Faceless captains of industry and confidential clerks do not generally enter the top echelons of British government unless they are first prepared to shed their anonymous career-styles and become parliamentarians.

The British cabinet and subcabinet are made up of professional politicians who, while they are in the ministries, more or less respect the rules of collective responsibility and confidentiality, though never to the extent of self-effacement and private diffidence to the Prime Ministers. When they leave the cabinet, they tend to revert to being politicians in the public arena: speaking up, championing causes, criticizing policies of the government—if necessary their own as well as the other party's. In the United States, by contrast, the cabinet member is first, last, and always a banker, industrialist, or corporate lawyer. And whenever he is not serving in government, he does not remain in politics but goes back to his bank, factory, or law firm. He vanishes from public view. He knows that the American insider, even when he is not in government, must always be seen to be playing the game by the rules, silently, never squandering his "effectiveness" on "florid" public gestures or the "immoderate" taking of public positions. Between government appointments he should continue to eschew public controversy, especially any public visibility, let alone the politics of public dissent. This prohibition applies not only to public opposition to the government in which he served but also to its successors, of whatever party. In this way, he remains eligible for service in either Republican or Democratic administrations. Indeed, a man who becomes ineligible to service with one party is probably ineligible for service with both. So, in power or out, he keeps his visibility low and reserves his thoughts for private consultations at the White House or for small board-room lunches with fellow insiders. To alter this style of Presidential advisement, to give the President a cabinet of autonomous individuals willing to assert their ethical autonomy, when required, for the well-being of the nation, it would be necessary to draw the cabinet from a pool of men and women who are—and intend to remain—*in elective politics,* whose concern for their fellow politicians and for the Chief would be tempered by concern for, accountability to, the public.

At present, the persons recruited to the upper echelons of the federal executive rarely have any experience at elective politics. Although they may earlier have served for a few years at middle-echelon positions in the federal bureaucracy, there are few who, like Cordell Hull, Elliot Richardson, Walter Hickel, and Melvin Laird, have had the experience of direct public accountability.

In the group of 389 "prime" resigners from top federal executive posts whose careers we studied, 289 were either big-business executives or lawyers, or both. These two professions thus account for 76.9 per cent of the total group of top federal officials, or more than three out of four. The large majority of businessmen come out of large manufacturing enterprises and financial institutions. The lawyers come disproportionately from big Wall Street or Washington firms. They serve for one or several brief periods in government, but their professional base, from which they come and to which, usually after two or three years, they return, is the large law firm or big business.[74] Public service may be perceived by them as a moral obligation, or as a steppingstone to advancement in the firm, or both. But in either case, it is no more than an exciting interlude in the pursuit of a private profession.

It seems inevitable that men and women who spend a part of their time in government but make their occupational base in the private sector will bring into public service some of the habits of thought and traits of personality developed while in their business or law firm. These strongly reinforce the tradition of discreet service to the Chief Executive and wholly discourage ever going public. Both law and big business, as it happens, have strong professional ethical commitments against public-protest resignation. Both permit quiet exit as a means of expressing dissent; but in neither occupation is it considered proper to combine exit with public voice.[75]

Given the predominance of businessmen (41.9 per cent) and lawyers (35.0 per cent) among the resigners we studied, it is not surprising that the statistical profile of resignation behavior should reflect the conduct of these two groups. Thus we find that only fifteen of the businessmen resigned with public dissent, or 9.3 per cent of the businessmen in the group we studied. This is very close to the average: resignations of public protest make up 8.7 per cent of the 389 resignations we studied. Lawyers, however, are even less inclined to speak out than the average. Although they constitute fully 35 per cent of the cases studied, only 5.9 per cent of these resigning lawyers chose to exit with public voicing of dissent.[76]

◇

The businessman who has advanced far enough up the corporate ladder to be eligible for a cabinet, subcabinet, or White House appointment must already long ago have internalized an ethic of corporate loyalty that makes any assertion of ethical autonomy highly unlikely. William H. Whyte's version of the businessman's litany is: "Be loyal to the company and the company will be loyal to you. After all, if you do a good job for the organization, it is only good sense for the organization to be good to you, because that will be best for everybody."[77] David Finn's study, *The Corporate*

Oligarch, leads him to conclude that executive loyalty in the modern American corporation is less to the firm than to the management team.[78] Stated either in terms of corporate *or* management team loyalty, the businessman's litany is easily adaptable to worshipful service in government.

Albert Hirschman has examined the penchant of businessmen, at the breaking point, for silent exit from their corporate jobs without any trace of public protest.[79] He notes that a businessman is more at home in the technology of quiet, dignified departure than in the messy, essentially political, technology of public protest. And the business community's own socializing rules of etiquette reinforce this predilection. If a vice-president of General Motors doesn't like the firm's response to the need for pollution-controlling or safety-inducing devices, he may, within the confines of the executive offices, urge a new policy; or he can resign and go to work for Ford. But if he decides to stay and fight, he must not allow his disagreement to become public. And, similarly, if he decides to go, he must go quietly. A failure to abide by the first part of this injunction would probably cause General Motors to fire him; and a violation of the second part would probably scare Ford away from offering him a job—since he might be "the kind of person" who would do "that sort of thing" to another employer. As Hirschman points out, "[o]nce you have exited, you have lost the opportunity to use voice. . . ."[80] If, after he leaves General Motors to work for Ford, our executive makes a point of firing public salvos at his former employer, he begins to be seen by the business community as an oddball, a sorehead, and fundamentally a "loner"—an embarrassment to old and new employers alike. Worse, he earns a reputation for disloyalty. Once that happens, his executive career is washed up, regardless of whether his public accusations against General Motors are valid or invalid.

The business ethic thus does not exclude dissent, but it rigidly requires that dissent be from *within:* that it be intended to effect change from within, and fought out exclusively within the sound-proofed walls of the executive suites. It also requires that even internal dissent be modulated and respectful of hierarchy. Finally, the business ethic demands that once a policy decision is made, those who argued against it unite to support and defend its implementation.

There are some practical justifications for this business ethic which compels a choice between either dissenting (inside) or resigning (quietly), but which prohibits a combination of exit with public voice. The free-enterprise creed assumes that our General Motors vice-president, when he goes to work for Ford, will have an opportunity to introduce his environmental and safety ideas to the marketplace. If these truly are better ideas, then, presumably, the growth in Ford sales will persuade General Motors either to follow suit or suffer lower sales volume. So long as the competitive-market mechanism combines a free flow of persons and ideas, the way for the best ideas to prevail is for them to be placed before the public in the form of competing products. The practice of unseemly verbal skirmishes between the competitors on the relative merits of their respective products is believed to be an inferior way of demonstrating product quality and runs the additional risk of turning the public off the products of both manufacturers. The idea that General Motors cars are dangerous cannot be unleashed by Ford without a chance that the public will also become afraid of Ford automobiles and will demand investigations and new laws which impose standards neither manufacturer really wants. Every "industry" has a sense of shared fate; a public outcry against one is likely to lead to undesirable consequences for all. An industry executive who helps raise such an outcry against one manufacturer is thus understandably perceived as an enemy to all.

This business ethic against going public prevails in the top echelons of the federal executive, brought there by the movement of hordes of businessmen to policy-making posts in Washington. So short is their public-service interlude that it cannot be expected that a banker or a corporate vice-president, in his three years as an assistant secretary, will develop a wholly new set of professional ethics. He has been a business executive, will shortly again be in the business world, and is surrounded, in the federal government, by other short-term recruits from the large firms.

British cabinets and subcabinets are also inhabited by businessmen and lawyers—although not to the same degree as in the United States. But the British, before entering government, take on a new career—elective politics—with its own ethics and its own lines of accountability. Once in, they serve, on the average, for about eight years in ministries and for twice that long in Parliament. Thus, while they may retain vestigial ties to their law chambers or bank, these tend to be overshadowed by their prolonged commitment to a quite distinct profession of Parliamentary politics. The American lawyer or businessman, when he takes a turn at federal government, enters it as an avocation, not a profession, and becomes for a brief time a member of a group whose members find the ethics of their private profession perfectly serviceable for their brief sojourn in Washington.

Yet the business ethic of silent exit has no logical application to Washington. The businessman who chooses to exit in a dispute over policy generally has the option to work for a competitor. This option does not exist in the case of the federal government. An Under Secretary of State who does not approve of American policy on Vietnam cannot, realistically, become Under Secretary in some other more amenable country. Therefore, the business option of reforming General Motors by working for Ford, or manifesting a policy preference by taking one's ideas to another firm, or even of starting a new competing business, is simply not available to those in the business of running a country.[81]

Not only does the business ethic incline against going public; it also militates against fighting too doggedly in the privacy of the board room or presidential suite. If an executive is unhappy with corporate policy, again the "decent" thing is for him to resign and go to work for a more compatible firm, not to continue to make life miserable for his superiors. This ethic, too, has also been transferred intact to the federal government, even though it has no place within it, because there is no compatible alternative government where a federal executive, having reached his ethical breaking point, can put his ideas to work.

John T. McNaughton, until his death McNamara's closest associate in the Defense Department, has told of a conversation with his friend and boss which illustrates this. As he did from time to time, McNamara had shared with his deputy some private misgivings about a policy to which he was publicly committed. "Why don't you tell the President?" asked McNaughton, a born infighter and Harvard academic with dovish tendencies.

McNamara reached back to his formative years. "When I was at Ford," he replied, "if I didn't like a policy, I used to take it up with the chairman. If he ignored my criticism, I would take it to him again. Then, if that didn't help, and if it were something I felt strongly about, I might even go back a third time. But after that, I'd never raise that particular issue again. I'd just tend to my knitting."

McNamara's perception of his role in government—and out— was deeply rooted in this corporate ethic, together with his concept of institutional loyalty.[82] In the end, it governed his way of leaving government even more than his performance as Secretary of Defense.

◇

Lawyers, who are the second largest occupational group in our survey (35.0 per cent) are even less inclined than businessmen to leave government with public expression of dissent over a policy difference. As noted, only 8 of the 136 lawyers in our "prime" group (5.9 per cent) resigned with any expression of public disagreement. All the rest left in silence.

Like the business community, but even more so, the lawyers have their professional ethics enforced by a stern code of conduct. The Canons of Professional Ethics of the American Bar Association, which have been adopted in the various states, include the following provision: "It is the duty of a lawyer to preserve his client's confidences. This duty outlasts the lawyer's employment. . . ."[83]

The lawyer is not only enjoined—on pain of disbarment—

from revealing his client's confidences, but state laws of evidence to varying degrees prohibit the admission into court of testimony which violates this basic norm of the solicitor-client relationship. And the lawyer's obligation to his client persists after the relationship has ceased. "The seal of the law, once fixed upon them, remains forever, unless removed by the party himself, in whose favor it was there placed."[84]

The reason for these rules is sound enough. It is, simply, to induce litigants to use lawyers instead of preparing and conducting their own cases, and, when they do hire a lawyer, to level with him or her so the case can be prepared properly. If the communications between clients and lawyers were subject to public disclosure, people would hesitate to use attorneys or would tell them only what they wanted the court to know. Thus the law requires that "the mouths of the attorneys shall be forever sealed."[85]

A study has shown that this particular ethic of their profession—the vow of silence—rates particularly high among the ethical values of lawyers.[86] It is especially popular among practitioners of the larger, well-established firms who are accustomed to dealing with corporate presidents, bankers, and other members of the Establishment in litigation over public-policy related issues such as taxation, antitrust, and the issuing of stocks and bonds.[87] It is also from among the partners of these firms, with their deeply internalized habits of keeping their important clients' secrets, that so large a proportion of the top federal executives are recruited.[88] In a recent upstate New York case, two lawyers *literally* knew where their client had buried the bodies. Corporate lawyers, figuratively, are expected to know the same thing and their silence is not merely tolerated but expected by the profession.

The vow of silence applies even to things a client may admit to a lawyer which are illegal or offend the lawyer's personal sense of ethics. In every such case, it is the lawyer's business to keep quiet and to do his best for his principal. But what is ethical for a lawyer in private practice may be quite unethical for the same man when he is an assistant secretary or a White House aide. Yet interviews with American lawyers who have resigned from public service confirm that they make no distinction between their Washington service and their Wall Street practice. They tend to regard their agency, department, or the President as a "client." And so it is natural that they would consider it unthinkable—a violation of a client's confidence—to go public under any circumstances. Canon 44 of the bar's rules of ethics permits the lawyer to withdraw from his client's case for "good cause" of "honor or self-respect." But to reveal what one has learned in the client's service is simply unthinkable.

George Ball's conduct is instructive of the legal ethic in the public service. As President Johnson's Under Secretary of State and, later, Ambassador to the United Nations, he became the "house dove," an early and frequent advocate against Vietnam escalation.[89] His advice was not taken, and yet it was inconceivable to him that he might turn public critic. His role was to advise his client, the President.[90] But when his advice was rejected, the counselor's role required him still to make every effort to defend his client to the best of his ability, no matter that he personally disapproved of what his client had done.[91]

This transference of the antidisclosure ethic from the professional to the public-service context is both fallacious and dangerous to democracy. Yet the Canons of Ethics fail to make clear the important distinctions between the private practice of law and being a government official with a law degree. The canons fail to emphasize the quite different ethical imperatives for a lawyer when he is in government service. As in the case of the business ethic against "exit" with "voice" so, too, the lawyer's vow of silence to his client is not appropriate to Washington. Most lawyers, when they enter an Administration, serve the President not as legal counselor but as adviser on such essentially nonlegal matters as national security, foreign relations, trade, welfare, and the budget. The secrecy vow of the lawyer was never intended to extend to such nonlegal work in the public political arena of Presidential policy-making. Nevertheless, it is inevitable that when men conditioned always to keep clients' confidences leave their law office and briefly enter the ranks of the federal executive, they will continue to perform in accordance with old habits. And, knowing that after a few years they will again be in Washington or New York practice, serving important corporate clients, prudence dictates that they preserve above all their reputation for being "the sort that can keep a secret." According to Ramsey Clark, a lawyer in government who speaks out in public "would damage not only his future chances for public service, but also his prospects in the legal profession."[92] Dean Acheson once remarked that "A 'sound' man is a more desireable lawyer than a 'controversial' one."[93]

Even in private practice, the rule of confidentiality has tended to assume an exaggerated priority which the Canons of Ethics do not support. Secrecy or confidentiality, among lawyers, has become so elevated a virtue as to have largely overshadowed the other ethical considerations that should, on occasion, induce public disclosure of a client's wrongdoing.[94] No lawyer is supposed to protect *only* his clients. "[T]he lawyer must decide whether the steps he should take, in serving a particular client, will also serve the best interests . . . of society as a whole."[95] The professional canons emphasize that there are circumstances in which a lawyer *should* reveal certain of his client's confidences,[96] as when his client has told him of an intention to commit a crime. Nor does he owe to his client any duty to assist in "deception or betrayal of the public."[97] If the lawyer discovers "that some fraud or deception has been practiced" by his client, it is his duty to bring it to light.[98] Above all, a lawyer must always "obey his own conscience and not that of his client."[99]

Unfortunately, these canons are too rarely heeded by the profession when they appear to conflict with client loyalty. This has come to light during the Watergate hearings. Senator Lowell Weicker asked former Attorney General John N. Mitchell whether he was not under a professional duty, after learning of the raid on Daniel Ellsberg's psychiatrist's office, to inform the judge in the

Ellsberg case. Should this not have taken precedence over loyalty to the White House? Mitchell agreed, in retrospect, that his social responsibility should have come first. But, in fact, the Attorney General chose loyalty to the President and the White House staff— his "clients"—over his responsibilities to the court and the Constitution.[100]

It is not the bar's professional ethics, but a widespread misinterpretation of them, that lawyers import into government service when they remain publicly silent in profound crises of conscience and in matters of legitimate public concern.[101]

But the lawyer who, in private practice, defines his role as the single-minded pursuit of his client's fortunes usually causes only minor damage to the public interest. The lawyer who, in government, sees his role solely in terms of responsibility to his superiors can do great damage to society. To abdicate personal conscience in favor of client loyalty in private legal practice may cause a guilty man to go free. But when high-echelon government officials abase their ethical autonomy and see their role exclusively in terms of loyal and confidential service, then the stage is set for a My Lai and a Watergate coverup.

The anti-public-disclosure ethic of business executives and lawyers is reinforced by a third recruitment pool for top federal executives: the federal bureaucracy. Although only 9 of the 389 top officials we studied had risen to senior Presidential appointments solely through the ranks of the career civil service, a much larger proportion of the total had, at some time during their careers, held an appointment in a middle-echelon federal bureaucratic position. Dean Mann's study of 800 assistant secretaries[102] found that fully one quarter of these had previously seen some service in a lower federal job. Many of the lawyers and businessmen who, in their forties and fifties, return to Washington as assistant or under secretaries may have spent two to four years during their twenties or thirties in lesser posts, at the G.S. 14-to-17 level, often as special assistants. Therefore, by the time a man is appointed from a corporate vice-presidency or senior partnership in a law firm to a policy-making position in the executive branch, he may already have spent some time internalizing the ethics of the federal bureaucracy, even though his principal ethical grounding will be in his own profession.[103]

This early exposure of future top officials to the ethics of "the service" takes place at a level which, in Britain, is called the administrative service and is staffed solely by civil servants.[104] In the United States, this same level is composed of a mixture of career and short-term political and professional personnel. But it is the professionals who shape its ethics. According to Charles Frankel, the public servant "lives by an unusual code. Assuming that the government for which he works is a constitutional one, a permanent official's conscience must not bleed when he is asked to carry out a policy that doesn't fit his own ideas. Indeed, he requires a conscience which tells him, except in extreme circumstances, to pipe down after he has had his say, and to get to work in support even of what he thinks is wrong."[105] The civil service ideal is the Vicar of Bray, who survived in his post by successively embracing the high-churchmanship of King Charles, the popery of James II, the protestantism of William of Orange, the Tory-ism of Queen Anne and the Whiggery of George of Hanover. Like the good ecclesiastical civil servant he was, he vowed:

> And this is law, I will maintain
> Unto my dying day, Sir,
> That whatsoever king shall reign,
> I will be Vicar of Bray, Sir![106]

This natural tendency on the part of the civil servant to defer to what in Britain is called his "political masters" is quite appropriate. The career public servant should have his conscience in harness and his tongue under a tight bit. Democracy links moral judgment with political responsibility; and the duty to exercise judgment in major questions of policy ought to be exercised by those who are endowed with responsibility. The system could not work if, as Harold Laski feared, passionately conservative civil servants refused to do the bidding of a Labour government. Thus, in America as in Britain, the career public servant is imbued with the ethic of service rather than of ethical autonomy. Resigning and going public is quite properly alien to the service ethic except in the direst circumstances.

In Britain, however, this service ethic tends not to be transmitted up to the political echelons of government for two reasons: *first,* because, in the U.K., only in the most extraordinary and rare circumstances is a civil servant ever promoted into the cabinet or subcabinet; and, *second,* because those few that do make the transition undergo a sharp break with their civil-service past. They must leave the civil service behind and strike out in a new direction, seeking election to Parliament, unless, as in the recent case of Lord Caradon, they are appointed to the House of Lords. They must forsake the tight-lipped life-style of the civil servant and, instead, learn to speak at rallies and make themselves accessible to aggrieved members of the public. And they must move out of the cloisters of Whitehall, or wherever they had been serving, and into the political hurly-burly of Parliament.

In America, on the other hand, the move up from career- or lower-public-service post to political appointment in the cabinet or subcabinet is both relatively frequent and requires only the barest change in life-style.[107] It does not require a mental adjustment to a new profession, a different ethic, as it would in Britain. An assistant to a commissioner or administrator can leave Washington for Wall Street, then return to become an assistant secretary. On his return, he will have moved only a few doors down the hall or, at most, a floor or two higher in the same building. Nothing much will have changed, except that more people will call him "Sir." Not surprisingly, although he now holds a policy-making "political" post in the federal government, he will probably not think of himself as a "political" person. His relations to his superiors will reflect the bureaucratic service ethic reinforced by the style of quiet confidentiality acquired in business or the law.

◇

Class, too, is a factor entrenching the insider ethic of acquiescent service and discreet entry and exit from the top jobs in the executive branch.[108] Various studies, using slightly different criteria, establish that approximately 20 to 25 per cent of the senior federal executives are of upper-class background.[109]

To examine the extent of the upper-class presence among top federal appointive officials, we tested our 389 "prime" resigners for three indicators of elite status which seem to us—despite some mixing of the less advantaged with the very advantaged around the edges of the indicators—still largely relevant. Simplified, these are: 1) entry in any of eleven city editions of the *Social Register,* 2) attendance at a selective, "name" prep school, and 3) membership in the most socially exclusive clubs.[110] Of the 389 resignations we studied, 93 (23.9 per cent) were by persons who satisfy one of these three upper-class criteria. Of these 93, only five (5.4 per cent) resigned in public protest, while the rest left silently. Among the 296 non-upper class, 29 (9.8 per cent) resigned and spoke up. Put another way, resignations by persons satisfying the upper-class criteria were 24.8 per cent of all silent resignations and only 14.7 per cent of all public-protest resignations. Either way, upper-class resignations are almost twice as likely to be silent as those of the non-upper-class group.

This ought not to be surprising. Almost above all other social characteristics, the upper class in the United States today prides itself, with cause, on being discreet. Theirs is certainly not the extravagant ostentation of the French court of Louis XIV. Great wealth and breeding are less and less publicly manifest in America. Most of the great châteaux of Newport stand empty and there are few replacements being built. Yet concentration of great wealth has not been abolished; rather, the style of the upper class has become anonymous, almost unnoticeable to the naked eye of the

◇
―――

middle-class observer. Members of the upper class know who they are, yet they not only do not flaunt their position to the populace but consider it in eminently bad taste to do so. They tend to avoid unnecessary publicity or exposure and frown on deviates who join the "jet set" or whose names appear regularly in the gossip columns. As noted, a small group within this class—W. Averell Harriman, Nelson Rockefeller, Franklin Roosevelt—do enter elective politics and it is grudgingly granted that they must, to a limited extent, expose their lives and thoughts to public scrutiny. The rest are expected to keep their thoughts and activities to the precincts of home and club.

Discretion of this sort—a deliberately low profile and a habit of discussing their affairs only among themselves—is dictated by a desire to avoid arousing the attention, envy, or antagonism of the majority of the populace. It was Beau Brummell's view that if one's elegance is noticed one has failed.[111] The social upper classes know that their survival chances increase if the public is not too aware of their affairs. In a republic like the United States, with a strong antiaristocratic philosophy of equal rights, the educational, financial, and cultural head-start programs of the hereditary rich are not advertised.

A further reason for discreet behavior among the upper class is that a degree of secrecy, of mysteries shared with one's equals but shrouded from everyone else, is itself a status symbol. The self-awareness of members of the select group *as* members is heightened by the psychological device of excluding others from information—often quite uninteresting in itself—which is available only to members of the group. To reveal such in-group information is to weaken the group's exclusivity. Gossip inside the group is one thing. But the only thing more unforgivable than publicizing one's own life is the public exposure of another's to the world at large.

The upper-class ethic of discreet reticence thus prepares one admirably for service in the President's inner circle. Also, an ability to husband inside information is as functional in Washington as in Grosse Pointe. Among the higher reaches of the government, confidential information, even if only exalted gossip—what the President said about a James Reston column, for example—is an important prestige symbol, a coin of power to be expended only where it is likely to buy equally valuable confidences or useful allies. It is not to be squandered in random public revelations.

The class-related style of perhaps a quarter of the top federal executives seeps down to those not of this upper-class background. Thorstein Veblen observed the extent to which "our standards" emulate "the usage of those next above us in reputability" with the eventual result that "all canons of reputability and decency . . . are traced back by insensible gradations to the usages and habits of thought of the highest social and pecuniary class. . . ."[112]

This general phenomenon of emulation is not explained by Veblen. But its operation among men who govern, and particularly among the young who wish to govern, is not at all mysterious, being made up of a composite of social snobbery, imitation for purposes of taking on "gilt by association," and a rather hard-headed understanding of the crucial role that can be played by an Establishment "sponsor" in advancing one's career. Sponsorship is particularly important, paradoxically, in a relatively open society because, unlike the British, Americans have no openly acknowledged, clearly marked steps to power. The talent search that led to the appointment by John Kennedy of Dean Rusk as Secretary of State is an excellent illustration. Born of a distinctly non-upper-class Georgia family, Rusk's career was substantially taken up by the Rockefeller family, and he became president of the Rockefeller Foundation. Kennedy had never met Rusk but his name was put forward by two eminent upper-class Kennedy talent scouts: Robert Lovett and Dean Acheson, and was endorsed by Rockefeller Foundation trustee Douglas Dillon.[113] Having this endorsement was enough for Kennedy to summon Rusk and, in Theodore Sorensen's words, the President-elect "talked briefly and somewhat vaguely with him about an article Rusk wrote on 'The Presidency,' and called him the next day to say the job was his."[114]

Key talent hunters mentioned by Sorensen—Robert Lovett, Chester Bowles, John J. McCloy, Dean Acheson, and, oddly, Dag Hammarskjöld—are all within the elite category,[115] and their power to place names before President Kennedy was matched by the power of virtually the same men, together with others like Douglas Dillon and Averell Harriman, to initiate promotions in other Presidential administrations. The word *patronage* in its literal sense reflects this notion of a guiding saint or upper-class *patron* giving a young comer his *laissez-passer*. In Britain, the road to politics leads past a "double first" at Oxford or Cambridge, the presidency of the Oxford Union, the presidency of the Young Conservatives, a seat in Parliament, a Private Parliamentary Secretaryship, etc. There are no comparable road markers in the United States to guide the steps of the hordes of young men and women in the country who are preparing themselves to be Secretary of State, Defense, or Treasury.[116] In selecting a cabinet, subcabinet, and White House advisers, each newly elected President must choose from among a large, random assortment of eager, more or less qualified candidates. In Britain, such choices are limited to a small number of eligibles who have already reached the requisite rungs on the ladder.[117] The very randomness of the American process inevitably puts a high premium on the cultivation of close personal contacts by the young with a few senior members of the upper-class Establishment. While Englishmen advance politically by steps, Americans vault upward in leaps, usually catapulting off the tall, broad shoulders of a patron.

Such close patronal contacts inevitably involve an emulation by the younger man of his patron's style. Most important, according to those who have succeeded in this process, is the development of a closeness that flourishes only in an atmosphere of strict respect for confidences. The younger man inevitably forfeits the support of his patron if he is perceived to be the kind that reveals to the public what has been disclosed to him in private. To contemplate resigning and going public is thus to abandon hope of advancement by patronal recommendation. The patron's protégé, like a client's attorney or business executive, is never absolved from his duty of silence about matters learned in the course of his privileged relationship.

In Britain, the upper class does not resign quietly. Fully 54.6 per cent of Ministers of the Crown in the group we studied satisfy our British upper-class criteria.[118] And of these, 51 per cent resigned with public statements of protest. This is only a slightly lower percentage than that of non-upper-class protest resignations (58.8 per cent). This certainly does not mean that the British aristocracy and gentry are by nature or social conditioning more garrulous or given to publicizing their affairs. It does indicate, however, that there is in Britain among the upper class a strong tradition of total immersion in elective politics and thus, when a scion—a member of the Marlborough clan like Winston Churchill, for example, or a Lord Salisbury—enters the House of Commons it is the ethics and responsibilities of elected public office, rather than those of his class, which govern his conduct.

◇

As long as the upper echelons of the federal executive in the United States continue to be filled with persons conditioned by the ethics of the practicing bar, big corporations, the civil service, and the upper class, it cannot be expected that the cabinet, subcabinet, or White House staff will develop a taste for doing serious battle with the Chief, in private or in public. If the survival of democracy, or even just good government, requires a system of effective checks and balances within the presidential branch, a radically different recruitment policy must be implemented that surrounds the President with men and women possessed of firm ethical autonomy, the pugnacious will to assert it, and the political instinct to do so effectively when and where it counts. Some of these might well come out of banking, the bar, or the civil service, but they will be persons whose commitment must first have been transferred to the public political process.

⋙ 6 ⋙

Saying Yes
to Saying No:
The Power of
Negative Thinking

A CABINET of "yea-sayers" is a profound danger in an era of wide Presidential discretion, particularly when the President, in his role as Commander-in-Chief, has life-and-death powers in matters of foreign policy and national security.

We have already speculated that, if there had been a tradition of protest resignation in the United States in 1967, those with misgivings about Vietnam policy in the Johnson Administration— McNamara, Ball, Moyers, Wirtz, Frankel, perhaps even Gardner and Katzenbach—might have been more effective in checking the President's discretion to send hundreds of thousands of men into an undeclared war.[1] As it was, their misgivings could too readily be dismissed. In the United States, the extent to which the Chief Executive takes his cabinet seriously, as a genuine check on his personal prerogatives, is, itself, almost wholly a matter of his personal preference. They cannot bring him down, nor, ordinarily, do him very serious harm. Johnson did become increasingly isolated within his own official entourage, but this did not pose the sort of threat to his grasp on the controls of government that similar isolation would be to a British Prime Minister.

Therefore, probably the most important cost of not having a

◇

tradition of public-protest resignation in the executive branch is that, in the absence of this ultimate deterrent to Presidential intractability, the cabinet and White House staff cannot constitute an effective *internal* system of checks and balances. A cabinet officer in conflict with the President over a matter of policy, particularly foreign policy, cannot expect to do much good because the President knows he will not do much harm.

A second cost is that the dearth of such resignations deleteriously affects the quality of the checks that are exerted on Presidential discretion from *outside* the executive branch. Again, in Britain, the resigner from the cabinet or subcabinet has an advantage. By his public rhetoric from the back benches, he can both mobilize and stabilize popular and Parliamentary opposition to a government policy, thereby nurturing the vitality of the adversary system that is the lifeblood of political democracy. In the United States, to the contrary, those top executives who do reach their breaking point over a question of policy and who choose to resign generally avoid all contact with the members of Congress, voters groups, students, and others who publicly espouse the very cause that induced their resignations.

This American executive style, exemplified by acquiescent, tight-lipped "public" service followed by mute departures from government, tends to polarize the society, alienating its critics not only from a specific government policy but from "the system" as a whole. Crises, in America, disrupt institutions and bring out revolutionary tendencies—precisely because dissent from within the system is suppressed in the name of loyalty. That leaves opposition to outsiders. An almost total absence of dissent among those who have been in the inner core of the government tends to magnify the intensity of dissent at the perimeters of the system. The lack of open politics around the precincts of the federal government's upper echelons aggravates the politics of the streets and the universities. Large segments of the U.S. population, remarking that not one senior member of the Kennedy, Johnson, or Nixon teams offered themselves as a leader in the fight against Vietnam escalation, concluded that the experience of being in government is, in itself, hopelessly corrupting. Why else would Robert McNamara refuse to assert in public what he was confiding in private? Citizens who, in the turbulent decade between 1960 and 1970, would gladly have rallied behind leaders experienced in foreign and defense policy, persons able to set out convincing alternatives, found no one of that group willing to lead.

Not only would the open advocacy of antiwar policies by a McNamara or Ball have rallied opposition but it would have insured institutional legitimacy and responsible leadership for the forces of dissent. Britain's Foreign Secretary Anthony Eden, after resigning from the cabinet, became the rallying point, with Winston Churchill, Duff Cooper, and Lord Salisbury, of those in the society who passionately opposed Chamberlain's policy of appeasing Hitler. This opposition, in its intensity and determination, is reminiscent of the forces in America opposing the Vietnam escalation. But the British system provides those who resign from the cabinet with an institutional base from which to oppose in public. In Parliament they can continue to make themselves heard, can lay their case before the public, and can confront and challenge those of their cabinet colleagues who choose to stay on. Opposition, in Britain, does not have to take to the streets, because the system provides a legitimate political forum for confrontation. And leadership of the forces of dissent does not pass to street politicians because the system permits experienced leaders to defect from the cabinet and lead the campaign against a controversial policy like appeasement. Eden, Churchill, and their colleagues knew that the British system could both accommodate their period of dissent and facilitate their eventual return to office. The system was able to contain both their dissent of conscience *and* their careerist ambition.

In America, the system forces men to choose between their consciences and their careers, compelling men with perfectly necessary and decent ambitions to make insufferable excisions that leave them psychically crippled. When Creon offers Antigone a comfortable life at his court if she will stop opposing his will, she replies: "Tell me: to whom shall I have to lie? Upon whom shall I have to fawn? To whom must I sell myself? Whom do you want me to leave dying, while I turn away my eyes?" The public silence of all those in the Kennedy, Johnson, and Nixon administrations who doubted or disagreed is the almost inevitable result of a system which compels a direct and irrevocable choice between principled autonomy and ambition. Forcing such a choice on its political leaders is highly dysfunctional and speaks of a system that is working against itself.

In Britain, even while appeasement was the official government policy, the system insured that the forces of antiappeasement were led by men of the same caliber, experience, and commitment to the system as were leading the government. This not only affected the quality of dissent—making it at once more credible and more responsible—but it also insured that when the government's policy of appeasement was eventually discredited, a team of respected public leaders within the system was ready to rejuvenate and sustain public confidence.

In the United States, because no insiders who had been at the font of foreign policy-making stepped forward to assume the leadership of those opposed to the Vietnam war, that leadership passed, by default, to persons who did not have the perspective of service at the inner core; and, more important, who did not expect ever to be invited to join a Presidential Administration. Their style, the "outsider" style, shaped opposition to the war. Dissent *leadership* was inevitably polarized and, in time, radicalized, because the system could not accommodate public dissent by insiders.

The outsider style also affected the quality of dissent *followership*. Those among the British public who supported the dissent of Winston Churchill and Anthony Eden firmly believed that their leaders would, in time, be proven right, and that the dissenters would then be recalled to power. The attitude of Churchill's and Eden's supporters toward the stern challenge of being outside power was thus quite different from that of Americans who, even while opposing Vietnam policy, must have known that neither

Senator William Fulbright nor Tom Hayden would ever become Secretary of State or Defense.

◇

When the leaders and followers of a dissent movement lose faith in the possibility of coming to power through the system, they must either be suppressed by the system or they will eventually try to overturn it. British dissent followers are able to work within the system to return their leaders to the helm of government. But American dissent followers know that their leaders cannot *come* to power through the system, so they are tempted to halt power *in its tracks*. The system itself becomes the enemy. Since their best strategy cannot be to *enter,* it must be to *prevent* the executive branch from functioning. The two-party system, as they perceive it, provides the people with no real alternatives in Presidential politics.[2] The Presidential candidates of both parties tend to rely on identical or frequently indistinguishable insider stereotypes in choosing their top associates and advisers.

It often seems to American dissidents faced with a choice (between, say, Hubert Humphrey and Richard Nixon) that while there is a make-believe two-party system in their country, the meaningful political alignment is not that of Democrats and Republicans, as it appears on the surface. Rather, the two-party system is one which runs under and across the visible institutions of U.S. politics. There is one alignment of insiders and another of outsiders, of "the yea-sayer and the nay-sayer" in Bertolt Brecht's phrase.[3] And the system insures that the insiders always retain control of executive power, from which the outsiders are perpetually excluded. Such a system precludes a real transfer of sharing of power and therefore, inevitably, comes to be perceived by those assigned to perpetual opposition not in parliamentary but in revolutionary terms.

Although guillotines are not yet working in the streets, revolutionary alternatives to the system are now emerging. We are witnessing the spontaneous appearance of organized alternatives to the processes of government, the springing up of institutions—

an entire system of antigovernment—operating alongside, and at cross-purposes to, the formal, constitutionally legitimate system. Americans, in substantial numbers, have created a response to the dysfunction of the system by beginning to constitute a countersystem. This countersystem, in its makeshift, unorthodox, and, at times, unlawful ways, seeks to provide what the official system denies the outsiders: access to policy-making (not, of course, access to the National Security Council, but to other makeshift entry points for influencing the President's decisions).

The requisite for changing policy is inside information. If critical debates affecting the lives and fortunes of the people are being carried on within the inner circles of executive power without any senior insiders dissenting and going public, then outsiders, if they are to affect policy, must devise alternative means for getting data. With so much government policy dependent on secret information gathered by government agencies, it becomes particularly essential for those outsiders who oppose a policy to lay before the public whatever data does *not* support the government's policy. Such data are usually secret. Opponents of government policy know that much official secrecy is directed toward denying information not to a foreign enemy, but to the internal opposition. This is not new, of course. Thoreau remarked that President Polk's war against Mexico was "the work of comparatively few individuals using the standing government as their tool; for, in the outset, the people would not have consented to this measure."[4] The public acquiescence in the Vietnam war, too, as the Pentagon Papers show, depended on careful "management" of what the public heard and read. McNamara's Defense Department spokesman, Arthur Sylvester, spoke for what has become—and remains—the prevailing view in Washington when he boldly asserted the government's right to lie to the people.

In Britain, inside information of this kind—indications of dissenting advice given the government by its own advisers or data which do not support a government initiative—is brought to light by resigners who speak up. In America, this route for public disclosure is blocked by the prohibition on public-protest resignations. A system which encourages McNamara's silent resignation and prohibits going public in the Anthony Eden style makes it inevitable that the countersystem will invent a Daniel Ellsberg. If top-echelon federal executives are precluded from resigning and alerting the public to information and issues about which they ought to know, then outsiders will find ways to recruit lower-echelon employees of the government to Xerox the documents in which the information is contained.

The Ellsberg phenomenon is the countersystem's makeshift equivalent to the information flow provided in crises by the British practice of resigning and speaking out. The media, in America, provide the countersystem alternative to the British Parliament's back benches. One way or another, in a democracy, dissent within government on issues of great public importance must make itself heard. If the system, as in Britain, provides the means for achieving this in an orderly fashion, most dissenters will choose to operate within that system; if not, then in all but the most efficient dictatorship they will create their own system. The theft of the Pentagon Papers, Kissinger Papers, and the growing flood of stolen executive memos being showered on the media are but the "tip of the Ellsberg."

The British system accommodates disclosure, but the resigning cabinet member's specific disclosures may be less important than are his credentials as an insider. A foreign minister speaking out against negotiations with Mussolini need not reveal much secret detail of Foreign Office transactions to arouse public interest in what he has to say. If he states publicly that the negotiations are ill-timed and dangerous it is probably not necessary to produce all the secret documents and statistics on which that judgment is based. By sacrificing high office in order to earn the right to criticize a policy in public, he has earned a certain credibility with the public which is further enhanced by public knowledge that the resigning minister was party to all the secret considerations that went into the decision he is opposing.

What the British resigner brings to the politics of dissent is his credentials as an informed critic. What an Ellsberg, operating at a lower level, brings—in the absence of such credentials—is copies of the actual documentary evidence on which to base dissent. The effect, in both cases, is to shake loose the hold that bland official reassurances have on the public conscience. It alerts the passengers on the ship of state that there is dissension on the bridge— something we passengers ought to know.

Key to the effectiveness of the American countersystem is the recent conversion of the media, and in particular of the Eastern Establishment press, to their cause or, rather, to several of their more recent causes: such as the ending of the Vietnam war and the exposure of White House "dirty tricks" and "horror stories." In a sense, the media have taken on the role of countersystemic Official Opposition. The press daily publicizes information which government seeks to withhold from the public. Relatively minor officials, like Gordon Rule and A. Ernest Fitzgerald, who defect and speak up are celebrated not because of who they are but because they are the only dissenters to have the courage to buck the President and to speak up.

By ceaselessly needling the Administration, prying into its files, publicizing and lionizing its defectors, the media, in the United States, have become politicized as the countersystem's instrument of dissent. Not only do they afford dissidents a platform but—at least in the most prestigious papers—the editorial writers have themselves become the leading dissenters. They and the columnists and correspondents tend to occupy, so to speak, most of their own back benches. They act in concert with those inside the Administration who would like to see a Presidential policy torpedoed, but dare not, themselves, go public, and with others, usually in the middle echelon, who are prepared to quit and speak up but do not, in themselves, have much public visibility until the press bestows it on them.

◇

The countersystem, however, is at most an unsatisfactory pallia-

tive for a serious systemic dysfunction. The militant politicizing of
the press, the stream of stolen secret documents, the polarization
of the society around professional "insiders" who always govern
and "outsiders" who always try to prevent government: these are
better than no effective counterbalance to Presidential power, but
they are also the symptoms of an ailing political process.

Nor can the cure be effected solely by a radical change in
dramatis personae. Let us stretch our imaginations to suppose that
those who currently dissent from the mainstream policies of American government were to succeed in electing the next President.
The countersystem might then succeed in transforming a range of
existing policies and of initiating new ones. In the short run, that
can be all-important. But it would not prevent the recurrence of
crises caused by an overconcentration of Presidential power, without effective checking and balancing. What of the men and women
the new President would select for his cabinet, for the upper
echelons of the federal departments and agencies, and for his
White House staff? Would not he, too, select persons with loyalty
solely to him, with consciences mortgaged to their careers? The
American countersystem has provided alternate ways of giving the
public some vital glimpses of the inner core's decision-making
process. It has developed ways to give public visibility to dissenters and credibility to their arguments. It has sometimes mobilized
public opinion to block Presidential policies. It has contributed to
the premature retirement of two Presidents. It may even influence
Presidential elections. What the countersystem does not have is
the capacity to effect fundamental change in the system itself—that
unsatisfactory part of the system where dissent confronts power.

Such basic system transformation may require a change in the
composition and constitutional status of the executive branch
itself. The failure, in America, of senior federal officials to resign
and speak up is really both a dramatic symptom and one cause of
the excessive gathering of power in the hands of the President.

There have been various proposals for breaking up this over-
concentrated Presidency. Barbara Tuchman has suggested a

Swiss-style collegial system. Pointing out that "Presidential government can get beyond control in the U.S. because the President is subject to no advisers who hold office independently of him," and that "too much power and too much risk has become subject to the idiosyncracies of a single individual at the top," she proposes instituting a cabinet directorate of six, nominated as a slate by each party and elected for a six-year term. The Presidency would rotate, with each of the six holding the post for one year.[5] In 1851, John C. Calhoun proposed a dual Presidency with all power shared by two elective officers who would have to agree to act in unison, to "effect an equilibrium" between encroaching Presidential power and the states.[6] Herbert Finer, in 1960, proposed that the "President and a cabinet of eleven Vice-Presidents shall be elected on the same ticket every four years. . . ."[7] The Finer proposal, in effect, parallels a suggestion considered, but not adopted, by Senator George McGovern in 1970: that the Presidential candidate name his key cabinet choices at the time he is nominated so that they could "run" alongside him. Each of these proposals has the merit of creating a Presidency in which there are a number of officials, each with a public mandate, each therefore able to restrain Presidential omnipotence.

As we have noted, the cabinet as presently constituted is not an effective check on Presidential discretion. The Constitution does not even recognize the existence of the institution and cabinet members, although their departments are established and funded by Congress, are in practice little but the extension of Presidential imagination. In the first century of the republic's history, Presidents tended to choose major political leaders for their subalterns, men like Hamilton and Jefferson. After Lincoln, however, Presidents began to choose bankers and lawyers, friends and "able administrators" who had no political experience or interest and who were unlikely to give their President the rough passage Lincoln's cabinet gave him. Rutherford B. Hayes wrested from Congress the right to choose his own cabinet with this in mind.[8] Under Grover Cleveland, the cabinet became an administrative, not a political, body. And its members, for the most part devoid of political clout, no longer constituted a really serious threat to the President's executive discretion.[9]

Today, a secretaryship—with the possible exceptions of State and Defense—is ordinarily no place to build one's political reputation or national visibility. John W. Weeks, Secretary of War from 1921–23, thought the public about as interested in the problems and accomplishments of his department as in "the geography and history of the Netherlands."[10]

In an interesting analysis of cabinet members' public exposure through the pages of *The New York Times,* Richard Fenno reports that, in the absence of a crisis in their departments, they rarely receive coverage. Except for the occasions of his appointment and resignation Wilson's Secretary of Agriculture, David F. Houston, appeared on the front page of the *Times* five times over a four-year period, and four of these stories concerned rumors—untrue, as it turned out—that he was about to resign. "It is a fair generalization to say," Fenno concludes from his survey of administrations back to 1913, "that what does interest the public more than anything else about a Cabinet member is his coming and his going, rather than what he does while he is in office."[11] Even senior officials in the executive branch thus are understandably loath to engage in a public contest of credibility and popularity with the elected Head of State. And most cabinet jobs are not likely to attract ambitious politicians, especially those holding senior elective office.

Among the top federal executives who did not resign, or who resigned without public disagreement during the Kennedy, Johnson, and Nixon administrations, a frequently cited reason for keeping quiet is that it would have been useless to speak up: "I'd have made the front page of *The New York Times* and *The Washington Post* once, and that's the last time anyone would ever have heard of me." Men of the rank of Assistant Secretary or below go further, believing like Roger Hilsman[12] (Assistant Secretary of State) and Robert Barnett[13] (Deputy Assistant Secretary of State) that they did not have the visibility to be heard even once, had they chosen to go public. White House staffers like William Watts similarly argue their own impotence: "the possibility of our influencing the Cambodian decision or the war in general [by resigning and speaking up] was absolutely minimal. If we had been Cabinet members or even sub-Cabinet members, our resignations might have had some impact—but not staff members, no matter how important we like to think we are."[14] Cabinet members say exactly the same thing. "Whatever became of Walter Hickel?" is a question that scores a not wholly invalid point. Another frequent comment is that "unlike the British, when they resign, we don't have a Parliamentary back bench to retire to, and from which we can make our criticisms heard. When a U.S. cabinet officer quits, he gets lost in the backwoods." If there is anything more nightmarish than letting out a scream in a room full of dignitaries, it is screaming to a crowd that cannot hear. The U.S. executive branch is deliberately constituted in such a way as to foster the inaudibility of its members, with the sole and major exception of the President.

When President Wilson fired Robert Lansing, Wilson's confidant, Joseph Tumulty, warned about a possible storm of public criticism should the Secretary of State choose to take his case to the people. "Of course, it will be another two-day wonder," Wilson replied disdainfully.[15]

British cabinets, by contrast, are made up of men who make themselves heard. Above all, they consist of seasoned politicians, not amateurs drawn for a few years of public service from business or law offices. This distinction is crucial. The few Americans who have braved the sanctions against quitting the cabinet and going public have mostly been scrappy politicians: Webster Davis, William Jennings Bryan, Henry Breckinridge, Mabel Willebrandt, Harry Woodring, James Farley, Henry Wallace, Harold Ickes, Harold Stassen, Edward Noble, John L. Sullivan, Walter Hickel, George Romney, William Ruckelshaus, Elliot Richardson. Historically, it is the politician who has the training, will, motive, and innate courage to speak up. That is why Presidents tend, where possible, not to select them.

◇

Yet, even were Presidents willing to populate their cabinets with more men and women grounded in politics, this would only go part of the way toward solving the problem. Politicians who have entered the executive branch have thereby tended to lose their political base. After a period in the cabinet they are little better positioned than their nonpolitical colleagues, as the uncharacteristic silence of Hubert Humphrey through the worst days of the Johnson era indicates. When Richard Nixon, at the beginning of his first Presidential term, introduced his new "team" he said, "We are not going to have a Cabinet that will be basically made up of yes men. Everyone is an independent figure."[16] Among the politically seasoned officials he recruited were men like George Romney, Melvin Laird, Walter Hickel, and Robert Finch. Yet all found themselves left with very little political clout by the time they fell out of Presidential favor.

In this respect, the politicians in the U.S. cabinet differ dramatically from their British counterparts. While U.S. cabinet members effectively become isolated from representative politics when they enter the cabinet, the British ministers all continue to have seats in Parliament. Most of them are, and remain, elected Members of the House of Commons. Many have important public followings throughout the country. Among them, almost invariably, are aspirant Prime Ministers.[17]

If members of the U.S. cabinet are to check Presidential power they ought to be persons *in,* not merely *from,* politics: persons with roots in their own political turf. Then, if they oppose the President, he will know that they speak as more than isolated individuals. It will no longer be true, to paraphrase the Book of Common Prayer, "that he has made them and not they themselves." If they threaten to resign, the President should know that they at least have the means to convoke a public inquest into the matter in dispute.

This can be accomplished in several ways, as the Tuchman and Finer proposals indicate. But the independence of cabinet members would be greater if they were not only elected but elected *on their own* rather than on a Presidential slate and if they were to hold elective office independent of their membership in the cabinet. This suggests that if the Constitution is to be amended, it should be in the direction of requiring the President to select his cabinet from among the Members of Congress and exempting these appointees from Article 1, section 6, clause 2 of the Constitution. That provision safeguards the separation of powers by insuring that "no Person holding any office under the United States, shall be a Member of either House during his continuance in office." It is conceivable, and has indeed been proposed by Thomas K. Finletter, Charles S. Hyneman, and Edward S. Corwin, that some form of a joint legislative-executive cabinet could be created without amending this provision of the Constitution.[18] But the difficulty with these proposals is that they envisage a cabinet in which the department heads are not in Congress and the Congressional Members do not head executive departments. While this obviates the need for constitutional amendment, it is also doubtful whether such a large and amorphous body would prove effective enough to act as a real check on executive power.

Woodrow Wilson, especially in his youth, was an ardent advocate of constitutional amendment to give the President a cabinet of congressmen.[19] His reasons, however, were quite different from ours and reflected the constitutional balance at the end of the last century, which he described as "the absorption of all power by a legislature which is practically irresponsible for its acts." "The legislature," he added, "has become the imperial power of the State."[20] As remedy for this condition of unruly legislative supremacy, of Congressional committees run as the fiefdoms of feudal, feuding, boss-ridden committee chairmen, he proposed the British cabinet system, with the cabinet in, and exercising party discipline over, the legislature. "[T]he safest course," he wrote with the persuasive logic of another era, "is to content ourselves with travelling ways already trodden and look to the precedents of our own race for guidance."[21]

The organization of Congress still leaves something to be

desired, but Congressional superiority over the Presidency is scarcely the current problem. The introduction of responsible cabinet government thus seems far less responsive to the constitutional ills of the republic in the 1970s than it did in 1900.[22] But the idea Wilson advocated, paradoxically, is as valid, today, as a way to weaken—rather than strengthen—Presidential supremacy.

A constitutional amendment requiring members to be selected from among the ranks of Congress need not erode the checks and balances of the system of separation of powers; neither need it implant British "responsible cabinet government." A mere handful of the 535 Members of Congress, perhaps fifteen, would be co-opted to serve as heads of the executive departments. This would not establish Presidential control over Congress of the kind enjoyed by British Prime Ministers over their followers in Parliament. Prime Ministerial control of the legislature depends on the control of a centralized, disciplined political party which, in turn, depends on the chief executive having the power to dissolve the legislative body and call elections—a trump card U.S. Presidents cannot play. The danger of the President, via his cabinet, capturing control of Congress, given his lack of disciplinary powers over its members and his party, would not be serious. Nevertheless, it can be further minimized if Congress' own rules insure that its members cannot simultaneously hold cabinet posts and committee chairmanships. So long as the chairmen are not co-opted, the independence of Congress is likely to subsist.

Nor, conversely, would the President become subservient to Congress. Its members would not have the powers of British Members of Parliament to vote the government out of office—short of Presidential impeachment for grave cause—nor the power of the British party caucus to precipitate the resignation of the Prime Minister. The essentials of the separation of legislative and executive powers would therefore not be abridged by the mere requirement that cabinet members be selected from among the congressmen and senators.

It would no doubt place something of a strain on the individuals concerned to occupy simultaneously a position as Presidential adviser, as head of an executive department, while also representing a state or a Congressional district. Yet ministers in Britain and other Commonwealth countries, as well as Israel, Germany, and Japan, manage to do this very thing.[23]

The cabinet as presently instituted has become a dangerously ineffectual anachronism. Hamilton described its role as that of "Constitutional advisers."[24] Washington convened it as an advisory council which, according to Henry Learned, was both "quite independent of the Legislature" and responsible "to the President alone."[25] True, Presidential nominations of "Officers of the United States" are, by Article 2(2) of the Constitution, subject to the "Advice and Consent" of the Senate, and U.S. cabinet departments are created not—as in Britain—by fiat of the head of government, but by act of Congress. Still, Congress does not effectively control the cabinet—the President does. And members of the cabinet have largely failed to establish a meaningful political role for themselves beyond that of high-level public administrators. As long as Presidents are free to choose Wall Street lawyers, academics, and business tycoons, all without political experience or independent base, there is little reason for them to seek trouble by including among their advisers a different breed more inclined and better positioned to say "no" at crucial junctures of policy-making.

Yet some effective nay-sayers are urgently needed in the executive branch, men, in Edward Corwin's apt phrase, "whose daily political salt did not come from the Presidential table, whose political fortunes were not identical with his, who could bring Presidential whim under an independent scrutiny today lacking."[26] No matter how brilliant the Chief Executive, regardless how overwhelming his electoral mandate, the expanded powers of the Presidency must not continue to be exercised so largely untested by steel on steel.

We are under no illusion that a constitutional amendment requiring the President to draw his cabinet from among elected members of Congress will be easily obtained. The amendment process is intentionally cumbersome and becomes particularly difficult to invoke when the beneficiary of the amendment is "the people" or "the system" in general, rather than a well-organized, highly motivated section of tenacious citizenry. As noted, various proposals with intent similar to ours have been around for a long time.[27] Are there, then, other, shorter range ways in which the objective of "politicizing" the cabinet could be achieved without a constitutional amendment?

One temporizing alternative is to have Presidential candidates name the key members of their cabinet at the party convention immediately after their nomination. The persons named would then be expected to run, informally, alongside the President during the campaign. Despite all Presidents' penchant to select team-playing nonpolitical "yes men" as their principal aides, the considerations that have made this inevitable would change if the candidates actually faced the prospect of having to run with their team. It would be embarrassing to face the voters with a slate of gray Wall Street eminences. The Presidential aspirants would certainly try to strengthen their campaign by naming influential political figures who could deliver votes, strong platform personalities who are experienced public campaigners. Such persons, however, would also tend to continue to be strong personalities after they entered the cabinet or White House. And the President would be politically beholden to them. They might not be quite as independent of the President as cabinet officials with seats in Congress, but they would carry a great deal more weight, and be likely to exercise far more ethical autonomy in their relations with the President, than most of the men and women who now occupy these posts.

As we noted earlier, this innovation was at one time considered by Senator George McGovern before his nomination for the Presidency in 1972, but it was finally discarded. One argument against it is that the Presidential nominee, by naming his key cabinet choices early in the campaign, would lose the advantage of being able to dangle hints of appointments before hordes of claimants. On the other hand, a candidate who presented the public with the opportunity to examine not only his, but also his key advisers', views in public during a Presidential campaign would undoubtedly capture the imagination of many citizens tired of the high-level brand of board-room politics that now characterizes the executive process. If adopted, the practice would, at least partially, politicize the cabinet without constitutional amendment.

Whatever the tools, a restructuring of the Presidency is long and dangerously overdue. The objective of such a reform must be to take the enormous executive power out of the hands of a single man, dispersing it in such a way as to create internal checks and balances within what has become the most powerful branch of the most powerful government. Such a dispersion of executive power comes down to this: the President must continue to be the embodiment of executive power, but he should be politically vulnerable to advisers who have the strength of character to say "no"—at first in private and, ultimately, also in public.

Currently, as we have demonstrated, hardly anyone says "no" very forcefully in private and just about no one says it in public.

≷ 7 ≷

Growing Up toward
Ethical Autonomy

NO CONSTITUTIONAL CHANGE, by itself, can transform a society's view of what constitutes appropriate behavior by its public officials. In positing as a positive good the willingness of some top officials to be publicly "disloyal" to the President, we cut across the deep grain of social decorum—what people have come to believe is "meet, right, and our bounden duty." It is this sense of what is fitting that must be reconsidered.

The social sense of propriety is one to which we are initiated early in life. Very soon we come to learn that decent, honorable persons do not betray the confidences of their peers, do not "squeal" or "tattle tell." This lays the groundwork for the conformist adult. It prepares us for the demands of our employers and our peer groups, convincing us that loyalty and cohesiveness is the highest value of all. Jean Piaget, the leading authority on child development, in an experiment told 100 Swiss primary school children of various ages the following story:

> Once, long ago and in a place very far away from here, there was a father who had two sons. One was very good and obedient, the other was a good sort, but he often did silly things. One day the father goes off on a journey and says to the first son: "You must watch carefully to see what your brother does, and when I come back you shall tell me." The father goes away and the brother goes and does something silly. When the father comes back he asks the first boy to tell him everything. What ought the boy to do?[1]

◇

Piaget posed this problem in order to discover whether the children believed that they should obey the adult and be loyal to the authority and law, or whether they should respect the principle of solidarity with their peers. He found that, among the younger subjects between the ages of six and seven, the predominant reaction was that the parent should be told everything. If the parent asks you to tattle, the small child believes, then it is right to submit completely to that wish. The adult looms larger in the child's life than the brother. Among older children between the ages of eight and twelve, however, the reaction was quite different. Predominantly, they indicated total solidarity with brothers and friends, their peers, against adult authority. Nothing should be volunteered to the parent or teacher. Some of the older children, when told Piaget's story, even felt that they should lie to protect the brother. They felt it wrong to betray an equal for the benefit of an adult.[2]

From this as well as other story-telling experiments with children, Piaget concluded that the more progressed the child's moral judgment, the less willing he is to engage in tattle-telling. The morally immature tattler breaks the solidarity of his peer group in favor of adult authority. Piaget postulates two personality types: *le petit saint,* who tattles and ingratiates himself with authority figures, and *le sport,* who sides with his peers and who is regarded by more mature children as a "moral" person.

Except among very young children, tattle-telling is regarded as a serious offense deserving punishment, particularly in the form of exclusion from the group. In the words of a British children's rhyme:

> I know a little girl, sly and deceitful
> Every little tittle-tat she goes and tells the people.
> If you want to know her name, her name is Heather Lee.
> Please, Heather Lee, keep away from me;
> I don't want to speak to you, nor you to speak to me.[3]

Even more venomous is this bit of children's doggerel:

> Tell tale tit,
> Your tongue shall be slit,
> And all the dogs in town
> Shall have a little bit.

Tom Brown's School Days, published in Britain in 1857, presents an excruciating example of a schoolboy's inability to break peer ranks by "squealing" on an older fellow student who has tortured him so severely as to warrant his hospitalization. Many other boys also witnessed the torture, yet though they disapproved, none reported it to the school authorities. This incident amply illustrates the power of the schoolboy peer group to enforce its rules of loyalty.

Children are not alone in deploring the tattler in their ranks. It is part of the adult world's perception of child-rearing that, at a certain state of maturity, children ought to balance respect for parental authority with loyalty to their neighborhood playmates or school chums. This is part of learning to develop reciprocal, mutually beneficial relations with peers. Parents, even at some cost to their own authority, generally want their children to be "in" with peer groups that can be useful to them, and tend to deem it important that they "get along" with the right pals, learning to recognize in them the potential allies needed to win the battles of life. Thus, after a certain age, parents often ally themselves with the child's peer group in disapproving of tattling. If a child's tattling persists at, say, the age of twelve, parents tend to be worried rather than pleased, fearing arrested development. In Piaget's words, such a child is in danger of becoming a "narrowminded moralist" with excessive deference to authority figures and no autonomous moral standards.[4]

The social disapproval of tattling remains a factor in group behavior past adolescence and into adulthood. Throughout literature, the "squealer" or tattler is the subject of an opprobrium which reflects this socialization theme. Judas Iscariot, Benedict Arnold, the war prisoner who sides with his captors are all objects of public loathing which attaches to adult tattlers. In the words of one observer of this phenomenon, "Martin Luther seems to be about the only figure of note to make much headway with public opinion after doing an inside job on a corrupt organization."[5] Ibsen's Dr. Thomas Stockmann, in threatening to expose the medical dangers in the therapeutic baths being developed by his enterprising fellow townspeople, is stoned as "an enemy of the people."

Life imitates literature. At the very least, tattlers are generally regarded with scorn. Persons who have "blown the whistle" by speaking up against an organization for which they had been working are perceived—and eventually report that they perceive themselves—as being on an ego trip. *The New York Times,* before committing itself to spreading the word of one adult tattler who had purloined government documents—Daniel Ellsberg—attacked another—Otto Otepka—by calling the latter's revelations to a Senate subcommittee a "dangerous departure from orderly procedures."[6]

In short, the lot of the tattletale in our society, child or parent, is not a happy one—not, that is, after about the age of eight.

This social conditioning against tattle-telling is deplored by some students of the subject. One authority cautions parents to distinguish between children who are merely ingratiating themselves with authority or trying to do damage to another child from those who are conveying valid information.[7] A child telling his parents that another child is in the process of setting fire to the garage is different from one revealing that his brother has not brushed his teeth after breakfast.

Among adults, it is far more inappropriate to lump together as tattlers all those who convey confidential information damaging to a peer, because in adult life tattling occurs in a different social context and often serves a different purpose. In an adult, tattling can be useful as a check on unbridled authority. It may be as significant a sign of the adult's ethical emancipation as tattle-telling in children may be indicative of arrested moral growth.

This different value that ought to attach to tattling in childhood and in maturity reflects its quite different function and social value at the early and at later stages in the individual's development. As we have seen, the animosity linked with tattle-telling in childhood serves as an indicator and aspect of the child's moral development, attesting to the growth of individuation and a degree of autonomy in place of authority fixation and favor-currying. By discouraging an infant's tendency to tattle, we encourage him or her to develop reciprocal relations with the peer group rather than continue excessive infantile dependence on the superior authority of the adult. Reciprocal dependence is the halfway house on the steep road from parent-authority dependence to ethical emancipation, mature individuation, and responsible self-determination. The child learns to broaden his universe and his sense of responsibility, coming to care about the effects of his conduct on the opinions and responses of both the parents and his peer group, rather than just the parents alone.

But in our society, the opprobrium against speaking out or going public, against telling tales out of school, lingers long after it has ceased to be socially functional. Even when most of us have already shed our dependence on parental authority and ceased playing up to mother, father, and teacher, we still feel constrained not to tattle-tell on fellow workers, neighbors, or superiors when we see them breaking the law or acting antisocially. Our peer group—the profession, club, team, office, social set, political party, White House staff, the President's "official family," or that vague but real establishment of "men who govern"—continues to demand group solidarity, even though such rigorous solidarity may have lost its positive, emancipating social function. Worse, this adult group solidarity tends to be regarded admiringly by the public at large, persons who are not members of the in-group, and who are too often victimized by the in-group's machinations. We tend mindlessly to admire the "virtues" of group loyalty and solidarity quite regardless of the social outcomes.

There are instances, of course, where it is quite appropriate for childhood values of group unity against parents and teachers to continue into adulthood. For example, in a society where a politi-

cal dictatorship replaces the parent, fostering a new but still immature dominance-dependence relationship with its citizens, a continuing conspiracy of silence, of tight peer-group solidarity against
tattlers, may continue to be functional. But in a democracy, where
the ultimate government is the people, a rigorous antitattling ethic
is socially dysfunctional. It is one thing to betray Jesus to the
Romans, but obviously quite another to report a fellow airplane
passenger to the San Francisco airport authorities for carrying a
concealed weapon. Whether adult tattling is very childish or very
mature depends on the specific circumstances. In a democratic
society, to disclose a fellow citizen's antisocial conduct may be the
highest manifestation of ethical autonomy, whether that citizen is a
fellow Rotarian, shopworker, the president of General Motors or of
the United States. This assumes, always, that the matter being
disclosed is one which is properly within the public-policy con-
cerns of the citizens of a democracy. If so, speaking up is an act of
courageous maturity, an emancipation from ingrained adolescent
peer-group pressures "not to rat."

The very groups of peers which, early in life, helped us
emancipate ourselves from infantile parent dependence fight to
hold us in the thrall of peer-group dependence. Some people
remain Choate old boys, sons of Eli, or Harvard men all their lives.
The social sanctions we have developed against those who "tell
tales out of school"—again the term is reflective of the level of
adolescent development it reinforces—can prevent the adult from
breaking out of dependence on his peer group to achieve a new
level of responsible reciprocal relationship with the community as
a whole. It may reinforce the adult's tendency, learned in childhood, to think of his responsibilities in terms of the team or clique,
without attaining a higher level of responsibility to a larger community consisting of his nation or, even, all humanity.[8] Serpico, the
New York cop whose revelations of police corruption triggered the
Knapp Commission, was led into a near-fatal ambush and hounded
out of the force by his fellows because "He had broken an unwritten code that in effect put policemen above the law, that said a cop

could not turn in other cops."[9] As he discovered, the road to ethical autonomy can be lonely and sometimes even dangerous.

A higher consciousness of one's wider responsibility to society—beyond the peer group—is, however, the apex of personal maturity. And it is equally functional to individual self-emancipation and to the collective survival of an interdependent world. Paradoxically, it is only through the extension of our individual sense of responsibility to an all-encompassing humanity that we attain true responsibility to ourselves—not in partiality, as son, fraternity member, or White House aide, but as a total, autonomous singular being. "The greatest thing in the world," Montaigne said, "is to know how to belong to ourselves." Each of us comes to belong to himself to the extent that he perceives himself as *one* of *all*. Our reciprocal special relations with "teams" are most mature if they are in the context of an overriding responsibility to our society and to humanity.

Professor Lawrence Kohlberg of Harvard has pointed out the flaw in Piaget's contention that the moral maturity of a person can be measured merely by his recognition of reciprocal relationships with his peer groups. Such reciprocal relations, he says, may play a role in emancipating a child from parent-authority dependence, but this progress is achieved by substituting group-authority dependence. It has been observed that the child learns to establish "I'll scratch your back if you'll scratch mine" relations with members of a gang, club, clique, and prep-school class, then carries this apparently successful way of "getting along" into his or her Ivy League college, fraternity, and sorority, and, even, in later life, the department where he works, or the Presidential Administration in which he serves.[10] Yet, the development of peer-group loyalty is only one step toward the ultimate goal of growing up, of self-emancipation, of becoming an autonomous being capable of making principled decisions on the basis of one's own internalized values without excessive fear of displeasing the authorities, the group, or the law. The final stage of the moral evolution of the individual, according to Kohlberg and others,[11] comes when life decisions and actions are rooted in an autonomous, principled judgment of right and wrong, in full consciousness of responsibility to the larger social community.

This definition does not prejudge the social utility of any particular decision made by an individual, but only the degree of genuine autonomy with which decisions are made and whether they are made by reference to generalized principles of right conduct that are genuinely those of the individual—i.e., which he has freely and deliberately chosen and made his own. In other words, adult tattle-tellers may be the most mature, the most autonomously principled, of adults if by going public they are breaking out of group conformity to inform the entire community of something it ought to know. But most members of society, still living in the early stages of the growing child's moral development, continue to regard the practice with disgust and disdain. Many an official who might have resigned from government in public protest against the Vietnam escalation has reported an unwillingness to be seen as a traitor by his "team" and a tattle-tale by his countrymen.

That no major figures in the Johnson or Nixon Administrations quit and spoke up in protest during the Vietnam war or Watergate is a comment, therefore, not solely on the ethical state of the men who occupy high office, but also on the ethical climate of the nation. We positively do not *want* to be told. We reject those who break faith with the system, even if they do it to keep faith with us. We prefer officials to be loyal to the President even if they are thereby disloyal to the Constitution and themselves. The men and women at the breaking point in the executive branch know this, and trim accordingly.

Obviously, going public is not invariably the mark of the ethically emancipated adult. A person may rightly be stigmatized for tattle-telling when he reveals confidential information the publication of which is not necessary to the well-being of those to whom it is revealed. An adult, like a child, may "rat" not out of a sense of obligation to society but solely in order to ingratiate himself with those in authority, for personal gain and publicity, or to damage rivals gratuitously. Those involved in the Watergate scandal who bargained for reduced sentences or immunity, in return for giving evidence against colleagues, are fairly stigmatized to the extent that they spoke up only because—and when—it served their personal interests rather than out of conviction that the nation needed to be told. But an official resigning over Vietnam and speaking out against the Kennedy, Johnson, or Nixon policies of escalation could not be suspected of doing so in deference to authority—the full weight of Presidential power would have come down against him or her—nor in the hope of personal gain. Only in the years after 1968 could a public antiwar stand be suspected of being politically opportune, and then only for persons intending to run for elected office from certain primarily urban parts of the country or seeking the favor of certain of the media. Yet officials like Charles Frankel who resigned and, to a limited extent, expressed their negative views of Presidential policies report the pressures from others, and from their own internal social conditioning, to maintain a "decent" silence about what they had seen and heard.

Social psychologists have begun to make some progress in the scientific measurement of our pilgrimage toward ethical autonomy. Kohlberg postulates six measurable levels which help us verify the relation between an individual's ethical maturity and, for example, his willingness to speak out against the team. Some further recent experiments conducted by New York University graduate students under our supervision indicate that, in a group of 96 law students at New York University, there could be found a distinct pattern of direct correlation between their willingness to go public in a dispute with authority and their level of moral development as measured by tests based on Kohlberg's theoretical six stages.[12] There thus appears to be a connection between the individual's stage of moral development and his or her ethical autonomy.

Kohlberg's work suggests that higher levels of moral development are more likely to be found in persons actively and broadly involved in social and interactional roles in the community.[13] Politicians, at least some of those who succeed in being elected to important state or Congressional office, fit this description. They have learned to listen to many points of view and many voices but have also acquired the habit of eventually making their own decisions, for which they are accountable not to a small, tightly knit organization or group but to a variegated public. This could conceivably be one more reason to surround the President with a political rather than a banker-lawyer cabinet.

Ultimately, however, a transformation in the structure of the executive branch depends upon a change in the level of moral maturity and ethical autonomy, not only of the cabinet but of the American public. The lesson of the Vietnam and Watergate eras is not merely that the government must be populated with ethically autonomous persons able to resist their President and, if necessary, to quit and take their case to the public. Of what use is it to go public if the public has been conditioned to despise and mistrust those who violate confidences, to turn a deaf ear to those who place the dictates of their own consciences before loyalty to "the Chief"? What hope is there for a true systemic transformation as long as the public extracts fearsome price from those who try to open crucial policy dialogues to the public? Not that Americans should line the streets to cheer anyone who quits the cabinet and tells everything he knows to *The Washington Post*. But acts of public protest should be judged on their merits, not by a reflexive social condemnation of tattlers.

Vietnam and Watergate: the names are synonymous with insufficiently fettered Presidential discretion. If America is ever to construct a working system of checks and balances within the executive branch, it will have to revise its judgment of those who exercise their option to "exit" with "voice." It will have to excuse, and even reward, that disloyalty to a President which bespeaks a higher loyalty to the democratic system.

Such a popular acceptance of disloyalty at the top will have to grow out of a much more universal inventory of the costs and benefits of the American emphasis on team play, at all levels of social and political organization. Our society will have to reconsider whether, and to what purpose, it wants to continue to reward nonautonomous and punish autonomous behavior in a wide range of institutional settings.

If we were to be asked by an official like George Ball whether, in 1966, after resigning, he should have led a public campaign against the Johnson Administration's Vietnam policies, our answer would be something like this: "Yes, for the sake of the republic, for the good of the democratic political system, as well as for the cause of Vietnam disengagement. It would have been very useful to have had you take a lead in the antiwar movement. It would have restored the faith of the young in the system, would have given credibility and weight to the war's opponents, would have created the basis for an informed, civilized public debate of the Vietnam issues. But it would also, in all probability, have ended your political career and led to your being ostracized by the professional and social circles in which you work and relax. It would have brought you to a severe crisis of self-esteem. You have spent your life as a team player, a loyal peer-grouper. You would suddenly have found yourself being categorized as a non-team-player by that small elite on whose amiability your professional and private life is built. The costs to you would have been enormous."

It has not been the point of this book that men like George Ball should pay these costs, although we would be less than candid if we did not admit to a vast admiration for the few, like William Jennings Bryan, who spent themselves heedlessly for the public weal and for their principles, without concern for the costs to their careers.

But it is unrealistic to expect many senior officials at the top of what Disraeli called "the greasy pole" to be unmindful of costs. Only a fanatic would climb to the top of that pole in order to immolate himself, no matter how brightly his light would shine. It would be unhealthy for the executive branch to be heavily populated by men and women of such unshakable ethical autonomy, for they would probably make government both more difficult and more dangerous in their unbending self-assertiveness and reckless ·rectitude.

It follows that, while we would applaud a higher incidence of strongly self-assertive consciences in the immediate vicinity of the White House, we believe that a better balance within the executive branch can best be attained not by surrounding the President with persons of iron principles, cheerfully willing to sacrifice everything, but by lowering the costs the ordinarily ambitious political aspirant must pay to have, and to manifest, a healthy amount of ethical autonomy.

We believe that, in a different institutional setting, the kinds of men and women who now elect to remain silent could persuade themselves to speak up. If, for example, John Gardner had been a senator from New York, as well as Secretary of Health, Education, and Welfare, it would have been politically astute, rather than suicidal, for him to have resigned and led the forces opposed to the war. The costs of ethical autonomy would probably have been well within his means.

And the costs of resigning would certainly be less if the public were to decide to lower them: by respecting the dissident, the man or woman who refuses to subordinate his conscience or his duty to the public, and by weighing thoughtfully what he has to say, rewarding or punishing in accordance with the social importance and political validity of his or her dissent.

"Unhappy the land that needs a hero," Brecht's Galileo says to us. Inevitably, the fate of the republic will, from time to time, depend on the emergence of a hero. And heroes will emerge, bidden or not. Yet the system ought not to be built on them, but on normally ambitious, reasonably benevolent, relatively mature persons who do the right thing because they are encouraged—or at least are not drastically discouraged—to live up to their own highest ideals and ethical standards.

Methodology for Selection of the American and British Executive and Ministerial Appointees Studied Statistically

TO MAKE statistical measurement possible, we defined the components of the question set out on page 59: (a) *senior political executives,* (b) *resignation as an act of personal volition,* (c) *reasonable prospects of return to office,* (d) *return to office,* and (e) *went public.*

We set the longitudinal range of our study: the years 1900–70.

(a) *Senior political executives.* We felt that the greatest moral dilemma was that of the man with a relatively large amount of responsibility and high political visibility. Thus we focused on only the upper echelons of government, omitting the "whistle-blowing" clerks and civil servants who, from time to time, take secret documents to Jack Anderson or *The New York Times.* Theirs is an important, but different, role and ethic.

In the United States, we limited our statistical survey to four top echelons, using the *U.S. Congressional Directory.*

i) *Echelon I* consists of all cabinet secretaries.

ii) *Echelon II* consists of under secretaries, deputy secretaries, or other second-rank posts in cabinet departments such as "chief clerk" or "assistant to the secretary" in the early years of the century.

iii) *Echelon III* consists of assistant secretaries, armed services secretaries (after unification), and other third-rank posts such as general counsel or legal adviser.[1]

iv) *Echelon IV* consists of senior White House staff, including, prior to the Reorganization Act of 1939,[2] only the very small number of "secretaries," but, thereafter, growing rapidly to encompass such diverse titles as press secretary, special counsel, appointments secretary, special assistants for national security, science and technology, and others.[3] Not included in this survey are the directors of the Budget nor members of the Council of Economic Advisers, nor the members of independent regulatory agencies.

In these four echelons, there were only 19 persons on whom we were unable to get complete data, and of these, there were only 11 we could not trace at all.[4]

We ran a check on comparable British data in order to have a different standard of behavior in a parliamentary democracy. The British group of *senior political executives* is much smaller, in part because, during the period studied, there is no equivalent in the Prime Minister's office to the U.S. White House staff (*Echelon IV*), but also because there is far less turnover in British cabinet and ministerial appointments. British *Echelon I* consists of all cabinet ministers, *Echelon II* of ministers not in cabinet, and *Echelon III* of junior ministers attached to a department, including ministers of state who are not heads of a department. We did not include in the survey certain regional law officers,[5] the Lord Advocate, the Lord Chancellor for Ireland, nor any Parliamentary secretaries. The last of these omissions also contributed to the comparatively smaller number of British officials surveyed.[6]

(b) *Resignation as an act of personal volition.* Having compiled the names and official data on virtually all persons in *Echelons I to IV* in the United States and in *Echelons I to III* in Britain, we realized that many of these persons were not relevant to our study of resignation ethics. What we wanted to know was how many persons leaving government *as a matter of personal choice* used the occasion of their departure to criticize the government and how this choice affected their political prospects. So we set about eliminating, first, persons who did not really resign at all, but were forced out by circumstances beyond their control. These necessarily included firings like those of Robert Lansing, Walter Hickel, and Henry Wallace, even though each involved a notable public protest. However, most firings are not of this order. They either preclude an ethical choice by the official being fired or else lead him to try to grasp for a bogus moral issue to cover up the real reason for his being sacked. Also excluded are persons who "resigned" only at the end of a Presidential term of office, or the death of a President, or after a change of Prime Minister. Such resignations, too, are really not matters of personal volition and so cannot involve the possibility of ethical choice. We also eliminated persons in Great Britain who were dropped from office in a major cabinet reshuffle, as, for example, often happens after a British election, even when a government has been re-elected. Occasionally, as in the case of Herbert Bowden's retirement from the British Labour government in 1967, such persons may be allowed to go through the motions of resigning, but it is clear from the circumstances that they have no real choice—they are really being terminated. On the other hand, group resignations from the cabinet based on a political split—the defection of pro-free-trade ministers from the British government in 1932, for example—are plainly instances of deliberate voluntary departure from government and must therefore be part of our study, even though they occasion a major cabinet reshuffle.

We also eliminated from consideration all those whose resignations were made necessary by personal scandal, as in the case of Britain's John Profumo or Hugh Dalton.[7] In Wallace's case, President Truman had publicly announced his discharge. But we also excluded persons who were not quite so openly fired: Harry H. Woodring, J. Howard McGrath, and Louis A. Johnson. Roosevelt in the case of Woodring and Truman in the instances of McGrath and Johnson had not publicized their demand that the aide resign; but the historical record makes clear that they cannot be included in a statistical study of how officials *choose* to depart because they were given no choice. Persons who are fired, or who leave under duress, are in a different position from those who have a choice whether to stay, to go quietly, or to go with public disclosure of their reasons. For example, a man being fired may be allowed to appear to resign in return for an implicit pledge of silence. At the other extreme, a man being fired or forced to resign may attack the government or the President to vent his anger or to draw attention away from his own shortcomings on the job. He may have nothing left to lose. Nothing so focuses the mind on moral issues as the rumor that one is about to be fired for incompetence. Since such a person is unlikely to have a bright future in government, the relationship between how he left—whether he went public or not—and his subsequent career in public service is likely to be quite tenuous. Though we excluded such departures from the statistical data we included many of the more interesting cases in our discussion in Chapters 1 and 2.

We also eliminated from our statistical study persons who resigned only to take up a comparable government post. These cannot be counted as genuine resignations as they are really reassignments. Among "comparable posts" we include not only the *Echelon I to IV* positions in the U.S. and *Echelon I to III* in Britain but also equivalent jobs outside these echelons, such as ambassadorships, appointments to fill Senate vacancies (but not elevations to the House of Lords), colonial governorships, judgeships (only federal ones in the U.S.), or full-time assignments to independent regulatory agencies. Chester Bowles's reappointment as the President's Special Representative for Asian, African and Latin-American Affairs and Lord Bowden's reassignment as chairman of the Independent Television Authority both come within this category: neither can truly be said to have made a decision to resign from government. They elected to stay in the service, accepting the favor of an appointment that was primarily within the President's or Prime Minister's power to bestow.

In several of these respects, Robert S. McNamara is a borderline case. His resignation had some elements of being compelled, but the evidence is not clear. He went on to a comparable position as president of the World Bank, which is not a U.S. government position, nor is it technically bestowed by the President. Thus he was not simply reassigned. Yet, in practice, once President Johnson had decided to nominate him, his election was probably assured. Given these balances, McNamara could have been regarded as a resignation, a firing, or a reassignment. We decided not to treat the case as a resignation but as a transfer. An official accepting such a transfer is making himself the object of a further Presidential or Prime Ministerial favor. He has therefore decided not to walk out.

There are a few other cases in which one suspects that a resignation was less the voluntary exercise of free choice than the only alternative to being fired. A British cabinet member who made a dramatic attack on government policy in the process of resigning was said to have heard that the Prime Minister's ax was being sharpened for him. But where the evidence is only gossip, we treat the case as a *bona fide* resignation.

We have also deleted from the statistical study those resignations that, in

Britain, were caused by electoral defeat in a constituency, and, in the United States, by election to some other office (but not resignations later *followed* by a decision to run for an elective office). In Britain, cabinet members must generally be a member of one or other House of Parliament. For a Member of the Commons, losing one's seat means resigning. In the United States, a member of the executive branch must resign if he is elected to the legislative branch. Again, there is no choice involved, and, in addition, such resignation after election is more analogous to a transfer within the government establishment. J. Mayhew Wainwright, for example, stayed on as Assistant Secretary of War in the Harding Administration until his election to Congress. His resignation suggests no more than a career advancement, certainly not a decision to get out of government. Similarly, James J. Davis resigned as Secretary of Labor in 1930 only after being chosen to fill an unexpired term in the Senate.

Men who stay in office until their resignation is made inevitable by election to Congress are almost certainly not asking themselves whether they should quit and go public or leave quietly. By running for elective office from the platform of their executive position, they seem to be endorsing the government and seeking the voters' endorsement as part of the President's "team." However, persons who resign and then run for office, like Clinton Anderson, may be in a different position. The circumstances are at least ambiguous. They could be running precisely to make a public case against a "team" with which they have become disenchanted: in any event, the act of resigning, in such cases, leaves open the choice between going quietly or speaking up, and so we left these cases in our data. In one instance, that of A. Piatt Andrew, Jr., who, in 1912, resigned as Assistant Secretary of the Treasury, an official blasted Administration publicly as part of the process of quitting and did run successfully for Congress—although not until 1921. There are no instances of a public-protest resignation in which the resigner runs successfully for Congress as part of his strategy of going public.

Finally, a very small number of deletions were occasioned by American interim appointees or nominees who failed to receive the requisite Senatorial confirmation; they, like defeated members of the House of Commons, also had no choice but to quit.

This left us with only those, in the United States and Britain, who could reasonably be expected to have resigned in circumstances which might conceivably have involved a choice between going and staying, as well as between speaking up and going quietly. We had eliminated those departures which could not possibly have involved an opportunity for going public, as well as those which were decided not by the retiring officials themselves but by circumstances or by higher authority.

(c) *Reasonable prospects of return to office.* We assumed that there were special, different considerations operating in the cases of persons who were too old to have much prospect of a return to political office or who left in ill health. Harold Ickes spoke up against President Truman at the age of seventy-one. His failure to be reappointed cannot reasonably be related to his decision to resign with a public blast: he was just too old to be a serious candidate. Moreover, his lack of future career prospects in government in view of his age makes his decision rather different from that of the ordinary person leaving government. To eliminate this factor, we decided to exclude from the statistical survey all persons who were *over sixty-two at the time of their resignations* or who *died within two years of resigning.*[8] In this way, we retained for statistical study only persons who, at the time of their resignation, could have expected to be called upon for further service. The Ickes resignation, however, is fully explored in the text.

(d) *Return to office.* By this we mean subsequent reappointment to an office of the same or higher echelon as the one resigned from. Also included among *returns* are appointments to ambassadorships, judgeships (federal, in the U.S.), full-time membership in independent government agencies, authorities, bureaus, offices or commissions of national (federal) standing. We are also interested in whether the resigner was subsequently offered part-time posts which are regarded as "plums" by lawyers, businessmen, and others and which serve as reassurance that one is still eligible for recall to be Secretary of State or Director of the Budget. These plums include many kinds of prestigious jobs within the gift-giving authority of Presidents and Prime Ministers: the part-time chairmanship of special commissions, task forces, departmental advisory committees, or assignments as special representatives (federal, in the U.S.). These are all posts that do not require resignation from, but add to one's prestige in, a law firm or bank. Return to full-time senior posts are classified as *Category I* returns; part-time plums, as *Category II* returns. In Britain, we include in *Category II* appointments to the House of Lords.

(e) *Went public.* As we have seen, there are many ways a resigner may communicate a certain disenchantment with his former team. George Ball gave private, not-for-attribution interviews. Harry Woodring wrote a letter of resignation so critical of Roosevelt that it could not be released. Robert Lansing, Roger Hilsman, and Richard Goodwin waited a respectful time and then published less than respectful books.

For purposes of the statistical survey, since we were dealing with hundreds of cases, an operational rule became necessary for defining and researching dissent behavior by resigners. We decided that a public protest, to be counted as such for the purposes of assessing the costs to the resigner's political career, ought to be something reasonably loud, clear, and, above all, attributable. We therefore define going public as *a criticism of government policy attributed directly to the resigner and reported in* The New York Times,[9] *for Americans, or* The Times *(London), for Britons.* That excluded George Ball, despite the articles by James Reston and others in *The New York Times* which purported to know how he was putting it to President Johnson, but always without attribution, so that the stories were just that, not reports. Even this rule, however, created at least one borderline case. James A. Farley, resigning as Postmaster General and chairman of the Democratic National Committee to run against Roosevelt for the party nomination, did not criticize F.D.R.'s Administration, nor did he publicly declare his opposition to a third term for the President. But he also refused to deny his opposition, and Senator Carter Glass of Virginia, chosen by Farley to place his name in nomination at the Democratic convention, bore down heavily on the third-term issue. We decided to count Farley's as a public-protest resignation, even though the criticism was technically attributable not to him directly but to persons who were, clearly, his authorized spokesmen.

In cases where someone resigns from office in a dispute—usually a dispute he is losing—against another department of the government, and he discloses the substance of the quarrel in order to continue his campaign publicly, this, too, we count as a public protest, even though it may not be a criticism of governmental or Presidential policy but only of the policies of one department. An example is H. Struve Hensel's public campaign, before and after resigning from the Navy Department, against the efforts of the War Department to achieve unification with Hensel's department, efforts which were in due course largely endorsed by President Truman. Truman also persuaded John L. Sullivan to aim his resignation blast not at him but at Secretary of Defense Louis Johnson.[10] On the other hand, the public airing of a dispute is not counted as going public if the public criticism is directed at a policy which has been proposed but not yet been adopted. In such circumstances, the President, or the head of the department, having not yet made a policy decision, usually is still encouraging (or at least tolerating) open attack and counterattack. For example, shortly after their respective noncontentious resignations, former White House adviser Jerome B. Wiesner and former Deputy Defense Secretary Roswell L. Gilpatric were asked by President Johnson to co-chair a prestigious defense review panel. Their report recommended a three-year moratorium on development and deployment of antiballistic missiles. This contradicted a policy of limited ABM construction favored by the Joint Chiefs of Staff. But the report is not treated as a public protest in our statistical study, because neither Secretary of Defense McNamara nor President Johnson had yet decided for, or against, the new system. Indeed, the Wiesner-Gilpatric report was specifically commissioned by the Administration to help it make up its mind. And the government, itself, made the report public.

In the first sections of this book we noted that a public protest tends to become less relevant the longer it is delayed. Spruille Braden's revelations, almost a quarter of a century after the event, were not meaningful inputs into the political/ethical system of the country. Robert Lansing's disclosures of Wilson's alleged perfidy at Versailles came three weeks after Wilson had left the White House, and after the Peace Treaty issue had been settled. John Gardner waited until a change in Administration, for two and a half years, to enter into open dissent over the Indochina war. "Effectiveness" is too subjective a test, so we opted for an arbitrary rule: to be counted as a public protest, the resigner's criticism must have been published within six months before, and two years after, the resignation.

Finally, there was a problem of whether a public protest ought to include only criticism of decisions made, and the handling of events that occurred, before the resignation, when the resigner was still in government. We would have preferred to exclude criticisms which a resigner directed toward events or decisions occurring after his resignation, since "team-playing" would no longer be quite so directly at issue. But this left too many borderline cases. Public dissent directed at policies responsive to postresignation events invariably seemed also to relate to, and to reflect, positions or attitudes which had their origins at least partly in an earlier period when the resigner was still in government. Thus the problem of "team play," loyalty, and confidentiality inevitably arose to some degree in every case of public criticism, whatever the issue. Within the two-year period after a resignation, therefore, all criticisms are counted as "going public." For example, we even count Senator Robert Kennedy's statement in May 1965, a year after his resignation as Attorney General, that the Johnson Administration's invasion of the Dominican Republic was a "misuse of power" because of failure to hold prior consultations with the Organization of American States.[11]

In a very few instances this rule produced unsatisfactory results. The Kennedy case may be one, Clinton Anderson another. There are two more. Sir Ellis Griffith resigned in Britain, in 1915, without public dissent. Six months later he made a stirring speech in Parliament calling for conscription. At the time, this was against official policy, but half a year later conscription had been adopted by the government. Robert V. Roosa resigned very quietly in 1964, but then chaired a study group formed by the United Nations Association (U.S. branch) which recommended membership for two Chinas in the U.N. At the time, this was contrary to State Department policy, but, as in the Griffith case, there were already many in government who agreed. One cannot be certain to what extent Griffith's speech and Roosa's report were genuine criticisms or were officially approved as trial balloons. In the event, we have retained both cases as public protests for purposes of the statistical survey.

One final point. Where a resignation was followed by a change of Administration or government prior to the expiry of the two-year period, we did not, for self-evident reasons, count as "going public" any public criticisms leveled by a resigner against a new "team" to which the constraints of loyalty did not apply.

After these exclusions, we were left with 389 Americans and 78 Britons, all of whom had served in the upper echelons of government, had resigned of their own accord, and could have reasonably looked forward to another chance to serve. The British group is much smaller than the American, in part because there is no British *Echelon IV* and also because the average Briton's tenure in office is much longer than in the United States.

This statistical survey group is rigorously controlled to test a single hypothesis which has to do with the political career-costs of going public. Excluded from it are a few of the most interesting dissidents in American and British political history, several of which we have analyzed in Chapters 1–3 of this book. The biographical sketches which comprise these earlier chapters are designed to portray the variety and texture of experience in the realm of political resignation and dissent. The departure from office of men like Henry Wallace, Harry Woodring, Harold Ickes, and Robert Lansing shed light on the phenomenon of exit with dissent; but for one or another of the reasons indicated, they could not be used in a rigorous statistical test of the career costs of public-protest resignations lest they skew the data. John Gardner and George Ball did, each in his own way, eventually register public dissent, and their style and ethic is discussed in the biographical analysis; but for the purposes of testing the career-cost hypothesis, the dissent of neither quite qualifies as an effective public protest.

We thus ended up studying a discrete statistical group of resigners. Although we gathered extensive biographical data on these persons, our principal interest was to discover: 1) whether they resigned going public or in silence, and 2) whether those who held their tongues did better than those who spoke up, in terms of subsequent opportunity to serve in full-time senior posts (*Category I*) and/or in part-time "plum" appointments (*Category II*). We also wanted to know whether the correlation was different in the United States and Britain; whether it changed over the seventy-year period; and whether it varied according to the party in office. We also asked whether going public tended to cluster around certain kinds of issues or events, and we wanted to correlate resignation style with the resigner's profession.

Resignation Statistical Charts

Figure 1
DISTRIBUTION BY DECADES, UNITED STATES*

	1900–09	1910–19	1920–29	1930–39	1940–49	1950–59	1960–69
Silent Resignations	23	21	34	18	58	93	104
Public-Protest Resignations	1	4	4	5	7	5	7
Total Resignations Studied	24	25	38	23	65	98	111
Public-Protest Resignations as Per Cent of Total Resignations Studied	4.2	16.2	10.5	21.7	10.7	5.1	6.3

*The statistics in other charts are based on 1900–70 inclusive (71 years) and totals are thus larger (34 growlers and 355 silent resignations, a total resignation studied of 389). In this chart, because we are using decades as our basic categories, our statistics only extend through 1969, one year less than the study as a whole. The total number of public-protest resignations and silent resignations in these seven decades is 384. There were, in addition, four silent resignations and one public-protest resignation in 1970, for a total of 389.

Figure 2
(A) DISTRIBUTION BY ADMINISTRATIONS, UNITED STATES

	Democratic Administrations	Republican Administrations
Public-Protest Resignations	24	10
Silent Resignations	218	137
Total	242	147

(B) PUBLIC-PROTEST RESIGNATIONS BY PARTIES AS PER CENT OF PARTY'S TOTAL RESIGNATIONS STUDIED

	Democratic	Republican
Public-Protest Resignations	9.9	6.8

◇

Figure 3
GROUPING OF ERAS BY ADMINISTRATIONS, UNITED STATES

(A) REPUBLICAN

Administration	Public-Protest Resignations	Total Resignations Studied	Per Cent
1900–13 McKinley/Roosevelt/Taft	2	28	7.1
1921–33 Harding/Coolidge/Hoover	3	36	8.3
1953–61, 1968–70 Eisenhower/Nixon	5	83	6.0
Total	10	147	

(B) DEMOCRATIC

Administration	Public-Protest Resignations	Total Resignations Studied	Per Cent
1913–21 Woodrow Wilson	5	28	17.9
1933–52 (Jan. 1953) Roosevelt/Truman	12	106	11.3
1961–68 Kennedy/Johnson	7	108	6.5
Total	24	242	

Figure 4
DISTRIBUTION BY DECADES, BRITAIN

	1900–09	1910–19	1920–29	1930–39	1940–49	1950–59	1960–69
Silent Resignations	2	9	2	8	3	10	2
Public-Protest Resignations	3	12	2	9	0	7	9
Total Resignations Studied	5	21	4	17	3	17	11
Public-Protest Resignations as Per Cent of Total Resignations Studied	60.0	57.1	50.0	52.9	00.0	41.1	81.8

◇

Figure 5
GREAT BRITAIN
PUBLIC-PROTEST RESIGNATIONS, SILENT RESIGNATIONS AND
TOTAL RESIGNATIONS STUDIED
DISTRIBUTION BY GOVERNMENTS

(A) NUMERICAL DISTRIBUTION

	Labour Government	Liberal Government	Conservative Government	Coalition* Government
Public-Protest Resignations	14	1	12	15
Silent Resignations	6	2	18	10
Total	20	3	30	25

(B) PUBLIC-PROTEST RESIGNATIONS BY PARTIES AS PER CENT OF ALL THOSE IN PARTY WHOSE RESIGNATIONS WERE STUDIED

	Labour Government	Liberal Government	Conservative Government	Coalition Government
Public-Protest Resignations	70.0	33.3	40.0	60.0

(C) NUMBER OF YEARS IN GOVERNMENT (ROUNDED)

Labour	15
Liberal	10
Conservative	29
Coalition	16

*Including "National" Government of 1931–35 but not of 1935–40, which is classified as Conservative.

APPENDIX C

Criteria for Measuring
Upper-Class Status

DOMHOFFF'S CRITERIA for upper-class membership, in G. William Domhoff, *Who Rules America?* (Englewood Cliffs, N.J.: Prentice-Hall, Inc., 1967), pp. 34–37, are:

1) A person is considered to be a member of the national upper class if he is in any *Social Register* other than the Washington edition. The Washington edition was not used by Domhoff because it includes persons by virtue of their being in the top political posts, making the category redundant for our purposes. Most other, nonpolitical Washingtonian listees are also listed in one of the other *Social Registers*. While the eleven city editions we use as criteria will include a few persons who are not long-standing members of the upper class, this merely reflects the relatively rapid mobility and assimilation that is characteristic of this country's business-oriented aristocracy. At the same time, it is also undoubtedly true that these volumes list a few families that have "lost their money," although it is difficult to assess what this statement means in terms of the net worth of the "impecunious families." However, we would estimate that the families worth tens of millions of dollars are the exceptions within the American upper class.

2) A person is also considered to be a member of the upper class if he has attended any one of these preparatory schools: Asheville (Asheville, N.C.); Buckley (New York, N.Y.); Choate (Wallingford, Conn.); Cranbrook (Bloomfield Hills, Mich.); Deerfield (Deerfield, Mass.); Episcopal High (Alexandria, Va.); Groton (Groton, Mass.); Hill (Pottstown, Pa.); Hotchkiss (Lakeville, Conn.); Kent (Kent, Conn.); Lake Forest (Lake Forest, Ill.); Lawrenceville (Lawrenceville, N.J.); Loomis (Windsor, Conn.); Middlesex (Concord, Mass.); Milton (Milton, Mass.); Pomfret (Pomfret, Conn.); Portsmouth Priory (Portsmouth, R.I.); St. Andrew's (Middletown, Del.); St. George's (Newport, R.I.); St. Mark's (Southboro, Mass.); St. Paul's (Concord, N.H.); Shattuck (Faribault, Minn.); Webb (Bell Buckle, Tenn.); Woodberry Forest (Woodberry Forest, Va.). Domhoff notes, "This list was compiled [as was the list of gentlemen's clubs] from the works of Baltzell and Kavaler. [See E. Digby Baltzell, *An American Business Aristocracy* (New York: Collier, 1962) and his *The Protestant Establishment* (New York: Random House, 1965); also, Lucy Kavaler, *The Private World of*

◇

High Society (New York: David McKay Co., 1960). For a supplementary discussion also consult Cleveland Amory's *Who Killed Society?* (New York: Harper & Row, 1960).] Exeter and Andover have been excluded from the list because of their large minority of scholarship students" (*ibid.*, p. 34).

3) A person is considered to be a member of the national upper class if he is a member of any one of the following "very exclusive" gentlemen's clubs: Boston (New Orleans); Brook (New York); California (Los Angeles); Casino (Chicago); Chagrin Valley Hunt (Cleveland); Detroit (Detroit); Eagle Lake (Houston); Everglades (Palm Beach); Harmonie (New York); Idlewild (Dallas); Knickerbocker (New York); Maryland (Baltimore); Pacific Union (San Francisco); Philadelphia (Philadelphia); Pickwick (New Orleans); Piedmont Driving (Atlanta); Rainier (Seattle); St. Cecilia (Charleston); St. Louis Country Club (St. Louis); Somerset (Boston).

The remaining criteria used by Domhoff, which we have not used,* are:

4) A person is considered to be a member of the upper class if his or her father was a millionaire entrepreneur or a $100,000-a-year corporation executive or corporation lawyer, *and* (a) he or she attended one of the 130 private schools listed in Kavaler, *or* (b) he or she belongs to any one of the exclusive clubs mentioned by Baltzell or Kavaler. The list of private schools and exclusive clubs can be larger here than for the second and third criteria above because it is known that the person is a member of the second generation of a wealthy family. Women's schools and clubs are included here because of the next criterion.

5) A person is considered to be a member of the upper class if he or she marries a person defined as a member of the upper class by criteria 1–4 above. Co-optation by marriage is one of the ways by which the upper class, whether its members are aware of it or not, infuses new brains and talent into its ranks. . . . *In the case of marriages into the upper class we are assuming that the person's interests and values will tend to become similar to those of the people with whom he mingles.* (Italics ours)

6) A person is considered to be a member of the upper class if his father, mother, sister, or brother is listed in the *Social Register,* or attended one of the exclusive private schools listed in criterion 2, or belongs to one of the exclusive gentlemen's clubs listed in criterion 3. This criterion allows us sometimes to obviate the reticence of some individual members of the upper class, especially those who refuse to list in the *Social Register.*

7) A person is considered to be a member of the upper class if he is a member of one of the old and still-wealthy families chronicled by Amory in *Who Killed Society?* or *The Proper Bostonians* (New York: E. P. Dutton, 1947). This criterion is based upon the assumption that Amory is an accurate ethnographer of the American upper class.

---

*These four criteria were not employed because they seemed to us either redundant or unduly to tend to inflate the category of upper class.

REFERENCE NOTES

Chapter 1. The Insider's Inner Conflict

1. David Riesman, in collaboration with Reuel Denny and Nathan Glazer, *The Lonely Crowd: A Study in the Changing American Character* (New Haven and London: Yale University Press, 1967), from the foreword, "Ten Years Later," p. xxi.

2. William H. Whyte, *The Organization Man* (New York: Simon and Schuster, 1956), p. 7.

3. The United Nations Secretariat is a particularly desperate case, its officials being pulled away from the direction dictated by individual conscience not only by the secretariat's own bureaucratic, hierarchic loyalty system but by the demands made on them by the governments whose citizens they remain. An excellent study of this subject is found in Shirley Hazzard, *Defeat of an Ideal: A Study of the Self-Destruction of the United Nations* (Boston: Atlantic, Little, Brown and Co., 1973).

4. Henry David Thoreau, *On the Duty of Civil Disobedience*, 8th ed. (New York: Rinehart and Co., 1958), pp. 283–84.

5. Solomon Asch, a pioneer in research on group conformity pressures, speaks, simply, of an individual's "independence" which he defines as his ability to resist or reject others by an open assertion of one's dissident personal judgment "as an ability which requires a strong assertion of the self and an ability to withstand attack without excessive rejection anxiety." Solomon E. Asch, *Social Psychology* (New York: Prentice-Hall, Inc., 1952), p. 498. For an analysis of autonomy in relation to the development of character in modern society see Riesman, *op. cit.*, Part III, "Autonomy," pp. 283–373.

6. Irving L. Janis, *Victims of Groupthink* (Boston: Houghton Mifflin Co., 1972). Groupthink is: "a mode of thinking that people engage in when they are deeply involved in a cohesive in-group, when the members' strivings for unanimity override their motivation to realistically appraise alternative courses of action. . . . Groupthink refers to a deterioration of mental efficiency, reality testing, and moral judgment that results from in-group pressures" (*ibid.*, p. 9).

7. *Ibid.*

8. Wayne C. Taylor to Henry M. Morgenthau, Jr. (Draft), February 7, 1939. Henry M. Morgenthau, Jr., *Diary*, Book 164, pp. 49–50, Franklin D. Roosevelt Library, Hyde Park, N.Y.; hereafter referred to as *Morgenthau Diary*.

9. Memorandum of Conversation, Henry M. Morgenthau, Jr., February 8, 1939, *ibid.*, pp. 47–48.

10. *Ibid.*

11. *Ibid.*

12. *Ibid.*

13. *Ibid.*

14. *Morgenthau Diary*, Memorandum of Conversation, February 9, 1939, Book 164, pp. 51–52.

15. *Morgenthau Diary*, February 16, 1939, as of February 7, 1939, Book 165, Attachment 65, p. 51.

16. *Morgenthau Diary*, Memorandum of Conversation, February 10, 1939, Book 164, p. 201; *Morgenthau Diary*, Memorandum of Meeting, April 11, 1939, Book 177, pp. 359–60.

◇

17. Sir Henry Newbolt, *Vitai Lampada* as cited in John Bartlett, *Familiar Quotations*, Emily Morison Beck, ed. (14th ed. rev.), (Boston: Little, Brown and Co., 1968), p. 865.

18. William L. Cary, "On Saying 'No' to a President," *Wall Street Journal*, July 30, 1973, p. 10.

19. *The New York Times*, June 26, 1915, p. 8.

20. *Ibid.*, June 29, 1915, p. 8.

21. Harold L. Ickes, *The Secret Diary of Harold L. Ickes: The First Thousand Days, 1933–1936* (New York: Simon and Schuster, 1953), p. 9; hereafter referred to as *Ickes Diary I*.

22. Dean Acheson, *Morning and Noon* (Boston: Houghton Mifflin Co., 1962), p. 191. Roosevelt claims to have fired Acheson. *Ickes Diary I*, p. 174.

23. Acheson to Roosevelt, undated, Private Secretary's File (hereafter referred to as P.S.F.): Treasury Department 1933–1937, Box 80, Franklin D. Roosevelt Library.

24. *The New York Times*, eleven days after the resignation, does report on a Treasury memo in which Acheson's dissent is noted. *The New York Times*, November 27, 1933, p. 2.

25. Acheson, *op. cit.*, p. 194.

26. *Time*, October 25, 1971, p. 19; also see Arthur M. Schlesinger, Jr., *The Age of Roosevelt*, vol. 2, *The Coming of the New Deal* (Boston: Houghton Mifflin Co., 1958), p. 242. Acheson also fondly recalls the incident. Acheson, *op. cit.*, p. 194.

Chapter 2. Fighting Back by Going Public

---

1. "Seemed to" in the sense that some of the tapes, when they were released, were so defaced as to be of little evidentiary value.

2. *The New York Times*, October 24, 1973, p. 32.

3. At the heart of their argument was a firm commitment by all three—Richardson has called it a "contract" (interview with Elliot L. Richardson, McLean, Va., December 7, 1973)—to the independence of the Special Prosecutor, a commitment Richardson and Ruckelshaus had specified to Congress at the time of their confirmation. This independence President Nixon had tried to abrogate by ordering Cox to "make no further attempts by judicial process to obtain tapes, notes or memoranda of Presidential conversations" (*The New York Times*, October 24, 1973, p. 33). Nixon himself admitted to Richardson that this was "intruding, to this very limited extent, on the independence which I promised you with regard to Watergate." (*Ibid.*) Richardson, even aside from his "contractual" obligation to protect Cox's independence, thought the ban on the release of further tapes to be a disastrously bad decision, probably sufficient in itself to warrant his public opposition and resignation. Also at stake was the Prosecutor's right to reject a compromise by which Senator John Stennis would listen to—and prepare a summary for Judge Sirica of—those tapes which the court had already ordered the President to produce in full.

4. *Ibid.*

5. *Ibid.*, p. 35.

6. The actual resignation was remarkable not only in the extent to which Richardson made public his disagreements with the President but in the firmness with which he refused to be drafted into the ranks of Nixon-haters. He steadfastly refused the invitation to describe the President as "paranoid" or to indicate that Cox had been fired because he was about to discover a big new scandal involving the President. Neither did he take the position that Nixon's refusal to reveal the tapes had been part of a cover-up nor that the President's offer to have the tapes audited by an impartial third party was legally unacceptable. In each of these matters he tried to stake out a position which separated him from the two large, organized groups of antagonists: the Administration and the Critics. "It won't be understood," a leading national television newscaster had warned him. "The image isn't clear. We're not in the business of reporting news but of projecting reality. You're not defining your reality

sharply enough for us to be able to put it across."

7. *The New York Times,* December 16, 1973, p. E2.

8. *Ibid.,* December 12, 1973, p. 30.

9. Interview with William D. Ruckelshaus, Washington, D.C., December 14, 1973.

10. *The New York Times,* January 20, 1946, p. 11, and January 27, 1946, section 4, p. 10. Confirmed in Margaret Truman, *Harry S. Truman* (New York: William Morrow and Co., 1973), p. 291.

11. *The New York Times,* February 2, 1946, p. 1.

12. *Ibid.,* February 6, 1946, p. 1.

13. Merle Miller, *Plain Speaking: An Oral Biography of Harry S. Truman* (New York: Berkley Publishing Corp., 1973), p. 210.

14. Margaret Truman, *op. cit.,* p. 291.

15. *The New York Times,* February 8, 1946.

16. Margaret Truman, *op. cit.,* p. 29.

17. Miller, *op. cit.,* p. 210.

18. Ickes to Truman, February 12, 1946, Official File, Papers of Harry S. Truman, Harry S. Truman Library, Independence, Missouri.

19. *The New York Times,* February 14, 1946, p. 1.

20. *Ibid.,* pp. 1, 21.

21. *Ibid.,* p. 1.

22. *Ibid.*

23. *Ibid.,* p. 21.

24. *Ibid.,* February 16, 1946, pp. 1, 3.

25. *Ibid.,* February 17, 1946, p. 33.

26. *Ibid.*

27. *Ibid.,* March 4, 1946, p. 24.

28. *Ibid.,* March 7, 1946, p. 52.

29. *Ibid.,* March 9, 1946, pp. 1, 28.

30. *Ibid.,* March 14, 1946, p. 1.

31. *Ibid.,* pp. 1, 11.

32. James A. Farley to F.D.R., August 7, 1940. P.S.F.: Post Office Department 1939–1940, Box 70, Franklin D. Roosevelt Library.

33. Rexford G. Tugwell, *In Search of Roosevelt* (Cambridge, Mass.: Harvard University Press, 1972), p. 291.

34. For a discussion of contending theories of public participation in democratic decision-making see, Elmer E. Schattschneider, *The Semisovereign People: A Realist's View of Democracy in America* (New York: Holt, Rinehart and Winston, 1960), and Peter Bachrach, *The Theory of Democratic Elitism: A Critique* (Boston: Little, Brown and Co., 1967).

35. Webster Davis, *John Bull's Crime or Assaults on Republics* (New York: The Abbey Press, 1901), p. i.

36. *Ibid.,* pp. 149–50.

37. William Roscoe Thayer, ed., *Life and Letters of John Hay,* vol. 2 (Boston: Houghton Mifflin Co., 1915), p. 221.

38. A.L.P. Dennis, "John Hay," in Samuel Flagg Bemis, ed., *The American Secretaries of State and Their Diplomacy* (New York: Alfred A. Knopf, 1929), pp. 152–53.

39. Davis, *op. cit.,* p. 159.

40. Davis noted that "The British government organized their police force by the appointment of Hottentots, the most contemptible of the natives, to the position of policemen. This action infuriated the Boers, for they regarded the Hottentots as much lower than themselves in the social scale," and that the British sent "missionaries from England to visit the natives of South Africa. . . . Some of these missionaries . . . married black women." *Ibid.,* pp. 154–55.

41. *Ibid.,* p. 151.

42. *The New York Times,* April 9, 1900, p. 3.
43. *Ibid.*
44. Davis, *op. cit.,* pp. 187–88.
45. *Ibid.,* p. 189.
46. *New York Daily Tribune,* January 27, 1900, p. 12.
47. Davis, *op. cit.,* p. 208.
48. *Ibid.,* pp. 209–10.
49. *Ibid.,* p. 213.
50. *Ibid.,* p. 215.
51. *Ibid.,* p. 219.
52. *The New York Times,* January 3, 1900, p. 1.
53. *Ibid.,* January 22, 1900, p. 2.
54. *Ibid.,* September 14, 1900, p. 1.
55. *Ibid.,* October 17, 1900, p. 5.
56. Davis, *op. cit.,* pp. 223–24.
57. Louis W. Koenig, *Bryan: A Political Biography* (New York: G. P. Putnam's Sons, 1971), p. 529.
58. *The New York Times,* May 14, 1915, p. 1.
59. Bryan to Wilson, May 12, 1915, Bryan Papers as cited in Koenig, *op. cit.,* p. 543.
60. *The New York Times,* June 1, 1915, p. 2.
61. *Ibid.*
62. Koenig, *op. cit.,* pp. 545–46.
63. William G. McAdoo, *Crowded Years: Reminiscences* (Boston: Houghton Mifflin, 1931), pp. 334–46; quoted in Koenig, *op. cit.,* p. 548.
64. *The New York Times,* June 9, 1915, p. 1.
65. *Ibid.*
66. *Ibid.,* June 11, 1915, p. 1.
67. *Ibid.*
68. *Ibid.,* June 12, 1915, p. 1.
69. *Ibid.,* June 18, 1915, p. 4.
70. *Ibid.,* September 21, 1915, p. 4.
71. *Ibid.,* October 16, 1915, p. 4.
72. *Ibid.,* October 18, 1915, p. 6.
73. *Ibid.,* July 5, 1916, p. 5.
74. *Ibid.,* November 6, 1915, p. 3.
75. *Ibid.,* November 7, 1915, p. 14.
76. *Ibid.,* p. 20.
77. *Ibid.,* November 8, 1915, p. 8.
78. *Ibid.,* November 11, 1915, p. 5.
79. *Ibid.,* February 26, 1916, p. 2.
80. *Ibid.,* March 6, 1916, p. 1.
81. Koenig, *op. cit.,* p. 564.
82. *The New York Times,* November 24, 1916, p. 4.
83. *Ibid.,* December 27, 1916, p. 2.
84. See comments in Miller, *op. cit., passim;* see, e.g., pp. 176–77.
85. Margaret Truman, *op. cit.,* p. 314.
86. *Ibid.*
87. Henry A. Wallace to Truman, July 23, 1946. Papers of Clark M. Clifford, Harry S. Truman Library.
88. Personal Memorandum of George Elsey, the White House, "L'Affaire Wallace," 17 September 1946. Papers of George Elsey, Harry S. Truman Library.
89. Press Conference No. 80 of September 12, 1946. Transcript in Papers of Clark M. Clifford, Harry S. Truman Library.

90. Margaret Truman, *op. cit.*, p. 316.
91. *Ibid.*
92. Press Release "Statement by the President," September 14, 1946. Papers of Clark M. Clifford, Harry S. Truman Library.
93. Margaret Truman, *op. cit.*, p. 318.
94. Press Release, "Statement by the President," September 20, 1946. Papers of Harry S. Truman, Official File, Harry S. Truman Library.
95. Margaret Truman, *op. cit.*, p. 343.
96. *The New York Times,* May 25, 1946, p. 7;.*ibid.,* April 13, 1947, p. 1.
97. *Ibid.*, December 30, 1946, p. 1.
98. *Ibid.*
99. *Ibid.*, September 13, 1946, p. 1.
100. *Ibid.*, April 1, 1947, p. 9.
101. *Ibid.*, April 15, 1947, p. 12.
102. *Ibid.*
103. *Ibid.*, April 10, 1947, p. 8.
104. *Ibid.*, April 24, 1947, p. 4.
105. *Ibid.*, September 20, 1947, p. 1.
106. Lewis W. Douglas, *The Liberal Tradition* (New York: D. Van Nostrand Co., 1935).
107. Interview with Lewis W. Douglas, Tucson. Ariz., May 16. 1973.
108. Joseph P. Tumulty, *Woodrow Wilson as I Know Him* (Garden City, N.Y.: Doubleday, Page and Co., 1921), p. 138.
109. *The New York Times,* February 4, 1915, p. 18.
110. See clipping in Garrison personal files of editorial in *The Evening Journal* (Wilmington, Del.), April 13, 1915. Garrison Papers, Princeton University Library.
111. W. W. Bailey to Mrs. Etta Blum, January 4, 1916. Warren Worth Bailey Papers, Princeton University Library, cited in Arthur S. Link, *Wilson: the New Freedom* (Princeton, N.J.: Princeton University Press, 1956), p. 120.
112. Memorandum for the President, Tumulty to Wilson, January 15, 1916. Papers of Joseph P. Tumulty, Manuscript Division, Library of Congress; see also Arthur S. Link, *Wilson: Confusions and Crises, 1915–1916,* IV (Princeton, N.J.: Princeton University Press, 1964), p. 40.
113. *The New York Times,* January 7, 1916, p. 6.
114. Hay to Wilson, February 8, 1916, Woodrow Wilson Papers, Series II, Frames 81961, 81962, Manuscript Division, Library of Congress.
115. *The New York Times,* January 9, 1916, section 2, p. 5.
116. Tumulty, *op. cit.*, p. 242.
117. Hay to Wilson, February 8, 1916, as above.
118. Wilson to Hay, January 18, 1916, Woodrow Wilson Papers, Series II, Frames 81500, 81501, Manuscript Division, Library of Congress.
119. *The New York Times,* January 18, 1916, pp. 1, 6.
120. David F. Houston, *Eight Years with Wilson's Cabinet, 1913–1920,* vol. 4 (New York: Doubleday, Page and Co., 1926), pp. 165–70.
121. Link, *op. cit.*, p. 120.
122. Houston, *op. cit.*, p. 168.
123. Wilson to Garrison, January 15, 1916, Woodrow Wilson Papers, Series II, Frames 81419, 81420, 81421, Manuscript Division, Library of Congress. This letter was sent, and is in other reproductions dated January 17, 1916.
124. *Ibid.*
125. Houston, *op. cit.*, p. 177.
126. *Ibid.*, pp. 177–78.
127. *Ibid.*, pp. 178–79.

128. Josephus Daniels, *The Wilson Era: Years of Peace 1910–1917* (Chapel Hill: University of North Carolina Press), 1944, p. 445.

129. *The New York Times*, February 13, 1916, p. 1.

130. *Ibid.*, February 12, 1916, p. 1.

131. Daniels, *op. cit.*, p. 448.

132. Address to New York Lawyers' Club, December 16, 1916, published in Addresses Delivered before the Lawyers' Club, New York, on the Subject of Nationalism, by Robert C. Morris, D.C.L., and Hon. Lindley M. Garrison, Saturday, December 6, 1916 (New York: Press of H. K. Brewer and Co., 1917), p. 16.

133. *The New York Times*, April 27, 1949, p. 6.

134. *Ibid.*

135. Interview with John L. Sullivan, Washington, D.C., March 21, 1973.

136. *The New York Times*, June 19, 1970, p. 51.

137. *Ibid.*, June 20, 1970, p. 10.

138. *The Washington Post,* July 10, 1970, p. A19.

139. *Women's Wear Daily,* July 15, 1970, p. 5.

140. *The New York Times,* May 7, 1970, pp. 1, 18.

141. Walter J. Hickel, *Who Owns America?* (Englewood Cliffs, N.J.: Prentice-Hall, Inc., 1971).

142. *The New York Times,* January 22, 1945, pp. 1, 30.

143. *Ibid.*, May 1, 1920, p. 7.

144. *Ibid.*, November 17, 1938, p. 37.

145. *Ibid.*, November 14, 1938, p. 31.

146. *Ibid.*, March 18, 1947, p. 1; *ibid.*, November 3, 1947, p. 5; *ibid.*, November 4, 1947, p. 15; *ibid.*, November 14, 1947, p. 17; *ibid.*, December 29, 1947, p. 14; *ibid.*, March 31, 1948, p. 32.

147. *Ibid.*, June 26, 1920, p. 7; *ibid.*, July 2, 1920, p. 10.

148. *Ibid.*, October 4, 1920, p. 2.

149. Memorandum of Conversation, December 3, 1933. *Morgenthau Diary,* Book 13, p. 4.

150. Memorandum of Conversation, April 30, 1935, *ibid.*, Book 5, Pt. 1, p. 61.

151. Memorandum of Conversation, May 1, 1935, *ibid.*, p. 62.

152. *The New York Times,* August 31, 1936, p. 14.

153. Memorandum of Conversation, September 20, 1937, *ibid.*, Book 89, pp. 72–73.

154. Press Release, August 14, 1940, President's Personal File (hereafter referred to as P.P.F.): 6793, Franklin D. Roosevelt Library.

155. *The New York Times,* August 17, 1940, p. 7.

156. *Ibid.*, July 24, 1940, p. 1.

157. *Ibid.*

158. Memorandum of Conversation, April 13–15, 1943, *Morgenthau Diary,* Book 625, p. 32.

Chapter 3. The Costs of Candor

1. Albert O. Hirschman, *Exit, Voice and Loyalty: Responses to Decline in Firms, Organizations, and States* (Cambridge, Mass.: Harvard University Press, 1970).

2. For the best collection of these stories see David Halberstam, *The Best and the Brightest* (New York: Random House, 1969), pp. 515–16, 616–17, 632–34, 644–45.

3. *The New York Times,* May 19, 1966, p. 11.

4. *Ibid.*, August 26, 1967, pp. 70–71.

5. Halberstam, *op. cit.*, p. 664.

6. *Ibid.*, p. 645.

7. In his capacity as Secretary of Labor, W. Willard Wirtz was placed in the difficult position of having to defend Administration policies while Great Society programs, specifically those beneficial to labor, were being curtailed or eliminated; see, for example, *The New York Times*, January 1, 1967, p. 42, where the President alleges that Wirtz will have an important role in determining budgetary priorities.

8. For a full discussion of the process by which the 389 persons were selected, of the reasons for selecting them, and of the way in which borderline cases were decided, see Appendix A.

9. These reappointments to equivalent or higher posts are referred to in the Appendices as Category I returns to office, to distinguish from reappointments to part-time positions in the federal government. See Appendix A for an explanation of this distinction.

10. The one instance is H. Struve Hensel, who resigned in 1946 from the post of Assistant Secretary of the Navy, spoke up against merger of the armed forces, and returned in 1952 as General Counsel and, in 1954, as Assistant Secretary of Defense. *The New York Times*, November 8, 1945, p. 6.

11. These discretionary political "plums" are treated as a separate Category II in the tables in Appendix B. Category II is more fully explained in Appendix A.

12. Benedict Crowell, T. Jefferson Coolidge, James R. Killian, and H. Struve Hensel.

13. The discrepancy between future career prospects of resigners and nonresigners would be even greater if the basis of calculation had been the *number* of full- and part-time posts to which each former official was subsequently appointed. Of the 127 quiet resigners, many subsequently received several full-time as well as several part-time appointments.

14. The exceptions are Webster Davis, Edward J. Noble, Robert Roosa, and Robert Kennedy.

15. *The New York Times*, February 5, 1917, pp. 2, 4.

16. Arthur W. Little, "Standing Back of the President," *Pearson's Magazine*, newspaper clipping, Woodrow Wilson Papers, Series 2, Folder dated Feb. 4–5, 1917, Manuscript Division, Library of Congress.

17. *The New York Times*, February 1, 1918, p. 8.

18. Archives of John Hay Library, Brown University.

19. Interview with John L. Sullivan, Washington, D.C., March 21, 1973.

20. Roger Hilsman, "Plea for 'Realism' in Southeast Asia," *The New York Times Magazine*, August 23, 1964, pp. 26, 32–36.

21. Roger Hilsman, *To Move a Nation* (Garden City, N.Y.: Doubleday and Co., 1967).

22. *Ibid.*, pp. 527–28.

23. *The New York Times*, June 10, 1915, p. 10.

24. *Ibid.*, June 12, 1915, p. 2.

25. *Ibid.*, p. 3.

26. *Ibid.*, June 13, 1915, p. 14.

27. *Ibid.*, June 14, 1915, p. 2.

28. *Ibid.*

29. *Ibid.*, June 27, 1915, p. 14.

30. Dr. Konstantin Theodor Dumba was the Austro-Hungarian Ambassador to Washington. After dispatch of the May 13, 1915, note to Germany, Bryan had a conversation which led Dumba to inform the Germans that the American note was not to be taken too seriously, that its "strict accountability" provision had been inserted for domestic consumption only. Bryan denied the story, asserting that he had been misunderstood by Dumba. He said that, once he became aware of the misunderstanding, he had called on Dumba to transmit an exact agreed text of what had actually been said, and that President Wilson had been fully apprised throughout. Nevertheless, the scandal did Bryan some damage, especially as he was reluctant to reveal just exactly what he did say to Ambassador Dumba. *The New York Times*, May 16, 1916, p. 5. Bryan eventually claimed he had merely tried to draw a

distinction for Dumba between U.S. reaction to British interference with U.S. trade and German actions which cost U.S. lives. The Providence *Journal* carried a story, widely reprinted, that the Bryan-Dumba conversation had been a move toward a tentative agreement between the U.S. and Germany, one being made behind Wilson's back. It was even reported that Mr. Bryan had actually got his "peace program" direct from Austria and Germany. *The New York Times*, July 4, 1915, p. 10. When, at last, the German government rejected Wilson's note of June 9, newspaper stories blamed German obduracy on encouragement received from Bryan. Like many another dissenter, his opposition was attacked as aid to the nation's enemy.

31. Louis W. Koenig, *Bryan: A Political Biography* (New York: G. P. Putnam's Sons, 1971), p. 569.

32. *Ibid.*, p. 570.

33. Koenig, *op. cit.*, pp. 592–660. "He brought upon himself a heap of ridicule and derision, and even to this day he remains buried under it." *Ibid.*, p. 655.

34. Merle Miller, *Plain Speaking: An Oral Biography of Harry S. Truman* (New York: Berkley Publishing Corp., 1973), pp. 116–17.

35. Solomon E. Asch, *Social Psychology* (New York: Prentice-Hall, Inc., 1952), p. 465.

36. *Ibid.*, p. 497.

37. *Ibid.*, p. 467.

38. Richard S. Crutchfield, "Conformity and Character," vol. 10, *The American Psychologist*, no. 5 (May 1955), p. 197.

39. For the resignation, see *The New York Times*, June 3, 1929, p. 12.

40. For a summary of these and of her ensuing book, see *ibid.*, November 21, 1929, p. 17; see also *The New York Times Index*, July–September, 1929, p. 400.

41. Mabel Willebrandt, *The Inside of Prohibition* (Indianapolis: Bobbs-Merrill, 1929).

42. See James J. Britt to Walter H. Newton, September 14, 1929, Memorandum for Commissioner Doran from Britt, August 12, 1929, Memorandum to Secretary Andrew W. Mellon from Britt, August 13, 1929, in File 21V, Presidential Papers, Cabinet Offices, Treasury: Commissioner of Prohibition, Correspondence, Herbert Hoover Presidential Library.

43. *The New York Times*, August 12, 1930, p. 22.

44. "Mitchell Foils Move to Make Mabel Dry Czar." Dispatch of Arthur Sears Henning, Chicago Tribune Press Service, June 2, 1929.

45. *Kansas City Star*, June 15, 1929, p. 2.

46. Letter from Clement H. Congdon to President Herbert Hoover, Philadelphia, Pa., October 21, 1929. Herbert Hoover Presidential Library, Presidential Papers, Cabinet Offices, Treasury, Prohibition Commissioner, Correspondence.

47. *Ibid.*, citing *Daily News*, October 19, 1929.

48. *Ibid.*

49. *The New York Times*, June 19, 1930, p. 10.

50. *Ibid.*, November 22, 1930, p. 2.

51. Henrik Ibsen, *A Enemy of Society*, William Archer, trans. (Boston: Walter H. Baker and Co., 1900), p. 110.

52. *Kansas City Star*, January 21, 1969, p. 26.

53. Rollin J. Britton, "Webster Davis, Sketch of Life," vol. 17, *Missouri Historical Review* (April 1923), no. 3, pp. 388–94; *Kansas City World*, February 28, 1901, p. 1; *Kansas City Star*, January 21, 1969, p. 26.

54. *The New York Times*, May 18, 1904, p. 3.

55. *The Kansas City Journal*, August 7, 1904, p. 1.

56. However, during the first decade of this century, the percentage of public-protest resignations was lowest: 4.2 per cent. This can be understood by reference to the breakdown by administrations and political parties, below. The statistics by decades with an explanatory note are set out in Appendix B, Fig. 1.

57. See Appendix B, Fig. 2.

58. This explains the seemingly inconsistent low rate of public-protest resignations during the first decade of this century; see Appendix B, Fig. 1.

59. See Appendix B, Fig. 3(A).

60. See Appendix B, Fig. 3(B).

61. Technically, the survey does not categorize its cases studied by the party affiliation of the resigners—since, in the American system, this is frequently difficult to establish—but by the political party in control of the Presidency.

62. There has, of late, been a small but highly visible increase in public dissension, of going public, among men who govern. This has followed in the wake of the Vietnam and Watergate disasters and is taking the form of various individuals' trying to establish their own innocence or mitigate their moral or criminal culpability by "fingering" colleagues. This is not a particularly edifying development. John Dean, Dwight Chapin, and Egil Krogh may now be willing to break the rules of the game and speak up. But not for the sake of a healthier democratic system did they volunteer to go public, but as part of their bargaining with the prosecutor's office—after the damage to the system had been done.

63. Franklin D. Roosevelt to Harry H. Woodring, September 25, 1936, P.P.F.: 663, Franklin D. Roosevelt Library. In his letter Roosevelt rather grudgingly states that "since you cannot remain as Acting Secretary of War beyond a period of thirty days . . . I am announcing the temporary selection of you as Secretary today."

64. "An American National Policy that is Unqualifiedly Pro-American," Statement by Harry H. Woodring, September 14, 1937, P.S.F.: Box 86, Franklin D. Roosevelt Library.

65. Roosevelt to Woodring, June 19, 1940, P.S.F.: Box 86, Franklin D. Roosevelt Library.

66. Woodring to Roosevelt, June 20, 1940, *ibid.*

67. *Ibid.*

68. Roosevelt to Woodring, June 20, 1940, *ibid.*

69. *The Kansas City Star,* June 22, 1940, p. 1.

70. Roosevelt to Woodring, June 25, 1940, P.S.F.: Box 86, Franklin D. Roosevelt Library.

71. Woodring to Roosevelt, January 15, 1941, P.P.F.: Box 663, Franklin D. Roosevelt Library.

72. Roosevelt to Woodring, January 21, 1941, *ibid.*

73. Woodring to Roosevelt, January 18, 1942, *ibid.*

74. Roosevelt to Woodring, January 29, 1942, *ibid.*

75. Woodring to Roosevelt, March 19, 1945, *ibid.*

76. Roosevelt to Woodring, March 24, 1945, *ibid.*

77. See *The New Yorker,* April 16, 1966, esp. p. 116.

78. Richard N. Goodwin, *Triumph or Tragedy: Reflections on Vietnam* (New York: Random House, 1966), p. 67.

79. Hans J. Morgenthau, "Room at the Top," *New York Review of Books,* June 23, 1966, p. 14.

80. Charles Frankel, *High on Foggy Bottom* (New York: Harper and Row, 1968).

81. *Ibid.,* pp. 56–57.

82. *Ibid.,* pp. 84–85.

83. *The New York Times,* January 26, 1968, p. 1; *Newsweek,* February 5, 1968, p. 25.

84. *Newsweek,* February 5, 1968, p. 25.

85. *Ibid.* Also *The New York Times,* January 25, 1968, pp. 1, 19.

86. *The New York Times,* January 26, 1968, p. 1.

87. *Ibid.,* p. 16.

88. *Ibid.*

89. Plato, "The Apology" in *Euthyphro, Apology and Crito,* F. J. Church, trans. (New York: The Liberal Arts Press, 1948), p. 45.

90. *The New York Times*, May 14, 1970, p. 22.

91. *Ibid.*

92. *Ibid.*

93. *Ibid.*, March 2, 1968, p. 30.

94. The 1958 resignation of Harold Stassen (*ibid.*, Feb. 16, 1958, p. 1; Feb. 26, 1958, p. 1; Feb. 27, 1958, p. 1) in a dispute with John Foster Dulles over disarmament policy is another study in the futility of making public general, rather than specific, differences.

95. Spruille Braden, *Diplomats and Demagogues* (New Rochelle, N.Y.: Arlington House, 1971).

96. *Ibid.*, p. 370.

97. Robert Lansing, *The Peace Negotiations: A Personal Narrative* (Boston: Houghton Mifflin Co., 1921), p. 165.

98. Josephus Daniels, *The Wilson Era: Years of War and After, 1917–1923* (Chapel Hill: The University of North Carolina Press, 1946), p. 521.

99. An exchange of angry letters surrounded this event. On February 7, 1920, Wilson wrote: "Is it true, as I have been told, that during my illness you have frequently called the heads of the executive departments of the Government into conference?" The President added ominously, "If it is, I feel it my duty to call your attention to considerations which I do not care to dwell upon . . ." (*The New York Times*, February 14, 1920, p. 1). Lansing responded that he had indeed held informal Cabinet meetings and offered to "relieve" the President of any further "embarrassment" by tendering his resignation if one was wanted (*ibid.*). Wilson declared that Lansing's reply "deepens a feeling" that the Secretary had accepted the President's instructions only "with increasing reluctance" and had, instead, "tried to forestall" his policies. "I must say," the President concluded, "that it would relieve me of embarrassment, Mr. Secretary, the embarrassment of feeling your reluctance and divergence of judgment . . ." (*ibid.*) if there could be a final parting of the ways. Lansing resigned the following day, on February 12.

100. G. B. Shaw, *The Revolutionist's Handbook and Pocket Companion*, "Maxims for Revolutionists (Decency)," *Man and Superman*, in *Selected Plays* (New York: Dodd, Mead and Co., 1948), p. 739.

101. Lansing, *op. cit.*, p. 4.

102. *Ibid.*

103. *Ibid.*, p. 5.

104. *Ibid.*

105. Daniels, *op. cit.*, p. 525.

106. Lansing, *op. cit.*, pp. 268–77.

107. *The New York Times*, March 26, 1921, p. 4.

108. Roosevelt's, "Organizer of the Braintrust," Rexford G. Tugwell, *In Search of Roosevelt* (Cambridge, Mass.: Harvard University Press, 1972), p. 125.

109. Telegram, Hull to Roosevelt, July 11, 1933, P.S.F.: State Department, 1933–1935, Box 70.

110. *The New York Times*, August 29, 1933, p. 16.

111. Raymond Moley, Letter to Thomas Franck, March 24, 1972.

112. *The New York Times*, December 15, 1933, p. 15.

113. Moley, *After Seven Years* (New York: Harcourt and Bros., 1939).

114. Letter from Roosevelt to Owen D. Young, August 9, 1939, P.P.F.: 61, Franklin D. Roosevelt Library.

115. *New York Herald Tribune*, September 24, 1939, part 9, p. 3.

116. Interview with Raymond Moley, Phoenix, Arizona, May 15, 1973.

117. A Roosevelt aide has elaborated this strategy: "Half of a President's suggestions, which theoretically carry the weight of orders, can be safely forgotten by a Cabinet member. And if the President asks about a suggestion a second time, he can be told that it is being investigated. If he asks a third time, a wise Cabinet officer will give him at least part of what

he suggests. But only occasionally, except about the most important matters, do Presidents even get around to asking three times." Jonathan Daniels, *Frontier on the Potomac* (New York: The Macmillan Co., 1946), pp. 31–32.

118. *Musarum Deliciae,* collected by Sir John Mennes and Dr. James Smith, 1656.

119. Eric F. Goldman, *The Tragedy of Lyndon Johnson* (New York: Alfred A. Knopf, 1969), p. 263.

120. In *The New York Times,* December 31, 1973, p. 1.

121. Townsend Hoopes, *The Limits of Intervention* (New York: David McKay Co., 1969), p. 163.

122. Charles Frankel, *op. cit.,* p. 136. One of the problems of staying on for as long as possible in an effort to prevent the worst is that it is often difficult to get off if the worst happens without seeming to repudiate both the colleagues and the policy with which the defector publicly appeared to have been in agreement. This appears to have been a part of Robert McNamara's decision not to go public. William Jennings Bryan, when he quit and criticized the sharp tone of the U.S. rebuke to Germany on the submarine-warfare question, was reminded that he had himself accepted authorship of an earlier, equally harsh note. "Mr. Bryan resigned somewhat too late to save his precious conscience," observed *The New York Times,* June 11, 1915, p. 14.

Chapter 4. Resignation British Style

---

1. Thomas Carlyle, *Heroes and Hero-Worship,* iv, "The Hero as King" (Philadelphia: Henry Altemus, 1920), p. 298.

2. See Chapters 5 and 6.

3. *The Times,* November 23, 1918, p. 7.

4. See Chapter 3.

5. For a discussion of the methodology used in arriving at the British group of resigners studied, see Appendix A.

6. This is a small group compared to the 389 "prime" American resigners studied. The reason why the British group is so much smaller illustrates one key difference between the political systems of the two countries. A recent survey indicates that senior federal political executives stay at their posts for only two to three years. See David T. Stanley, Dean E. Mann, Jameson W. Doig, *Men Who Govern: A Biographical Profile of Federal Political Executives* (Washington, D.C.: The Brookings Institution, 1967), p. 56. They may have served for one or two years, earlier, in a lesser post. They may return again, later, for another stint of two years. But they base their careers on a business or a profession, and government service is regarded more as an avocation, perhaps a duty, and frequently a way to advance careers in law or industry. Thus, resignation from the U.S. government is a frequent, ordinary occurrence and it carries no implication of political dissent or disloyalty, or of moral choice. In Britain, by contrast, politics is in itself frequently a career; members of the government tend to stay at their posts much longer and to have a much greater stake in returning to office as soon and as often as their party's fortunes allow. A person would ordinarily be more careful to preserve his vocation than his avocation. Thus one would expect the Americans to be less fastidious about fouling the nest in the process of making grievances public than their British counterparts, who know no other nest but politics. But the opposite is true. We wanted to know why.

7. There are instances of relatively silent resignations, or public protests postponed until long after the event, but these are rare. Viscount Morley permitted the publication of his eloquent *Memorandum on Resignation* only after his death, fourteen years after he had

resigned from the Asquith government, in August 1914, in passionate opposition to British entry into the war. (John Viscount Morley, *Memorandum on Resignation*, New York: The Macmillan Co., 1928). Anthony Nutting, during the Suez crisis of 1956, permitted himself to be persuaded to postpone going public until the military phase of the crisis was over.

8. 77 H. C. Deb. (5th ser.) 1646, January 12, 1916.

9. The Rt. Hon. Viscount Simon, *Retrospect* (London: Hutchinson and Co., 1952), pp. 107–108.

10. Roy Jenkins, *Asquith: Portrait of a Man and an Era* (New York: Chilmark Press, 1964), p. 388.

11. Hans Daalder, *Cabinet Reform in Britain, 1914–1963* (Stanford, Calif.: Stanford University Press, 1963), pp. 33–34.

12. 75 H. C. Deb. (5th ser.) 535, November 2, 1915.

13. *Ibid.*, 1555, November 15, 1915.

14. *Ibid.*, 536, November 2, 1915.

15. *Ibid.*, 537, November 2, 1915.

16. 77 H. C. Deb. (5th ser.) 240, December 22, 1915.

17. 75 H. C. Deb. (5th ser.) 536, November 2, 1915.

18. J. A. Spender and C. Asquith, *The Life of Herbert Henry Asquith, Lord Oxford and Asquith*, Vol. II (London: Hutchinson and Co., 1932), p. 267.

19. *The Times*, November 9, 1956, p. 10.

20. *Ibid.*, December 15, 1956, p. 2.

21. Anthony Nutting, *No End of a Lesson* (London: Constable and Co., 1967), p. 162.

22. Lord Salisbury resigned in public protest a second time in 1957 from the post of Lord President of the Council and Leader of the Lords, this time in open protest against the release of the leader of the Cypriot decolonialization movement, Archbishop Makarios. *The Times*, March 30, 1957, p. 6.

23. Iain Macleod, *Neville Chamberlain* (London: Frederick Muller Ltd., 1961), p. 211.

24. Anthony Eden (Lord Avon), *Facing the Dictators* (Boston: Houghton Mifflin Co., 1962), p. 563.

25. 332 H. C. Deb. (5th ser.) 49, February 21, 1938.

26. *Ibid.*

27. *Ibid.*, 48.

28. *Ibid.*, 52.

29. 339 H. C. Deb. (5th ser.) 87, October 3, 1938.

30. 345 H. C. Deb. (5th ser.) 461, March 15, 1939.

31. 339 H. C. Deb. (5th ser.) 232–33, October 4, 1938.

32. 341 H. C. Deb. (5th ser.) 214, November 9, 1938.

33. 339 H. C. Deb. (5th ser.) 36, October 3, 1938.

34. *Ibid.*, 40. Another "resigners' creed" was the affecting statement of Mr. Henry G. Strauss, who, on March 1, 1945, resigned from the Churchill government with the words: "I found it impossible to approve of the treatment of the Polish people by the Crimea conference. . . . I hate disagreeing with colleagues with whom I have worked so happily, but, holding the convictions that I hold, I could not honestly take a different course" (*The Times*, March 2, 1945, p. 2). Addressing his constituency party organization he confessed, "My own decision was simple but painful. Simple, because I was asked to approve of an agreement [Yalta] the essential parts of which seemed to me to be unprincipled and wrong; painful because my decision involved giving up work that I loved, ending a happy collaboration with Ministerial colleagues and sacrificing personal ambitions." He added, "Russia respects strength, and not least strength of character" (*ibid.*, April 7, 1945, p. 2). The Prime Minister replied, "[Y]ou have taken an appropriate and becoming course . . ." (*ibid.*, March 2, 1945, p. 2). Strauss's constituency party voted to support his right to act "according to his sincere convictions" (*ibid.*, March 23, 1945, p. 2).

35. *Ibid.*, August 10, 1917, p. 6.

◇

36. Doves as well as hawks have resigned in vigorous protest against the policies of their own governments. The most recent British cabinet "dove" resignation in protest concerning matters of defense and national security was by Christopher Mayhew. Regretting that he must "embarrass an admirable government" (*ibid.*, February 21, 1966, p. 7), he nevertheless openly opposed Prime Minister Wilson's decision to continue to operate a defense establishment "East of Suez" but on a much reduced budget and scale. This, he thought, was the worst of both worlds, producing "an in-between role East of Suez which is still extremely expensive, involves us in serious risks, and makes no equivalent contributions to our national interests" (*ibid.*, February 21, 1966, p. 7). Mayhew made his arguments in the Parliamentary statement, which he called "an old and generous custom" (725 H. C. Deb. (5th ser.) 254, February 22, 1966) and in extensive interviews with the media. In a little over a year, Prime Minister Wilson rescinded Britain's commitments East of Suez. Particularly dramatic among doves is the second resignation of Lord Cecil in August 1927. In resigning, Cecil, then Chancellor of the Duchy of Lancaster in charge of disarmament negotiations, stated that his differences with his government had led him to feel that he could better advance that cause by leaving the cabinet (*The Times*, August 29, 1927, p. 10). He asserted that he was "out of sympathy with the instructions I received" for the Naval Limitations Conference at Geneva and believed that "an agreement might have been reached on terms which would have sacrificed no essential British interest" (*ibid.*, August 30, 1927, p. 10) but that this had been prevented by the cabinet's obdurate nationalism. For a further discussion of the Cecil case, see Chapter 4.

37. 339 H. C. Deb. (5th ser.) 88, October 3, 1938.

38. 144 H. C. Deb. (5th ser.) 1491, July 14, 1921.

39. *Ibid.*

40. *Ibid.*, 2509–2510, July 21, 1921.

41. *Ibid.*

42. *Ibid.*, 2511.

43. *Ibid.*, 2517.

44. Lord Beaverbrook, *The Decline and Fall of Lloyd George* (New York: Duall, Sloan and Pearce, 1963), p. 133.

45. *The Times*, April 23, 1951, p. 4.

46. 487 H. C. Deb. (5th ser.) 37, April 23, 1951.

47. *Ibid.*

48. *Ibid.*, 38.

49. *Ibid.*

50. *Ibid.*, 41.

51. *Ibid.*, 42. Bevan's attack from the left is matched by other fighting resignations from the political right. In 1958, Peter Thorneycroft, the Conservative Chancellor of the Exchequer in the Macmillan government, resigned together with his ministers at the Treasury, J. Enoch Powell and Nigel Birch, over excessive spending on *both* guns and butter. "We have," he said, "been trying to do two things at the same time. First, we have sought to be a nuclear power, matching missile with missile and anti-missile with anti-missile and with large . . . conventional forces in the Far East, the Middle East and the Atlantic at the same time. . . . At the same time we have sought to maintain a Welfare State at as high a level as—sometimes at an even higher level than—that of the United States of America" (580 H. C. Deb. [5th ser.] 1295, January 23, 1958).

52. C. R. Attlee, *As It Happened* (London: William Heinemann, 1954, p. 206). Some sources have suggested that Bevan's resignation was based not on principle but on personal and careerist considerations, a view one of his fellow resigners has described to the authors as part of the truth.

53. *The Times*, April 24, 1951, p. 4.

54. There was, in fact, a third "false dentures" resignation from the Attlee government. John Freeman, the Parliamentary Secretary to the Ministry of Supply, left with Bevan and

Wilson. In his published letter to Wilson he declared himself "deeply disturbed [by] the beginning of a real reduction in our social services. I do not believe," he added, "that a rearmament programme, on anything like the present scale, can be carried out in prevailing conditions, except by the use of measures of priority which would do grave—perhaps permanent—damage to our civil economy. I do not believe it can be right for us . . . to foster a policy which is calculated to rob us of our viability as a nation, to cause a great degree of avoidable hardship among our people . . ." (ibid., April 25, 1951, p. 4). Freeman's subsequent career veered away from government but not, he asserts, because of his resignation. When Harold Wilson became Prime Minister he offered him a cabinet post (interview with Rt. Hon. John Freeman, London, June 6, 1973), which he declined, preferring to represent his country as High Commissioner in India and Ambassador in Washington.

55. 239 H. C. Deb. (5th ser.) 404–405, May 21, 1930.

56. 790 H. C. Deb. (5th ser.) 388, 390, October 30, 1969..

57. See, for example, the resignation and angry polemics concerning the right to strike of Hon. Ray Gunther in 1968 (The Times, July 3, 1968, p. 2).

58. Chancellor of the Exchequer Charles Ritchie resigned, in 1903, to protest against the proposal of Prime Minister Arthur Balfour, not then implemented, to abandon free trade in favor of some measure of imperial preference. Lord Hamilton, the Secretary of State for India, and Lord Balfour of Burleigh, the Secretary for Scotland, joined him in the attack (130 H. L. Debs. (4th ser.) 150, 158, and 162, February 18, 1904). At the same time, Joseph Chamberlain resigned as Colonial Secretary in order to be able to push for imperial preferences (The Times, September 18, 1903, p. 7). In 1932, the imperial preference issue, focused on the Ottawa Agreements, provoked the breakup of the Liberal party, half of their number remaining in the National (Coalition) government and the other half going into opposition. Sir Herbert Samuel, the Home Secretary, was joined in resigning by seven other members of the cabinet and Ministers. Their public attack against the abandonment of free trade was prolonged and relentless.

59. Ibid., September 29, 1932, p. 15.

60. Not going public immediately allows for second thoughts. When Lord Rothermere resigned as Secretary of State for Air in 1918, he at first submitted a stinging letter attacking two fellow Members of Parliament, Sir John Simon and Lord Hugh Cecil, over their criticisms of his dismissal of Lord Trenchard as Chief of Air Staff. Lord Beaverbrook, then Minister of Information, considered this would exacerbate the government's problems and helped Rothermere to draft an innocuous letter, instead. See R. K. Alderman and J. A. Cross, The Tactics of Resignation (London: Routledge and Kegan Paul, 1967), p. 47.

61. Morley, op. cit., pp. 29–30.

62. Randolph S. Churchill, Winston S. Churchill: Youth, 1874–1900 (Boston: Houghton Mifflin Co., 1966), pp. 81–82.

63. The Times, December 15, 1956, p. 2.

64. Ibid., November 17, 1956, p. 3; December 8, 1956, p. 3; interview with Sir Edward Boyle, London, June 8, 1973.

65. The Times, November 7, 1956, p. 6.

66. Ibid., November 15, 1956, p. 6.

67. Interview with Anthony Nutting, London, June 5, 1973. During the Munich prewar days, Lord Cranborne's constituency stood by him. The Council of the South Dorset Conservative and Unionist Association, having heard his explanation, were satisfied that "he had no option but to resign," given his views on the matter (ibid., February 28, 1938, p. 9). Duff Cooper, on the other hand, merely scraped by. His constituency executive committee agreed to "respect his action" in resigning, but also made it a point to "declare themselves in complete agreement with the action of the Prime Minister and with the policy of the Government . . ." (ibid., October 12, 1938, p. 14). Duff Cooper did not, however, consider it incumbent on him to resign his seat. At times, the constituency organization can become fiercely divided over the protest resignation of its member, as did the Leyton

Division Liberals over the decision of Sir John Simon to oppose conscription in World War I. An unofficial group tried but failed to organize a postcard vote campaign to disown their Member (*ibid.*, January 10, 1916, p. 10).

However, the return to the constituency may be merely *pro forma*. The general secretary of Aneurin Bevan's constituency, Ebbw Vale, stated at once that the "resignation of Mr. Bevan from the Government is a matter for Mr. Bevan himself and not for the Ebbw Vale Labour Party to decide" (*ibid.*, April 24, 1951, p. 4). Nevertheless, he welcomed Bevan's desire to discuss his decision with the local party members. Frank Cousins' constituency positively pressed him not to resign from Parliament when he left the government (*ibid.*, July 5, 1966, p. 1; July 7, 1966, p. 1). When Nigel Birch resigned and explained his action to his West Flint organization, he "was given a standing ovation and the meeting was over in 50 minutes" (*ibid.*, January 16, 1958, p. 6). Occasionally, as in the cases of C. Ritchie and Lord George Hamilton, the passionate Free Traders who resigned from the cabinet in public protest in 1903, their return to the constituency took the form less of a seeking after absolution than of a boisterous kickoff in a national campaign to change the policy that precipitated their resignations, complete with mayors, overflow crowds, and ritual singing of "For he's a jolly good fellow!" (*ibid.*, October 10, 1903, p. 10; October 23, 1903, p. 8).

68. Aneurin Bevan, 487 H. C. Deb. (5th ser.) 34, April 23, 1951.

69. *Ibid.*

70. Macleod, *op. cit.*, pp. 60–67.

71. Neville Chamberlain to Hilda Chamberlain, letter, January 7, 1917, in *ibid.*, pp. 66–67.

72. *The Times*, October 7, 1903, p. 4.

73. *Ibid.*, March 30, 1957, p. 6.

74. *Ibid.*, January 10, 1958, p. 8.

75. *Ibid.*, April 23, 1951, p. 4.

76. *Ibid.*, April 25, 1951, p. 4.

77. A full account of Bevan's resignation is in Michael Foot, *Aneurin Bevan: A Biography, 1945–1960* (New York: Atheneum, 1973), pp. 283–349.

78. Permission to reveal secrets, given by the Crown as a courtesy to a resigning minister, is in theory applicable only to the issues immediately relevant to the resignation. The Prime Minister complained to Queen Victoria that he had had to interrupt Mr. Chamberlain during his resignation speech to inform him that he had gone too far and was discussing a subject not within the scope of the permission granted him by the Queen. The Queen, in the instance, replied that Mr. Chamberlain's conduct had been "most proper." (See G. E. Burkle, ed., *Letters of Queen Victoria*, 3rd series, vol. 1 [London: John Murray, 1930], pp. 100–105). However, Victoria was stricter with Lord Derby in enforcing another rule: that permission given to reveal secrets in connection with a resignation are for one Parliamentary debate only and "that the permission thus given should only serve for the particular instance and [should] not be considered an open license." Burkle, *op. cit.*, 2d series, vol. 2 (1928), pp. 631–32.

79. Winston S. Churchill, *Lord Randolph Churchill*, Vol. 2 (New York: The Macmillan Co., 1906), pp. 255–56.

80. Discussed above, pp. 99–100.

81. 75 H. C. Deb. (5th ser.) 1499–1521, November 15, 1915.

82. In another case, Labourite Minister Arthur Henderson, resigning during World War I (1917) in disagreement with the Lloyd George Coalition government's opposition about his participation in a meeting of Socialist parties at Stockholm, made equally indiscreet public statements. The Stockholm meeting had been intended as an unofficial effort to end the war and Henderson, in defending it, revealed top-secret communications from, and initiatives by, the Russian government which he considered helpful to his case. He also revealed the content of discussions on the subject of the Conference held by the War Cabinet, acknowl-

edging only: "I know that I am treading on delicate ground" (97 H. C. Deb. [5th ser.] 913, August 13, 1917).

83. *The Times*, August 30, 1927, p. 10.

84. Viscount Cecil of Chelwood, *All the Way* (London: Hodder and Stoughton Ltd., 1949), p. 191.

85. 69 H. L. Deb. 91, November 16, 1927.

86. *Ibid.*

87. *Ibid.*, col. 92.

88. *Ibid.*, col. 90.

89. Macleod, *op. cit.*, pp. 213–14.

90. 332 H. C. Deb. (5th ser.) 48, February 21, 1938. See also *The Times*, February 28, 1938, p. 9, in which Cranborne further discloses the "take it or leave it" nature of Mussolini's invitation to Chamberlain.

91. Simon, *op. cit.*, p. 244.

92. Official Secrets Act, 1911, s. 2.

93. See Harry Street, "Secrecy and the Citizen's Right to Know: A British Civil Libertarian Perspective," in Thomas M. Franck and Edward Weisband, eds., *Secrecy and Foreign Policy* (New York: Oxford University Press, 1974), ch. 19, pp. 332–50.

94. Cmnd. 5104, Departmental Committee on Section 2 of the Official Secrets Act, 1911 (The Franks Report), September 1972, London, H.M.S.O.

95. The existence of a formal exception has been denied by Prime Minister Asquith. 73 H. C. Deb. (5th ser.) 1160 (1915). However, the practice denies Asquith's view. The vivid public disclosures of ministers quitting Lloyd George's wartime Coalition and the Labour government of 1929–31 were not prosecuted. See 86 H. L. Deb. (5th ser.) 522 (1932). Mr. Swift MacNeill observed in a speech to Parliament that in "the whole history of the criminal law a cabinet minister has never been betrayed for giving away secrets, or how many guilty men there would be!" See 82 H. C. Deb. (5th ser.) 1411 (1916).

The *de facto* immunity of Parliamentarians was further and dramatically illustrated when an OSA prosecution was brought, in 1934, against the son of the former Minister, George Lansbury. He was fined for violation of section 2 of the Act, having published hitherto secret cabinet information in a biography of his father. In the terse words of the Franks Committee, "His father was recognized as having given them to him, but was not prosecuted." See Cmnd. 5104, *op. cit.*, p. 116.

These incidents raised, but did not finally resolve, the issue of the scope of the OSA in relation to Parliamentary Privilege. That issue was resolved in 1939 as a result of what came to be known as the "Sandys Storm." Duncan Sandys, then a young backbench MP, and a captain in the territorial Army as well, had received information from a superior officer concerning the sparsity of antiaircraft guns in the vicinity of London. Sandys drew up a proposed Parliamentary Question in the course of which he would have revealed these figures. He sent the proposed Question off to the War Department in an attempt to provoke them into rectifying the situation. The question was never publicly asked, but the government's response was a request by the Attorney-General—citing the then section 6 of the 1920 OSA duty to disclose who had revealed secret information—that Sandys divulge the source of his data. Sandys declined and complained to the House of his own government's threat to prosecute him under the OSA. 348 H. C. Deb. (5th ser.) 207 (1939). In the aftermath of a heated debate the issue was referred to a Select Committee of the House. That Committee made two reports, the first of which dealt with the conduct of Sandys and the Attorney-General and the facts of the immediate cause of the dispute. *Report and Proceedings of the Committee of Privileges;* 1937–38 (146) vii. 591. The second dealt with the effect of the OSA on Parliamentary Privilege. *Report of the Select Committee on the Official Secrets Acts;* 1938–39 (101) viii. That report, which was agreed to by a House resolution, concluded that no disclosures by Members of Parliament during debates or proceedings in Parliament, nor disclosures made between Members relating to House of Commons business—whether in the House or not—could ever be made the subject of proceedings under the OSA. 353 H. C. Deb. (5th ser.) 1084 (1939). The House of Lords was even more blunt. It resolved "that the extent to which privilege extends immunity to members of the House of Lords from prosecution is not affected by the operation of the Official Secrets Acts of 1911 and 1920." 114 H. L. Deb. (5th ser.) 315–16 (1939).

96. Title 18, U.S. Code, §793, 794.

97. See Benno Schmidt, "The Espionage Statutes and Publication of Defense Information," in Franck and Weisband, eds., *op. cit.*, ch. 11, pp. 179–201.

98. *United States* v. *New York Times Corporation,* 403 U.S. 713 (1971).

99. See Appendix B, Fig. 4.

100. See Appendix B, Fig. 5.

101. *Ibid.*

Chapter 5. A Cabinet of Yea-Sayers

---

1. Alexander Galech, *The New York Times,* February 12, 1972, p. 29.

2. James Madison in The Federalist No. 51 in Henry Steele Commager, ed., *Selections from The Federalist: A Commentary on the Constitution of the United States* (New York: Appleton-Century Crofts, Inc., 1949), p. 86. Also sometimes attributed to Hamilton; for example, see Edward Mead Earle, ed., *The Federalist* (New York: The Modern Library, 1937), p. 335.

3. *Ibid.*

4. For an excellent historical survey of this process, and its acceleration in recent years, see Arthur M. Schlesinger, Jr., *The Imperial Presidency* (Boston: Houghton Mifflin Co., 1973).

5. Woodrow Wilson, "Cabinet Government in the United States" (1879), in Arthur S. Link, ed., *The Papers of Woodrow Wilson,* vol. 1, 1856–80 (Princeton, N.J.: Princeton University Press, 1966), pp. 493–510 at 495.

6. Interview with William C. Clark, formerly Member of the Staff, the Prime Minister's Office, New York, February 24, 1973.

7. *The Times,* March 16, 1968, p. 1.

8. Patrick Gordon Walker, *The Cabinet* (rev. ed., London: Fontana/Collins, 1972), p. 93.

9. Stanley A. deSmith, *Constitutional and Administrative Law* (Harmondsworth: Penguin Books, 1971), p. 168.

10. Walker, *op. cit.,* pp. 93–94.

11. *Ibid.,* p. 96.

12. Harry M. Daugherty, *The Inside Story of the Harding Tragedy* (New York: The Churchill Co., 1932), pp. 71–72.

13. *Ibid.,* p. 209. The Daugherty references are cited in Richard F. Fenno, Jr., *The President's Cabinet* (Cambridge, Mass.: Harvard University Press, 1963), pp. 57, 66.

14. Robert Keith Gray, *Eighteen Acres under Glass* (New York: Doubleday and Co., 1962), p. 258; Gray served in the Eisenhower Administration as Secretary to the Cabinet.

15. Theodore C. Sorensen, *Kennedy* (New York: Harper and Row, 1965), pp. 251–90.

16. Charles Frankel, *High on Foggy Bottom* (New York: Harper and Row, 1968), p. 53.

17. Bill Moyers as cited in Charles Roberts, *LBJ's Inner Circle* (New York: Delacorte Press, 1965), p. 50.

18. Irving L. Janis, *Victims of Groupthink* (Boston: Houghton Mifflin Co., 1972), p. 12.

19. *Ibid.,* p. 13. Italics deleted.

20. Thomas M. Franck and Edward Weisband, "When It's Time to Leave," *The New York Times,* July 27, 1973, p. 31.

21. *The Washington Post,* August 2, 1973, p. A22.
22. Pierre Salinger, *With Kennedy* (New York: Doubleday, 1966), p. 63.
23. Sorensen tells a story—one he evidently considers amusing yet essentially illustrative of an admirable ethic—about Dean Rusk's loyalty to Kennedy, how it overrode even common sense or the natural urge to protest against an apparently outrageous Presidential foray into foreign relations: "His [Rusk's] loyalty was early demonstrated when I solemnly handed him . . . a clipping from a Costa Rican newspaper which contained, on that nation's equivalent of April Fool's Day, a faked photograph and news story to the effect that President-elect Kennedy, 'on his way' to Palm Beach, had stopped off in San Jose to promise an outsized foreign aid grant. Rusk looked at the bogus clipping and nodded gravely that any commitment made would have to be kept. Although he later proved to possess a wry sense of humor, he looked more reassured than amused when I confessed it was a hoax" (Sorensen, *op. cit.,* pp. 270–71).
24. *Ibid.,* p. 256.
25. *Ibid.* The speech is in Shakespeare's *Henry V,* Act IV, Scene 3.
26. Sorensen, *op. cit.,* p. 304.
27. Schlesinger, *A Thousand Days* (Boston: Houghton Mifflin, 1965), pp. 258–59.
28. Janis, *op. cit.,* p. 42, quoting (but not citing) Schlesinger.
29. Eric F. Goldman, *The Tragedy of Lyndon Johnson* (New York: Alfred A. Knopf, 1969), pp. 262–63.
30. *Ibid.*
31. United States, Senate Foreign Relations Committee, *U.S. Commitments to Foreign Powers: Hearings,* 90 Cong., I Sess. (1967), pp. 82, 141.
32. Interview with Nicholas deB. Katzenbach, New York City, April 15, 1971.
33. For the pre-eminent role of President-elect Kennedy in selecting second-echelon personnel for his departments, see Sorensen, *op. cit.,* pp. 254–55.
34. *The New York Times,* August 25, 1974, p. 33.
35. George E. Reedy, *The Twilight of the Presidency* (New York: The World Publishing Co., 1970), p. 14.
36. *Ibid.,* p. 169.
37. Sorensen, *op. cit.,* p. 256.
38. Frankel, *op. cit.,* p. 109.
39. Reedy, *op. cit.,* p. 196.
40. Emmet John Hughes, *The Ordeal of Power* (New York: Atheneum, 1963), p. 73.
41. Sorensen, *op. cit.,* p. 256.
42. *Ibid.,* p. 264.
43. Harry McPherson, *A Political Education* (Boston: Little, Brown and Co., 1972), p. 252.
44. Frankel, *op. cit.,* pp. 85–86.
45. *Ibid.,* p. 108.
46. *Ibid.,* p. 57.
47. Theodore J. Lowi, *The Politics of Disorder* (New York: Basic Books, 1971), p. xiv.
48. *Ibid.*
49. *Ibid.*
50. *Ibid.,* p. xvi.
51. *Ibid.,* p. xv.
52. Chester Bowles, *Promises to Keep: My Years in Public Life, 1941–1969* (New York: Harper and Row, 1971), p. 354.
53. *Ibid.,* p. 343.
54. Thomas Babington Macaulay, "On John Dryden," in *Edinburgh Review* (January 1828).
55. Reedy, *op. cit.,* pp. 77–78.
56. Walker, *op. cit.* pp. 91–95, 107–111.

57. Edward George Bulwer-Lytton, *What Will He Do with It.* Bk. III, ch. 15.

58. McPherson, *op. cit.,* p. 258. Verification has been obtained in numerous interviews.

59. Reedy, *op. cit.,* p. 80.

60. Interview with George W. Ball, Washington, D.C., May 1, 1973.

61. Cordell Hull, *The Memoirs of Cordell Hull,* vol. 1 (New York: The Macmillan Co., 1948), pp. 196, 199.

62. *Ibid.*

63. Gray, *op. cit.,* p. 262.

64. Sorensen, *op. cit.,* p. 262.

65. Salinger, *op. cit.,* p. 74.

66. Sorensen, *op. cit.,* p. 283.

67. *Ibid.*

68. Reedy, *op. cit.,* p. 73.

69. By 1878, Prime Minister Lord Salisbury was able to state: "For all that passes in Cabinet, each member of it who does not resign is absolutely and irretrievably responsible. . . ." Lady Gwendolyn Cecil, *Life of Robert, Marquis of Salisbury,* Vol. 2 (London: Hodder and Stoughton, 1921–1931), p. 219.

70. Interview with Anthony Nutting, London, June 5, 1973. Eden has subsequently attributed the transfer to solicitude over Monckton's failing health (Anthony Eden, *Full Circle: Memoirs* [Boston: Houghton Mifflin Co., 1960], p. 580), while, paradoxically, Monckton, during the crisis, believed that the Prime Minister "was a very sick man" (Anthony Nutting, *No End of a Lesson* [London: Constable and Co., 1967], p. 107). He appears also to have hinted to U.S. Ambassador Winthrop Aldrich before the actual outbreak of hostilities that a great blunder was afoot. (Kennett Love, *Suez: The Twice-Fought War* [New York: McGraw-Hill Book Co., 1969], p. 447). After the Suez debacle, Monckton went quietly from the Commons to the House of Lords and, although he never spoke publicly of the matter, his dissociation from the disastrous Eden policy was generally known in British political circles.

71. See note 69.

72. Jesse Jones and Edward Angly, *Fifty Billion Dollars* (New York: The Macmillan Co., 1951), p. 303.

73. *The Times,* July 4, 1966, p. 1.

74. According to another study of top federal executives, the median period of service of these men and women is 37 months; see David T. Stanley, Dean E. Mann, Jameson W. Doig, *Men Who Govern: A Biographical Profile of Federal Political Executives* (Washington, D.C.: The Brookings Institution, 1967), p. 56.

75. A pioneering development of concepts of *voice* and *exit* is to be found in Albert O. Hirschman, *Exit, Voice and Loyalty: Responses to Decline in Firms, Organizations, and States* (Cambridge, Mass.: Harvard University Press, 1970).

76. On the other end of the scale, academics and educators, who make up the third largest occupational group (11.1 per cent), provided 26.5 per cent of all American public-protest resignations. Of the 43 academics and educators in the total group studied, slightly more than one in five (20.9 per cent) resigned and spoke out. Although the propensities of trade unionists and journalists to go public seem statistically high, they make up only an insignificant percentage of the group studied, as do all other professional categories. Only a very small number—2.4 per cent—of the "prime" resigners we studied are professional civil servants. None of these ever resigned with public protest.

77. William H. Whyte, *The Organization Man* (New York: Simon and Schuster, 1956), p. 129.

78. David Finn, *The Corporate Oligarch* (New York: Simon and Schuster, 1969), p. 153.

79. Hirschman, *op. cit.,* pp. 15–19.

80. *Ibid.,* p. 37.

81. Another, related reason why the business-resignation ethic is inappropriate to government is that no one can truly exit from the latter. In the realm of public goods, we are all consumers, and none can boycott the producer or go comparison shopping. The Secretary of the Treasury who resigns in protest against a fiscal policy and returns to his banking career continues in private life to be subject to that policy, only with the difference that he can no longer hope to affect that policy from within. But the silence of a resigner from government cannot be justified on the ground that the policy with which he disagreed is "no longer any of his business." On the contrary, it crucially affects his business, probably more than when he was temporarily out of banking and his private investment portfolio was being held in trust.

82. Interview with Townsend Hoopes, New York City, December 9, 1971.

83. American Bar Association, *Canons of Professional and Judicial Ethics,* adopted in 1908 and updated to 1965 (Summit, N.J.: Martindale-Hubbell, Inc.), p. 6.

84. For discussion see Gleason L. Archer, *Ethical Obligations of the Lawyer* (Boston: Little, Brown and Co., 1910), p. 132.

85. George W. Warvelle, *Essays in Legal Ethics,* 2nd ed. (Chicago: Callaghan and Co., 1920), p. 168.

86. Joel Carlin, *Lawyers' Ethics* (New York: Russell Sage Foundation for the City Bar of New York, 1966), *passim;* also see other basic texts on lawyers' ethics which illustrate this point, e.g., Henry S. Drinker's authoritative work *Legal Ethics* (New York: Columbia University Press, 1953); Josiah Henry Benton, *The Lawyers Official Oath of Office* (Boston: The Boston Book Co., 1909); Corrine Lathrop Gilb, *Hidden Hierarchies: The Professions and the Government* (New York: Harper and Row, Inc., 1966); Gerald A. Davis, "The Attorney-Client Privilege: The Remedy of Contempt," *Wisconsin Law Review,* Winter 1968, 1195; Edwin Bolte, *Ethical Success at the Bar* (Baltimore: Waverly Press, 1925); Henry Wynans Jessup, *The Professional Ideals of the Lawyer* (New York: G. A. Jennings Co., Inc., 1925); William Howard Taft, *Ethics in Service* (New Haven: Yale University Press, 1915); Warvelle, *op. cit.;* and Edward P. Weeks, *A Treatise on Attorneys and Counselors at Law* (San Francisco: Sumner, Whitney and Co., 1878). For behavioral oriented studies of the attitudes of attorneys consult Orie L. Phillips and Philbrick McCoy in *Conduct of Judges and Lawyers: A Study of Professional Ethics, Discipline, and Disbarment* (Los Angeles: Parker and Co., 1952); Joel F. Handler, *The Lawyer and His Community* (Madison: The University of Wisconsin Press, 1967); and Albert P. Blaustein and Charles O. Porter, *The American Lawyer* (Chicago: The University of Chicago Press, 1954).

87. Several studies have examined "role-strains" and the problems created by conflicting obligations in the legal profession. Edwin M. Schur in *Law and Society* (New York: Random House, 1968), pp. 172–75, for example, describes the dilemmas arising out of the circumstances of representing a corporate client and exposing information which may protect the securities-buying public, or between acting as a "free professional" and a public servant; also see Talcott Parsons, "The Law and Social Control," in William M. Evan, ed., *Law and Sociology* (Glencoe: The Free Press of Glencoe, 1962), and Martin Mayer, *The Lawyers* (New York: Harper and Row, 1966).

88. Dean E. Mann, *The Assistant Secretaries: Problems and Processes of Appointment* (Washington, D.C.: The Brookings Institution, 1965), pp. 31–32.

89. David Halberstam, *The Best and the Brightest* (New York: Random House, 1969), p. 497; *The New York Times,* March 12, 1971, p. 37, column of C. L. Sulzberger; James C. Thomson Jr., "How Could Vietnam Happen? An Autopsy," *Atlantic Monthly* (April 1968), p. 49.

90. Ball often spoke warmly of the adversary system within the Johnson White House which cast him in the role of dove's advocate. *The New York Times,* June 27, 1966, p. 6.

91. Viewed from the outside, however, Ball's role was to convince the public that the continued escalation of the Vietnam war after 1965 had only been undertaken after all the evidence to the contrary had been fully presented and weighed by the President. While

briefly out of office, in 1968, Ball published a book which received much attention. But its ground rules are set out in the introduction: "this is not a memoir. It reveals no state secrets. It discloses no personal confidences" (George W. Ball, *The Discipline of Power* [Boston: Atlantic Monthly Press, 1968], p. 3) and, more seriously, it offers no criticism. "I shall shoot no bullets or even arrows at my old colleagues, for whom I have both affection and respect," he wrote; "criticism is easy . . . and it would unfairly disparage the intelligence and imagination of the men and women I worked with . . ." (*ibid.*, p. 344). In the book, he admits differing with Johnson over the efficacy of bombing the North and believes it to have "impaired the moral authority of the United States . . ." (*ibid.*, p. 321). But he is equally willing to concede that from the President's perspective, bombing may have been his only viable option. "I know," he wrote, "that the actions we are now taking were decided by the President only after the most searching and prayerful study of all the alternatives" (*ibid.*, p. 308). The bombing was ordered only after "all the issues were exposed to the full benefits of an adversary process" (*ibid.*, p. 321).

92. Interview with Ramsey Clark, New York City, October 10, 1973.

93. Dean Acheson, *Morning and Noon* (Boston: Houghton Mifflin Co., 1962), p. 195.

94. See Blaustein and Porter, *op. cit.*, p. 44.

95. *Ibid.*

96. Canons, *op. cit.*, number 37, p. 6.

97. *Ibid.*, number 32.

98. *Ibid.*, number 41.

99. *Ibid.*, number 15.

100. Senate Judiciary Committee Hearings on the Watergate Matter, July 11, 1973. *The Washington Post*, July 12, 1973, p. A13.

101. Eulau and Sprague, however, state that a confidential communication "must not be made public even if . . . the public interest might require it." Heinz Eulau and John D. Sprague, *Lawyers in Politics* (New York: The Bobbs-Merrill Co., 1964), p. 89.

102. Mann, *op. cit.*, pp. 27–30.

103. For a confirmation of the finding that the large preponderance of the appointees to these upper echelons have preponderant careers outside government, see Harold Seidman, *Politics, Position and Power: The Dynamics of Federal Organization* (New York: Oxford University Press, 1970), pp. 104–106.

104. For recent studies of the British civil service, see R. H. S. Brown, *The Administrative Process in Britain* (London: Methuen, 1970); G. A. Campbell, *The Civil Service in Britain* (London: Penguin Books, 1955); of particular interest is C. K. Fry's *Statesmen in Disguise: The Changing Role of the Administrative Class of the Home Civil Service* (London: Macmillan and Co., Ltd., 1969). For a discussion of the classical role of the British civil servant as nonpolitical, consult C. H. Sisson, *The Spirit of British Administration*, 2nd ed. (London: Faber and Faber, 1966). The organization of the British civil service for much of the period under review is conveniently depicted in F. M. G. Willson, *The Organization of British Central Government, 1914–1964*, 2nd ed. (London: Allen and Unwin, 1968). For an analysis of the relative political influence in British government of members of the civil service as opposed to elected officials, see Richard Rose, "The Variability of Party Government: A Theoretical and Empirical Critique," *Political Studies*, 17 (1969), pp. 413–45. In this regard also see James B. Christoph, "Political Rights and Administrative Impartiality in the British Civil Service," *American Political Science Review*, 51 (March 1957), 67–87.

105. Frankel, *op. cit.*, p. 109.

106. The version cited is from *The Oxford Book of Light Verse* (New York: Oxford University Press, 1938), pp. 260–62.

107. See Frederick C. Mosher, *Democracy and the Public Service* (New York: Oxford University Press, 1968); Francis E. Rourke, *Bureaucracy, Politics and Public Policy* (Boston: Little, Brown and Co, 1969); David T. Stanley, *The Higher Civil Service* (Washington, D.C.: The Brookings Institution, 1964); Lloyd W. Warner, Paul P. Van Riper, Norman H. Martin, and Orvis F. Collins, *The American Federal Executive* (New Haven: Yale

University Press, 1963); also consult Seidman, *op. cit.;* Michel Crozier, *The Bureaucratic Phenomenon* (Chicago: The University of Chicago Press, 1963); and Robert Presthus, *The Organizational Society—An Analysis and a Theory* (New York: Alfred A. Knopf, 1962).

108. The composition, character, and influence of the upper class in America has been the subject of considerable study and debate. C. Wright Mills in his pioneer study *The Power Elite* (New York: Oxford University Press, 1956), p. 11, observes: "The people of the higher circles may also be conceived as members of a top social stratum, as a set of groups whose members know one another, see one another socially and at business, and so, in making decisions, take one another into account. The elite, according to this conception, feel themselves to be, and are felt by others to be, the inner circle of 'the upper social classes.' They form a more or less compact social and psychological entity; they have become self-conscious members of a social class. People are either accepted into this class or they are not, and there is a qualitative split, rather than merely a numerical scale, separating them from those who are not elite. They are more or less aware of themselves as a social class and they behave toward one another differently from the way they do toward members of other classes. They accept one another, tend to work and to think if not together at least alike." A more reserved appraisal is that of Arnold M. Rose in *The Power Structure: Political Process in American Society* (New York: Oxford University Press, 1967), who observes (p. 2) that "Segments of the economic elite have violated democratic and legal processes with differing degrees of effort and success in the various periods of American history, but in no recent period could they correctly be said to have controlled the elected and appointed political authorities in large measure. . . . Further, neither the economic elite nor the political authorities are monolithic units which act with internal consensus and coordinated action with regard to each other (or probably in any other way). In fact there are several economic elites which only very rarely act as units within themselves and among themselves. . . ." Also see Robert A. Dahl, "A Critique of the Power Elite Method," *American Political Science Review,* 52 (June 1958), 463–69, and Dahl's *Who Governs?* (New Haven: Yale University Press, 1961); finally, for a general review, consult T. B. Bottomore, *Elites and Society* (Baltimore: Pelican Books, Inc., 1966), pp. 126–27.

109. Stanley, Mann, and Doig found that at a time when only 6 or 7 per cent of the United States population went to private schools, over 20 per cent of the top federal executives had done so. Nearly half of these attended one or more of the best-known prep schools in the East. Stanley, Mann, and Doig used the following schools for this category: Avon Old Farms, Choate, Deerfield, Groton, Hill, Hotchkiss, Kent, Lawrenceville, Loomis, Middlesex, Milton, Phillips Andover, Phillips Exeter, St. George's, St. Mark's, St. Paul's, Taft, and Thatcher. *Op. cit.,* pp. 20–21.

110. These are the most rigorous of Domhoff's seven criteria of upper-class status. G. William Domhoff, *Who Rules America?* (Englewood Cliffs, N.J.: Prentice-Hall, Inc., 1967). These indicators are explained in Appendix C.

111. The reference is cited in Nicholas Tomalin, "Yesterday's Fad," *New Statesman* (June 29, 1973), pp. 959, 960. The article deals amusingly with the phenomenon of the upper class's dilemma.

112. Thorstein Veblen, *The Theory of the Leisure Class: An Economic Study of Institutions* (New York: The Modern Library, Inc., 1931), first published in 1899, p. 104.

113. Sorensen, *op. cit.,* p. 271.

114. *Ibid.*

115. *Ibid.,* p. 255.

116. Interview with Thomas L. Hughes, New York, April 20, 1971.

117. For the classic if brief comparative analysis of the British and American "ladders" to high position in government, see Richard E. Neustadt's "White House and Whitehall," no. 2, *The Public Interest* (Winter 1966), pp. 55–69.

118. A person is in the upper class in Britain for the purpose of this study if he or she attended one of four exclusive public schools: Eton, Harrow, Winchester, or Rugby; or if

he or she holds a hereditary peerage or any title derived by virtue of being the child of a hereditary peer.

Chapter 6. Saying Yes to Saying No: The Power of Negative Thinking

---

1. In Townsend Hoopes's opinion, McNamara "could have split government bureaucracy had he wanted to take really public issue with the President about the war." Interview, New York City, December 9, 1972.

2. For an exposition of the failure of the parties to offer meaningful choices to the public see David S. Broder, *The Party's Over: The Failure of Politics in America* (New York: Harper & Row, 1971).

3. *"Die Ja Sager und die Nein Sager."*

4. Henry David Thoreau, *On the Duty of Civil Disobedience,* 8th ed. (New York: Rinehart and Co., 1958), p. 281.

5. Barbara Tuchman in *The New York Times,* February 13, 1973, p. 37.

6. John C. Calhoun, *A Discourse on the Constitution and Government of the United States* (New York: D. Appleton and Co., 1853), pp. 392–93.

7. For a full discussion in reference to this proposal, see Herman Finer, *The Presidency: Crisis and Regeneration* (Chicago: The University of Chicago Press, 1960), pp. 303–318.

8. See James McGregor Burns, *Presidential Government: The Crucible of Leadership* (Boston: Houghton Mifflin Co., 1965), p. 48.

9. This evolution is traced in Woodrow Wilson, *Constitutional Government in the United States* (New York: Columbia University Press, 1908), pp. 74–77.

10. Richard F. Fenno, Jr., *The President's Cabinet* (Cambridge, Mass.: Harvard University Press, 1963), p. 164.

11. *Ibid.,* pp. 164–67. Only persons with highly specialized interests in government ever mastered the distinction between Charles E. Wilson of General Electric, who was Truman's Director of Defense Mobilization, and Eisenhower's Secretary of Defense, Charles E. Wilson of General Motors. Perhaps that is not surprising. But opinion polls also show that 55 per cent of the public in 1937 had "no opinion" of Harry H. Woodring, Roosevelt's then-incumbent Secretary of War; and in 1943, 34 per cent had never heard of the Secretary of Agriculture, Claude R. Wickard. After four years in office, 72 per cent of the public did not know of George M. Humphrey, Eisenhower's rather active Secretary of the Treasury. (These statistics are cited in *ibid.,* p. 165.)

12. Interview with Roger Hilsman, New York City, April 5, 1971.

13. Interview with Robert W. Barnett, New York City, October 27, 1970.

14. Quoted in Charles Peters and Taylor Branch, *Blowing the Whistle: Dissent in the Public Interest* (New York: Praeger, 1972), p. 283.

15. Joseph P. Tumulty, *Woodrow Wilson as I Know Him* (New York: Doubleday, Page and Co., 1921), p. 445.

16. *New York Post,* August 30, 1973, p. 28.

17. In Canada, to take the British case to a further level of development, the cabinet is an extraordinarily complex balance of regional, religious, and ethnic factors. Thus, a Canadian Prime Minister should always strive to have a balance of cabinet members from the Maritime Provinces, Quebec, Ontario, the Prairies, and British Columbia. Within these categories, he must strive to appoint an English-speaking member from French Quebec, a Catholic from Protestant Ontario, and a woman or two. Each cabinet member thus "represents" a large "constituency" in a "federation" of regional, religious, ethnic, and gender interests, wielding independent power accordingly.

18. Thomas K. Finletter, *Can Representative Government Do the Job?* (New York: Reynal and Hitchcock, 1945), see esp., chapter 11, "A Joint Executive-Legislative Cabinet," pp. 88–105; Charles S. Hyneman, *Bureaucracy in a Democracy* (New York: Harper and Bros., 1950), pp. 571–74; Edward S. Corwin, *The President: Office and Powers, 1787–1957* (New York: New York University Press, 1957), pp. 297–98.

19. Woodrow Wilson, "Cabinet Government in the United States," in Arthur S. Link, ed., *The Papers of Woodrow Wilson*, vol. 1, 1856–80 (Princeton, N.J.: Princeton University Press, 1966), p. 494.

20. *Ibid.*, p. 497.

21. Woodrow Wilson, "Committee or Cabinet Government?" (c. Jan. 1, 1884) in Link, ed., *op. cit.*, vol. 2, 1881–1884 (1967), pp. 614–40 at 627. For further elaboration of the case for "responsible cabinet government" of the British model, see Henry Hazlitt, *A New Constitution Now* (New York: McGraw-Hill Book Co., 1942), pp. 107–187; C. Perry Patterson, *Presidential Government in the United States: The Unwritten Constitution* (Chapel Hill: The University of North Carolina Press, 1947), esp. pp. 245–66.

22. For an incisive elaboration of the arguments against "responsible cabinet government," see Don K. Price, "The Parliamentary and Presidential Systems," 3, *Public Administration Review*, no. 4 (Autumn 1943), 317–34.

23. The burden of multiple tasks would reinforce, however, the position that cabinet posts not be held simultaneously by senior members of the Congressional establishment: the party leaders and whips, committee chairmen, and ranking minority members.

24. Henry Barrett Learned, *The President's Cabinet: Studies in the Origin, Formation and Structure of an American Institution* (New Haven: Yale University Press, 1912), p. 5.

25. *Ibid.*, p. 4.

26. Corwin, *op. cit.*, p. 298.

27. See note 14.

Chapter 7. Growing Up toward Ethical Autonomy

---

1. Jean Piaget, *The Moral Judgment of the Child* (New York: The Free Press, 1965), p. 290.

2. *Ibid.*, pp. 290–293.

3. Dorothy Barclay, "What Tattling Really Tells," *The New York Times*, August 12, 1962, Section VI, p. 46.

4. Piaget, *op. cit.*, pp. 294–95.

5. Charles Peters and Taylor Branch, *Blowing the Whistle: Dissent in the Public Interest* (New York: Praeger, 1972), p. 19.

6. *Ibid.*, p. 230.

7. Lawrence Kohlberg, "The Development of Modes of Moral Thinking and Choice in the Years 10 to 16" (Ph.D. dissertation, University of Chicago, 1958), pp. 339, 346.

8. Pressures to uniformity in groups is comprehensively analyzed in Dorwin Cartwright and Alvin Zander, eds., *Group Dynamics*, 3rd ed. (New York: Harper & Row, 1968), esp. pp. 139–51.

9. Peter Maas, *Serpico* (New York: The Viking Press, 1973), p. 23.

10. Barclay, *op. cit.*

11. See, for example, Piaget, *op. cit.*, and the works of Kohlberg, including *op. cit.*, and "Development of Moral Character and Moral Ideology," in M. L. and L. W. Hoffman, *Review of Child Development Research* (New York: Russell Sage Foundation, 1964); "Stage and Sequence: The Cognitive-Developmental Approach to Socialization," in David Goslin, *Handbook of Socialization Theory and Research* (Chicago: Rand McNally, 1969); for other writers that differ in some respects with Piaget and Kohlberg but confirm the

validity of their observations as stated above regarding the nature and development of principled autonomous judgment in children, consult Robert Peck and Robert Havighurst, *The Psychology of Character Development* (New York: John Wiley and Sons, 1964); Havighurst and Hilda Taba, *Adolescent Character and Personality* (New York: John Wiley and Sons, 1967); Elizabeth B. Hurlock, *Child Development*, 4th ed. (New York: McGraw-Hill, 1964); William A. Kay, *Moral Development: A Psychological Study of Moral Growth from Childhood to Adolescence* (New York: Schocken Books, 1969).

12. Joseph H. Moskowitz and Bertram I. Spector, "Profiles of the Growler and the Insider: Two Styles of Dissent in Government," New York University Center for International Studies, unpub. manuscript, 1974.

13. Kohlberg, dissertation, pp. 140–142: Richard Kramer, "Changes in Moral Judgment Response Patterns During Late Adolescence and Young Adulthood: Retrogression in a Developmental Sequence" (Ph.D. dissertation, University of Chicago, 1968), p. 44; Kohlberg and Kramer, "Continuities and Discontinuities in Childhood and Adult Moral Development," *Human Development*, vol. 12, 1969, 100–101.

Appendix A. Methodology for Selection of the American and British Executive and Ministerial Appointees Studied

---

1. The number of Echelon II and III personnel in government is very small at the beginning of the century and rises rapidly after the first half of the period we have studied. The first undersecretaryship was created in 1919. In 1933 there were only four undersecretaries and 25 assistant secretaries; by 1961 there were 17 and 64 respectively. Dean E. Mann, *The Assistant Secretaries* (Washington, D.C.: The Brookings Institution, 1965), p. 66.

2. 53 Stat. 561.

3. In 1901 the White House staff consisted of only three secretaries—plus six clerks and a few doorkeepers and messengers whom we omit from the survey. Leonard D. White, *The Republican Era* (New York: The Macmillan Co., 1958), p. 102. The Executive Office of the President was established only in 1939 by F. D. Roosevelt's Plan No. 1 under the Reorganization Act of 1939.

4. Andrew Geddes (Agriculture); W. Blair Taylor (Post Office); James R. Riggs (Agriculture); Thomas J. Howell (Post Office); Carl Schuneman (Treasury); Garrison Norton (State); R. E. Short (Agriculture); A. Gilmore Fleus (Treasury); Norman Ross Abrams (Post Office); Frank Barton (Commerce); Ramsey S. Black (Post Office); Moris Burge (Interior); William F. Cronin (Post Office); Thomas W. S. Davis (Commerce); Boyd H. Gibbons III (Interior); Archibald Owen (Navy); George H. Revercomb (Attorney General); Harry Shoosham (Interior); and Samuel R. Young (Post Office).

5. Solicitor-General for Scotland, Solicitor-General for Ireland, Attorney-General for Scotland, Attorney-General for Ireland.

6. Also excluded are Junior Lords of the Treasury and members of H. M. Household, who ordinarily appear on lists of "the government."

7. In Britain, resignations are usually classified as being based on *ministerial responsibility* or *personal responsibility*. Cf. David Butler and Jennie Freeman, *British Political Facts, 1900–1960* (London: Macmillan and Co. Ltd., 1964), pp. 52–53. Ministerial responsibility denotes an unwillingness on the part of a minister to continue to share collective responsibility for a government policy with which the minister disagrees. Personal responsibility denotes a minister resigning in order to relieve the government of blame for a failure attributed to his department or a scandal involving the minister. It is only in the case of a scandal actually involving a minister that the case has been deleted from our survey on the ground that the resigner had no real choice. In other cases of so-called personal (i.e.,

departmental) responsibility the minister is usually free to refuse to resign and, in recent years, has usually refused to pay for mistakes made by subordinates.

8. I.e., a mathematical age of 63 or over derived by subtracting year of birth from year of resignation.

9. For the period from July 1905 through December 1912, there is no *New York Times Index*. This presented research problems. For this period we have examined the *Times*, page by page, day by day, but only for a period of one week before and one month after a resignation.

10. Interview with John L. Sullivan, Washington, D.C., March 21, 1973.

11. *The New York Times*, May 8, 1965, p. 1.